KITCHENER PUBLIC LIBRARY
3 9098 00642172 0

D1272175

Original Painting by Ed Hill

BROKEN WING

Stewart Dickson

KITCHENER PUBLIC LIBRARY

BROKEN WING

Stewart Dickson

Publisher

Copyright 1990 Stewart Dickson

All rights reserved. No part of this publication may be reproduced or transmitted in any form or by any means, electronic or mechanical, including photocopy, recording, or any information storage and retrieval system, without the permission in writing from the author.

All characters in this book are fictitious, and any resemblance to actual persons, living or dead, is purely coincidental.

Canadian Cataloguing in Publication Data
Dickson, Stewart, 1924-
Broken Wing
ISBN 0-9692807-6-9 (bound). — ISBN 0-9692807-5-0 (pbk.)
I. Title
PB8557.134B7 1990   C813'.54   C90-091478-5
PB9199.3.D53B7 1990

Graphics and layout by John D. Weyburg

Cover artwork by Ed Hill and Angel Strehlen.

Typesetting by Vancouver Typesetting Co. Ltd.

Printed by Hemlock Printers Ltd., Vancouver, B.C., Canada

Bound by North-West Books Co. Ltd., Surrey, B.C.

Distributed by Raincoast Books Ltd.,
112 E 3rd., Vancouver, B.C. V5T 1C8, Canada

Published by SummerWild Productions Ltd.
#2202 1275 Pacific Street, Vancouver, B.C. V6E 1T6

Produced by Talking Stick Productions Ltd.,
Box 1016, Gibsons, B.C. V0N 1V0 Canada

Prints of the original cover artwork by Ed Hill available on request. Correspondence concerning this or other matters pertaining to the book should be addressed to Talking Stick Productions.

Printed in Canada

To my family,
    native Indian brothers,
    and former colleagues
    with whom
    I have shared the skies.
Without them there would be no story.

BROKEN WING

Chapter One

Dawn was just breaking as the two heavily-laden freighter canoes set out across Tatlatui Lake, knifing through the ghost-like wisps of fog hanging over the water and leaving ever-widening vees in their wakes on the glassy surface of the lake. The four occupants of the canoes, two in each, huddled low against the bitter chill of the late autumn morning. The wind created by the forward speed of the outboard motors humming smoothly on the sterns of the canoes increased the cold. The lone woman glanced back at the rapidly fading lights of the reserve. They would not see it again until the next April.

She was crouched as low as she could get in the bow of the leading canoe, bundled up in heavy clothing. In her early thirties, she was now known as Suzanne Pierre, although as a child she had had an Indian name, Washababino. At an early age her parents had deserted her and she was raised by her maternal grandmother until she was ten. Then, like many of her native brethren, she was taken from the reserve to a convent school in Prince George. She had endured incredible hardships at the convent that had left an indelible scar, making her somewhat bitter and yet compassionate with her fellow man. She was undertaking this arduous journey with her uncle, Willie Bearpaw, as much to cleanse her soul as to partake in the trapping trip for the winter.

Her kindly uncle, Willie Bearpaw, who was running the outboard motor of their canoe, had taken pity on her and given her refuge in his house after her traumatic experiences and he prevailed upon the elders to reinstate her Indian status. He was delighted when she had offered to accompany the three trappers to their winter traplines on the Stikine Plateau knowing that the product of their labours would benefit the whole tribe.

Willie Bearpaw was a big hulk of a man with a happy disposition who had never married. He had the typical round features and stocky build of the Kwakwala tribe. He was secretly delighted when Suzanne had come to live with him in his small house on the reserve. Being a typical bachelor, his home was in total disarray until Suzanne set about washing and cleaning and rearranging. Although he grumbled about being disturbed from his routine he took great pride in what Suzanne had accomplished and even agreed to remove his boots before entering the house. He was a widely respected elder of the tribe and noted for his skill as a trapper; his furs brought premium prices on the market and money for improvements that benefited everyone on the reserve. Suzanne's offer to accompany him and the other two trappers for the winter was a total surprise but he agreed without hesitation. She was still ostracized by many of the band members and he felt better about her being with him than staying alone on the reserve. Her domestic and nursing skills would be invaluable on the trapline although he had warned her that the trapping cabin was much worse than his house.

Willie skillfully navigated the canoe across the wide expanse of water to an unseen destination, seemingly guided by a built-in compass, a sense developed after a lifetime in the wilderness. The only deviation he made was to investigate an object on the surface of the water which invariably turned out to be a solitary loon or duck which had not yet left for southern wintering grounds. As the canoe approached at high speed they were momentarily transfixed before finally diving beneath the surface leaving only a circle of ripples. Suzanne was not sure if Willie was being playful or following his innate hunting instinct, but it did provide some diversion from the bitter cold. At one point Willie spotted a huge bull moose swimming across the lake to a small island, probably enroute to its winter habitat. Willie brought the canoe alongside and slowed the motor down until they were keeping pace in formation. It was the first time Suzanne had been so close to a moose and she was awed by the massive antlers. She felt some apprehension that it would turn and attack the canoe but Willie finally resumed his heading for the unseen destination at the end of the lake. Willie thought wistfully how the moose would have provided their winter meat but it was still too far from the camp and they had no free space in their fully loaded canoes.

In the bow of the second canoe was a man who was a total enigma and somewhat feared on the reservation. He refused to be known by anything but his native name of Mye-Ook and usually grunted only in monosyllables when spoken to. Like Suzanne, he had been taken away to an Indian school as a young boy and it was rumoured that he had been sexually abused for a number of years before he finally tried to commit suicide in desperation. Subsequently he was transferred from the school to an insane asylum and incarcerated until he was twenty-seven before being released to return to the reserve. He had developed an obsessive hatred of all white men and became physically violent if provoked. Willie Bearpaw had many misgivings about bringing him along on the trip but Mye-Ook had much respect for Willie. Mye-Ook was also a skilled woodsman, with great endurance, which was of considerable value on the trapline. Again, Willie felt that he was doing Mye-Ook a favour by taking him from the reserve where he was sometimes the butt of cruel teasing. He was known for his tremendous strength; and this coupled with his fearsome countenance earned him grudging respect.

The fourth member of the small band was Paul Joe, Willie's lifelong friend and his usual trapping partner. He was a very quiet individual who spoke little, but when encouraged he was a skilled story teller. He had memorized the oral history of the tribe that his grandfather had told him when he was a small boy and was now recognized as an authority on the Kwakwala tongue and origins. He was skilled at recounting many of the old fables which made the long nights in the trapping cabin more endurable. For this reason he had been given the Indian name Swakium, meaning storyteller. In contrast to Willie he was a tall, wiry individual. He was also a steadying influence on Mye-Ook.

The trip across the lake took almost an hour before they turned due north into the mouth of the Tucho River and headed directly for the mountain range that was already adorned with a cap of white snow. It had been a dry fall and the flow of water was lower than normal. Slowing down considerably, Willie called out to Suzanne, "Watch for rocks." There were many just below the surface of the swift-flowing river. She hung out over the bow and signalled by hand the direction to take to avoid rocks or deadfalls in their path while the second canoe followed closely in their wake. The massive spruce trees came right to the banks of the river and created the impression that they were entering an enormous cathedral with Goat Mountain serving as the altar. Since it was still early in the morning, the sun had not risen enough to penetrate the forest but sparkled on the fresh snow on the peak, giving it a luminous quality. Even though Suzanne was overwhelmed by the beauty of the scene and the majesty of the forest she dared not relax her vigilance for a moment and signalled frantically whenever a hazard loomed. There were some close calls when the canoe brushed against underwater rocks or logs and Suzanne realized the peril if they were thrown into the icy water that came from the mountain towering above them.

Suzanne was becoming quite exhausted from the intense concentration when, almost as if he had sensed her plight, Willie pointed the nose of the canoe into a small sandy beach and stopped the motor. The sudden silence was awesome as the motor of the second canoe was shut down and it crunched on the sand alongside them.

"Make tea," Willie announced without elaboration. He was never one to make useless conversation and his brief statement conveyed all that was necessary.

The men collected small branches and soon had a hot fire going over which they hung a smoke-blackened tin into which Suzanne threw a handful of tea.

When the pot was boiling they each dipped in a tin mug and munched on pieces of bannock that Suzanne had baked before leaving. There was total silence in the forest except for the murmur of the river as it meandered past. Even the whiskey-jacks had migrated or they would have appeared as if by magic when food was available and added their raucous squawking. It was almost as if the forest was preparing for the onslaught of winter and was in a peaceful, resting period. The scenery was breathtakingly awesome in its splendour and Suzanne could sense the change in the men as they returned to their beloved environment. She too was overwhelmed by the majesty and tranquillity of the forest.

Suzanne broke the silence by asking how much further they had to travel to the camp, and was rewarded with a curt "A fair ways" from Paul who was packing up the tea mugs and tin pot. Being no wiser, she dutifully followed Willie into the canoe and the other two men pushed them off into the current. She resumed her vigilance as soon as the motor burst into life. Paul and Mye-Ook poured water on the embers of the fire and pushed off into their wake.

They penetrated farther and farther into the forest until Suzanne thought they would become grounded in the shallow river. The shallows were alive with huge steelhead trout performing their ritual mating frenzy as they deposited their eggs in the clean gravel of the bottom. The big males with

15

their hooked noses were battling to deposit their milt and fertilize the eggs laid by the does. When Willie whistled, Suzanne looked back to see him making eating motions and pointing to the fish indicating that they would catch some of them for the camp when they stopped, which was just around the next bend. There was a broad sandy beach and a well-worn path leading off into the forest to a clearing that was just visible through the trees. In the clearing stood a small log cabin with a moss-covered roof that was to be their home for the next few months.

As soon as they had beached the canoes they started packing supplies up to the cabin, but were stopped in their tracks when they saw the inside of the cabin. It was in shambles. Articles were strewn all over and the air reeked with a pungent odour. It smelled like formaldehyde and made their eyes water.

"Wolverine," grunted Willie in disgust, as he gasped for air.

"My God," exclaimed Suzanne, "I've never seen anything like it before. You mean that one small animal could cause all this damage? They must be some vicious!" She had heard stories told of wolverines, how animals many times their size were terrified of them and when they marked out their territory with their pungent urine, all other animals stayed well clear. This was the first time she had seen the destruction they could create.

The men set to work repairing the damage to the cabin to make it weatherproof before night while Suzanne started the disheartening task of cleaning up the mess in the cabin. The first priority was to set the stove upright again and reconnect the chimney that had been knocked askew. Only then could they get a fire going. Fortunately, the bedding had been suspended from the rafters and had not been damaged, but some of the bunks were virtually destroyed.

While the men worked on the cabin Suzanne walked back to the river with a bucket for more water and took with her a net that was hanging on the wall, hoping to catch some of the trout for their first dinner. At first she was reluctant to take off her heavy wool slacks and enter the icy river but finally she took the plunge and managed to net three good-sized trout that would make a delicious dinner. She thought that they all needed a boost of morale at this point so she cleaned the fish and carried them back to the cabin, where she was relieved to see smoke rising from the chimney.

As Suzanne made her way back up the trail to the cabin with her bucket of water and load of fish, a large bushy-tailed squirrel ran out on an overhanging branch and chattered its disapproval of her intrusion into his world where he was busily preparing a store of food for the imminent winter. When Suzanne made the same chattering sounds back at him it cocked its head quizzically and listened in silence to this large animal mimicking its call. Suzanne had learned a great deal about wild animals from her grandfather, who seemed to have a magical rapport with all wild animals and birds. As a little girl she accompanied him into the forest and sat enraptured as he made bird and animal calls that always elicited a response. He would hold a piece of bread in his mouth and the birds showed no fear of him as they pecked the bread right out of his mouth. He had a mystical quality about him that allowed him to communicate with animals and birds and overcome their natural fears. Suzanne had inherited a measure of this native intuition and knew that she would soon have the squirrel eating out of her hand.

The sounds of the men pounding nails into the cabin jolted her from her reverie and she hurried along the trail with her burden not wanting to be seen as a slacker on her first day. She entered the cabin and found the stove burning well. The heat it gave off was sufficient to keep the door open and air out the cabin which had sat vacant, apart from the wolverine's unwanted visit, since last spring and which had a decided musty smell. The cabin consisted of one room about fifteen by twenty feet. Six bunks were ranged around the outside wall in two tiers. As soon as they arrived Suzanne placed her meagre belongings on the bottom bunk in the far corner, reasoning that she would enjoy most privacy there even though it was the most remote from the stove, possibly a problem in the colder weather. She also found an old bedspread that she could hang from the top bunk to provide her with a curtain separating her from the men. She was certainly no prude but her feminine sensitivity required a measure of privacy in the intimacy of the small cabin.

While the men continued to repair the cabin and chinked the walls again, Suzanne got down a big old cast iron frying pan and heated it with some oil. She took a sharp knife and filleted the fish, rolling them in corn meal, and fried them to a crisp golden brown. When they were cooked, there was no need to call the men who laid down their tools and sat around the big rough table with their tin plates in front of them. Suzanne loaded the plates with fish and fresh bannock and watched with satisfaction the men wolf down the meal, their first of the day. Finally, Willie Bearpaw pushed himself away from the table and unabashedly let out a large belch of satisfaction. Even Mye-Ook had the glimmer of a smile on his face as he wiped his plate clean with a piece of bannock.

"Some good, Suzanne," Willie announced as he headed for his bunk. "We eat like that all winter we'll be four fat Indians by spring."

Suzanne grinned with pleasure. "I'm going to catch a load of trout and smoke them for the winter. I figure I can get the smoker working again."

As she was about to dump all the scraps into the stove, Paul stopped her and said, "Give me those. I'm gonna set out a trap for that evil beast that wrecked everything 'cause it will keep terrorizing us all winter. He's called the Carcajou and one of the devil's helpers. If we don't catch him he'll stay in the area 'cause he has marked out his territory and won't leave even with humans here. Another thing, I sure hate to use our valuable kerosene but it's the only thing that'll get his stink out of the cabin."

As they sat around the table after dinner Suzanne surreptitiously scanned the faces in turn of each of her companions of the next few months in the confines of this tiny cabin. They were a diverse group, each distinctively different in appearance and personality, and yet they shared a strong common bond — a respect for the wilderness and the bounty it could provide.

Willie's face epitomized the typical western native Indian, dark brown and deeply etched with wrinkles. He had an aquiline nose and high cheekbones topped by a shock of unruly black hair with a few traces of gray starting to show at the temples. He only stood about five feet eight inches tall but was stockily built with powerful legs, slightly bowed, the result of years of travel in the forest and carrying enormous burdens. He was a natural leader despite his taciturn manner and the other two did not question his judgment or directions. Even Willie was not sure how old he was but estimated he was about forty-five.

Paul Joe was the antithesis of Willie and stood well over six feet tall. His hawklike face was rough and leathery and his misshapen hands like the gnarled branches of a tree. His most startling feature was his blue eyes, obviously a throwback to the introduction of white blood somewhere in his past, probably a passing fur trader or explorer. His black hair stood straight up, making him look even taller and emphasizing his lean, craggy look. Paul rarely spoke unless encouraged, but once started, the flood gates opened and a wealth of history and myth poured forth, justifying his Indian name of Swakium. He was probably a few years older than Willie.

Mye-Ook was like a child locked in a strong man's body. He had a powerful build that belied his apparently docile nature and instilled respect even among those who mocked him for his obvious mental deficiency. He wore a permanent frown on his face that had created deep furrows in his brow and he rarely spoke more than a few syllables. He never took off the fur hat that was adorned with claws and other talismen, not even in bed. In the cabin he never joined in the conversation but sat and rocked on his bunk. He treated Willie with great deference and responded immediately to any directions given by him. Mye-Ook was about the same age as Suzanne and it

19

was obvious that he felt a great empathy with her and treated her with kindness and respect. This undoubtedly stemmed from their both being removed from the reserve as children. Even though it was still early, the men rolled into their bunks for the night as Suzanne cleaned up the dinner residue. From his bunk Willie called, "Up early tomorrow and get the traps out to the trapline before the snow comes." Walking on bare ground was much easier and faster than on snowshoes, and the task could be accomplished in half the time. The trapline was almost twenty miles long and they would require Suzanne's help to place the traps at strategic places along the line ready to use at the first heavy snowfall. "Snow's not far off," predicted Willie with conviction. After that there was no more conversation and a chorus of snores filled the cabin after their long and exhausting day. Suzanne also immediately fell asleep when she rolled into her sleeping bag and pulled her curtain over in front of the bunk.

Suzanne was still sleeping soundly the following morning when she was awakened by the sound of pots rattling on the stove. Pulling aside her curtain she looked out to see that the three men were all dressed and had a kettle steaming on the stove for tea. She hurriedly dressed behind her curtain and gave her hair a few quick strokes with a brush before stepping out into the cabin, embarrassed that she had overslept. "Sorry, guys," she said sheepishly. The men grunted acknowledgement of her apology and went back to getting breakfast. Suzanne hurriedly mixed up some bannock batter and put it on the hot stove to cook. The touch of treacle that she added gave it an aroma that soon had the men salivating and her tardiness was immediately forgotten. They sat around the table drinking tea in anticipation of the fresh hot bannock. When Suzanne placed the steaming bannock on the table with a jar of treacle, they ignored their burning fingers and wolfed down the entire loaf. The smiles on their faces were adequate thanks for Suzanne and she felt that she had more than compensated for her lateness and resolved that it would never happen again. She wanted badly to justify her uncle's faith in her before the other two men.

After breakfast Willie and Suzanne took half the traps while Paul and Mye-Ook took the rest. They started out in different directions, from each end of the trapline, so that they would meet about the middle and return to the cabin before nightfall. It was a raw, cold morning but Willie cautioned Suzanne not to wear too much clothing. He knew they would become heated on the trail and clothing drenched in sweat would be chilling later in the day. She was in good physical condition and her lithe frame carried no excess weight to burden her. Willie was nevertheless careful to give her less than half of the heavy traps to carry as they started off up the trail towards Goat Mountain.

"Snow tonight," Willie said, sniffing the air. "That's good. Makes the animals get moving." Suzanne felt the little thrill she had experienced ever since she was a young girl when the first snowfall arrived, but she was sure that she would see more than she wanted before this winter was over.

Although Willie Bearpaw was at least twenty years her senior, Suzanne had great difficulty keeping up with him on the trail. He moved with an easy, loping gait that carried him great distances with apparent minimum of effort. When Suzanne tried to emulate him her feet became tangled and she ended up almost running to stay within sight of him. His old and grubby Trapper Nelson packboard was filled with traps, and a battered .22 rifle was slung over his shoulder with a makeshift sling of heavy string. His moccasins were laced up to his knees and he moved silently through the forest with his head slightly bowed but constantly alert. From time to time he stopped to deposit a number of traps, cutting a blaze into the tree with his knife. Wordlessly, he took the traps from Suzanne's pack and it became progressively lighter, which helped her to keep up with his relentless pace. On one occasion he stopped abruptly and unslung the old rifle, pointing up into the branches of a tree at a target Suzanne could not see. There were two sharp cracks from the rifle and two fat spruce partridge fluttered down. Now Suzanne saw that there were many more, but Willie just took the two, saying, "Supper," as he tied their necks together and slung them over his shoulder.

The trapline was about twenty miles in length and made two loops of about equal distance from the cabin. The half that Willie and Suzanne were travelling went directly towards the foot of Goat Mountain and was quite steep in parts. Suzanne was overwhelmed by the spectacular scenery even though she was puffing badly to keep pace. Goat Mountain dominated the area with its massive, treed slopes. The cap of early snow was like icing on a beautiful cake. Some of the trees must have been centuries old and they rose majestically hundreds of feet in the air. The undergrowth was a dense, virtually impenetrable tangle that extended to the sides of the well-worn trail, obviously used by a variety of animals each leaving its distinctive imprint. Willie could have read the trail like a book, but they were travelling too quickly to examine the spoor closely.

They had been travelling for a good two hours, depositing traps as they went along, when suddenly the silence of the forest was shattered by a cacophony of howls and yelps. Willie stopped dead in his tracks saying over his shoulder, "Wolves." Suzanne stood paralyzed, never having heard wolves so close nor so many of them. Although she had spent her early days on the reserve she had never before experienced the sights and sounds of the wilderness in such dramatic realism. The Indian boys were indoctrinated at an early age to the hunting rituals of their ancestors, but girls were limited to dressing and preparing the game after the hunt. For Suzanne it was a totally new dimension that she could not have imagined from the tales of the hunt that she had listened to as a little girl.

The wolves appeared to be running back and forth along a ridge just above them, and their terrifying howls were punctuated by a pitiful bawling.

"They've cornered a moose," said Willie as he unslung his old rifle. He took his pack off and laid it at the foot of a tree. "Sounds like they're closing in for the kill."

He stood silently for a few minutes until the wild symphony of sound concentrated in one place just above them. Suzanne was terrified as she stood behind Willie, not sure what to do. She resisted the urge to run back down the trail but realized safety was in remaining close to Willie and his rifle. When he started up the ridge to the source of the ruckus, she followed closely on his heels, her heart pounding in her chest.

Willie cautiously crept up the steep incline, keeping his rifle in front of him as he approached the source of the fearful wild animal sounds. After a hundred yards they were finally able to catch a glimpse of the horrifying sight of some twenty wolves biting and tearing at a cow moose that was lying down and bellowing at the top of her lungs. The wolves were so intent in their task that they did not notice the approach of Willie until he was a mere thirty yards from them. Suddenly he stood up and fired a number of shots into the pack of wolves, yelling at the top of his voice. Taking her cue from Willie, Suzanne also started screaming at the top of her voice. The wolves broke off their attack and ran off into the timber yelping and howling. Willie reached into his pocket and handed Suzanne a whistle. "Keep blowing it as long as you can. It will frighten the wolves and the guys will hear it. They shouldn't be too far away, on the other loop of the trapline."

The moose lay on its side with its head held up, its eyes already beginning to glaze. The wolves had hamstrung it and the animal was bleeding profusely from tears around the jugular vein. It was mortally wounded and Willie moved quickly to put it out of its misery. It did not struggle when Willie walked up and placed the rifle behind its ear, squeezing off three rapid shots. The moose shuddered briefly and lay still on its side.

"Oh, the poor beast," gasped Suzanne as Willie lowered his rifle.

"This is a gift from the Spirits, Suzanne. We got our winter's meat thanks to those wolves. But first we gotta get it back to the cabin. Paul and Mye-Ook shouldn't be far from here so go back down to the trail and head towards them. Blow the whistle, three blasts at a time, and when they hear it they'll know we need help. I'll stay here and start cleaning the moose and keep the wolves off till you get back."

Suzanne struggled to regain her composure but realized that she had to prove her worth and was reassured when Willie told her that the wolves would not come near her if she kept blowing the whistle and shouting. "It'll also keep away bears that might come when they scent a fresh kill on the wind," he added.

Summoning every ounce of courage she had, Suzanne started back down the hill, blowing the whistle every few minutes. When she reached the trail she broke into a full run in the direction she expected the other two men to approach, stopping only to blow the whistle at regular intervals after she had caught her breath.

When she finally felt as if her legs would not carry her another step, her heart leapt when she heard three short blasts on another whistle somewhere up ahead. Mustering what seemed like her last breath, she blew the whistle as hard as she could before collapsing in a heap at the foot of a tree, panting like a dog. From time to time she could hear the whistle getting progressively closer but was totally incapable of going another step to meet Paul and Mye-Ook.

After what seemed an hour, the pair of them came loping around a corner in the trail and she was relieved to see that Paul was carrying a heavy hunting rifle over his shoulder.

"What's happening?" asked Paul, also out of breath from running.

"The wolves killed a moose and Willie has scared them off and is cleaning it now. He needs help in a hurry 'cause the wolves are still in the forest all around."

Without waiting for any more explanation, Paul and Mye-Ook ran back up the trail, leaving Suzanne alone. Finding

24

hidden reserves of adrenalin and energy, she started off after the men.

Paul and Mye-Ook found Willie's pack lying beside the trail and followed his tracks up onto the ledge where he was busy gutting the moose and firing intermittent shots at the wolves that were watching from the forest and howling their dismay at being robbed of their feast. When the three men got together again they embraced and whooped and did a little war dance around the moose carcass. A winter's supply of moose meat was an unexpected bonus that was going to make their life a lot easier.

While they worked with their knives skinning and cutting up the moose they discussed their plan of action. It was getting too late to pack it all back to the cabin that day so they agreed that Mye-Ook would stay with the carcass while the other two carried as much as possible back to the cabin. They would come back the next day for the rest. In order to appease the wolves they dragged the offal back into the trees and collected a large pile of firewood so that Mye-Ook could keep a good fire going all night. Suzanne busied herself collecting more firewood while the men skinned and cut up the moose into packable pieces. When they had finished, Willie and Paul strapped large pieces of the meat on to their packboards while Suzanne loaded the fresh heart and liver into her pack. In addition, Willie skillfully removed the tongue and nose, considered to be rare delicacies. They left the hide, which was still supple, for Mye-Ook to put over himself that night and skewered some tenderloin on green sticks for him to cook for his dinner. Paul also left the hunting rifle and a whistle with Mye-Ook as they started their long journey of two to three hours back to the cabin with their prized load.

The trip back to the cabin was long and arduous with the extra burden of the meat. When they had to rest, they did not remove their packs or sit down; instead they leaned against a tree to shift the load and relieve the agonizing pressure on their shoulders. In the end they fell into an automatic pace and tried to think of other things to divert their attention from the pain. On one occasion another diversion came along in the form of a high-flying bush plane and they rested and watched as it crested the peak of Goat Mountain and disappeared from view. "Headin' for Sustut," surmised Willie who had guided hunters into that area when he was younger. Sometime later the plane reappeared, heading in the opposite direction, and again they took the opportunity to rest while they watched it pass almost overhead.

As they got closer to the cabin, the first flakes of snow appeared, just as Willie had predicted. In the forest, protected from the influence of the wind, they floated lazily down and Suzanne playfully stuck out her tongue and caught some of the flakes. Not only did it offer a diversion but a small measure of refreshment for her parched mouth. She noted that the men breathed through their noses but she could not master the technique and continued to breathe through her mouth which added to her thirst. She could not banish the image of the cold river rushing past the cabin and was sure she would drink gallons when she finally arrived there.

At last the terrain started to look familiar and Suzanne began to anticipate seeing the cabin around every corner. Instead, they were greeted by a piercing scream that was heart-stopping in its intensity.

"Wolverine," said Paul. "Guess he's in the trap I built. I'll drop my load here and take the rifle to check it out." He struggled out of his pack and lifted the rifle off Willie's shoulder and cautiously crept forward. He had set the trap intentionally a good distance from the cabin so that there would be no fear of the wolverine inflicting more damage to it in their absence.

As he rounded the next curve he saw the wolverine in the trap furiously trying to bite its way out, all the while emitting fearful screams. Ancient Indian folklore said the wolverine was known as the incarnation of the devil so they treated him with great respect, believing that he had the power to take them back to his lair at the entrance to Hades. Even though Paul was a brave and skilled trapper, the sight of the raging, frothing animal filled him with fear, and he approached the cage with great caution. When he was close enough, he stuck the barrel of the rifle through the bars. The wolverine immediately seized it in its mouth and started shaking it violently. Overcoming his terror Paul, squeezed the trigger of the rifle three times in rapid succession. Even though it was mortally wounded the wolverine kept biting at the rifle and screaming in unholy defiance at its tormentor. The forest echoed with its dying screams and Willie and Suzanne huddled close together in terror at the sound of one of the most feared animals in the forest. Slowly the sounds subsided to a low growl; they moved cautiously forward until they could see Paul and the cage with the dying animal. Even then they did not approach until the animal lay inert on the bottom of the cage and Paul withdrew the rifle, its barrel scarred from the vicious teeth of the wolverine.

"We'll skin him out and hang his pelt on the cabin to keep the evil spirits away," said Paul when he had caught his breath. "Must have been sent to take our furs this winter but we've given the devil a setback by killing one of his disciples."

Suzanne was a mixture of faiths and beliefs. Inculcated with Christianity as a child in the convent, she still clung to a deep respect for the ancient ways of her people. Somehow, even when they were in conflict, she held them both within her heart. She still religiously said her prayers to the Christian God every night and invoked his blessing on everything she did. She wore a small gold crucifix on a chain around her neck and had unconsciously found herself fingering it during the terror with the wolves and the wolverine.

While the men packed the meat up into the meat cache they had built in the branches of a big spruce tree near the cabin, Suzanne got a good fire going in the stove and prepared a gourmet dinner in celebration. She skillfully skinned out the moose nose, and fried it with some of the heart and liver in the big skillet, flavoured with some of the precious onions they had brought with them. She mixed up a fresh batch of bannock to go with it and the whole cabin smelled of its delicious aroma. The men had been splitting more firewood and washing up at the river, but when the aroma started drifting outside they came and sat at the table impatiently until the feast was cooked. As Suzanne served it they started eating before the next item had been placed on their plates. They did not notice that she quietly bowed her head and said grace before starting her own meal. She also gave thanks that so far she had been able to pull her weight and felt an equal partner in the venture.

They were sitting in quiet contentment after the meal when Paul started speaking in a low voice. "Once there was a young Indian boy who went into the forest to go hunting but he got separated from his father and lost. He ate berries and drank water from the streams, but he became weaker every day." A quiet fell over the listeners as they became enraptured with the cadence of the old stories. The warmth of the cabin, an occasional hiss or pop from the stove, and Paul's slow, measured tones combined to mesmerize Suzanne and Willie.

"One day a pack of wolves came along and were going to eat him up, but the leader of the pack said no, that they should take him into the pack with them and teach him to be a great hunter like them. They brought him food and he got stronger and learned to run as fast as the wolves. When he reached manhood he mated with one of the wolves and they produced half wolf and half man. To this day his descendants still roam the forest and if an Indian is lost or hungry they will give him food and guide him home. They're called the Wuwukw-Nach-Em and they're the ones who've provided us with this fine cache of meat for the winter."

Even though his tale was fascinating, Paul's voice droned on and Suzanne and Willie found themselves nodding off. They rolled into their bunks and were soon fast asleep.

Suzanne vowed that she would never be late up again and spent a fitful night checking the luminous face of her watch. Even though every bone and muscle in her body ached she dragged herself out of bed at 4:30 a.m. and had the stove well going with tea brewing and moose tenderloin frying before the men woke up. She was not looking forward to the trip back to pick up the rest of the moose and she was delighted to hear Willie decide that she should stay around camp while he and Paul went back to pick up Mye-Oook. They would bone out the rest of the meat and between the three of them they could carry all they needed. Anything that was left over would soon be picked over by the animals in the forest. As they left with their empty packs on their backs they made tracks in the fresh snow that had fallen overnight and as soon as they were out of sight Suzanne went out in the sparkling snow, making snowballs and falling on her back and making angels with her arms and legs as she did when she was a child. The white snow that had blanketed the forest overnight seemed to muffle every sound and brought with it a new peace and tranquillity that Suzanne had never before experienced. It seemed that her soul was being renewed after the tragedies of her earlier life and her mind was being purged of evil memories.

After she had satisfied her childish urges she suddenly felt a strong sense of guilt and hurried back into the cabin, tidying up and sweeping and cleaning to make the cabin as presentable as possible. She then lifted the big hoop net off the wall and made her way down the trail to the river to see if there were still any trout in the bay. She was delighted to see the large fins slicing through the black water as they continued their ritual of spawning and mating. Unlike the salmon, steelhead prepared themselves for another hazardous journey to the ocean when spawning was completed and their bodies were still in fairly good physical condition, except for the doe fish who had lost their bloated bellies after depositing their eggs in the clean gravel of the river bed. Suzanne reluctantly peeled off her moccasins, wool pants and underwear, leaving her naked from the waist down, and stepped hesitantly into the frigid water. At first the water felt as if it was burning her skin but it quickly turned into a numbing cold that made her gasp for air. As she waded deeper to reach the fish, a flood of memories came back of the young males of the tribe who had to go through a ritual initiation when they were fourteen to prove their manhood. The ritual included being completely immersed in icy water in mid-winter. Little did she think that one day she would experience the same torture that all the boys bragged about after their initiation, but she wanted to experience all the rigours of the trapping trip that her uncle had allowed her to join. She had built a good fire in the cabin and the thought of its warmth sustained her while she netted the big trout, some of which would hardly fit into the mouth of the net. After half an hour she had twenty-two fish on the bank. She was totally numb from the waist down and shivering violently.

Suzanne scooped up her clothes and ran through the ankle-deep snow to the cabin, not stopping to even put on her underwear. For a fleeting moment she burst into a gale of laughter as she pictured herself dashing through the forest like a semi-naked nymph, but the thought sustained her until she burst through the door of the cabin into the almost sickening heat.

She wrapped herself in her sleeping bag and poured a good portion of oolichan oil into a pan on the stove. As soon as it was hot she gulped it down, searing her throat and not noticing the pungent, fishy taste. She still shivered violently but the hot oil and the warmth of the sleeping bag and the stove were overcoming the pain in her frozen limbs. She started to become drowsy, and reluctantly she fought off the urge to climb into her bed and sleep. She wanted to deal with the trout before the trappers came back.

Finally she found the strength to get dressed and went out to light the smoker which the men had repaired. Mye-Ook had made her a big pile of bark chips from an old cottonwood snag that he had felled near the cabin and they were soon glowing and smoking while giving off a pleasant, sweetish odour. It took five trips to the river to retrieve the fish and another two hours to clean them all and butterfly them for smoking. Suzanne was careful to observe the native custom of preserving all the scraps and bones that were of no value and carried them back to the river where she deposited them in the black water to be regenerated into new fish. She also took a drink of clean water to cleanse her soul. Despite all the years she had spent with the white man she still carefully observed all the native customs and beliefs.

Meanwhile, Mye-Ook had spent a cold night guarding the rest of the moose carcass against predators. He kept a big fire going, stirring it from time to time to send showers of sparks heavenward to let the spirits know he was there. On his head he wore the skin hat adorned with grizzly bear teeth and claws, which he knew would ward off any evil spirits that were present. The moose hide had not yet stiffened and he pulled it over his shoulders as he sat cross-legged in front of the fire. Although he still had Paul's hunting rifle he did not shoot at the wolves that paced around the perimeter all night, in case he shot the benevolent wolf-Indian who had provided them with their store of meat for the winter, and relied on the fire to keep the pack at a distance. As soon as it was dawn he started to bone out the rest of the moose and threw the bones to the wolves who fought furiously over them. When Paul and Willie finally appeared he had all the remaining carcass ready to load onto their backpacks. "Good work, Mye-Ook," said Willie who noted the trace of a smile that passed over his face in response to the praise.

It was mid-morning before the three trappers left with their heavy burden, but not before Mye-Ook insisted they load the moose hide on top of what was an already great weight. He refused to explain why he wanted it, but the other two knew better than to anger him and finally agreed to load it on top of his pack. Without hesitation Mye-Ook started down the trail at a brisk pace, leaving the other two well behind. Quite apart from his younger age, Mye-Ook was known for his great strength and this was one of the major reasons for his presence on the trapping trip. He finally disappeared from view as his stout legs carried him and his load at a relentless pace towards the cabin, without stopping for a rest as did the other two at regular intervals.

The smell of the smoking fish permeated the forest and could be sensed by the trappers a considerable distance from the cabin, spurring them on with their heavy loads. They had not eaten since morning, except for a handful of pemmican to sustain them, and the delectable odour almost made them drop their packs and break into a run. Mye-Ook was first back to the cabin and Suzanne greeted him with a piece of hot smoked trout. He wolfed it down, licking his fingers for the after-taste. "Good, Suzanne," he grunted in Kwakwala. "I've got a gift for you," he added, pulling off the moose hide from the pack. "Make a jacket for you and new moccasins for us guys."

"Thank you, Mye-Ook. It was nice of you to think of me. It must have been very heavy to carry," Suzanne answered in Kwakwala. She always respected his wish to never speak English and was delighted to see him smile at her obvious pleasure with the gift. She went to the smokehouse and brought him another large piece of hot smoked trout on a skewer which he quickly ate even though it burned his mouth.

It was at least half an hour before Paul and Willie arrived at the cabin. They were also greeted with generous pieces of smoked trout which they consumed before even taking off their packs. "Boy, some good," they both exclaimed. "How about some more?"

"No way. I've got a big stew on the stove as soon as you've packed the meat up into the tree cache," she explained. Thus motivated, they forced their tired muscles to one last exertion for the day.

That night they ate their fill and rolled into their bunks, satisfied that they were well provisioned for the onset of winter. Suzanne felt a warm glow of satisfaction that she had also contributed substantially to the storehouse and their comfort in the long winter to come. As soon as she had cleaned up the cabin and stoked up the stove for the night, she crawled into her bed behind her curtain and was asleep instantly.

Chapter Two

The clatter of the alarm clock shattered the early morning stillness and jolted Bill Headingly awake. For a few seconds he lay immobile, heart pounding, trying to collect his thoughts. He felt the warm body of his wife, Jennifer, hesitantly stir beside him as she too was brutally brought back to reality from her dreamworld. Instinctively she snuggled up to Bill and wrapped her arms around him.

Switching on the bedside light, Bill saw by his trusty old alarm clock that it was 4.30 a.m. and the start of another day of indeterminate length. He had always been a heavy sleeper, but the combination of the tranquillizing effect of the pure, unpolluted air of Buffalo Narrows and days ending in utter physical and mental exhaustion had turned him into a virtual Rip Van Winkle. Conventional alarm clocks could not even penetrate his deep sleep, and he had finally resorted to an old-fashioned, windup bell alarm placed on a tin pie plate which generated enough din to raise the dead.

Bill luxuriated for a few more moments in the warmth of the big double bed with the goose feather eiderdown. He was tempted to respond to Jennifer's advances but murmured, "No time for that now, unfortunately." Still, he didn't get up immediately, but lay still, thinking about the circumstances that had lured him and his family into this semi-wilderness, and the nagging doubts rose once again as to whether or not he had done the right thing. Although Jennifer had supported him loyally, and the children were ecstatic in their new environment, he could not eradicate the fear of failure in his venture which could spell disaster for the entire family.

"Do you think we did the right thing, Jennifer?" Bill asked tentatively.

"About what?"

"Burying ourselves in here with the kids and trying to make a go of bush flying."

"Too late to be thinking about that now," Jennifer responded, suddenly wide awake when she detected the note of concern in Bill's voice. "We went into this with our eyes wide open and I support you wholeheartedly. Mind you, there were some misgivings when I had to give up my beautiful house and belongings, but I love this place and the kids are crazy about it. So, get out of this bed and get your aeroplane into the air to pay off the mortgage. We'll continue where we left off tonight when you get back," she added seductively.

* * *

It had started eight years earlier when, as a young air force captain, he had dreamed of satisfying his three all-consuming passions — flying, independence and the outdoors — by starting his own bush flying business.

Ever since he was a small boy, Bill had avidly read every book and publication about flying that he could lay his hands on. His room had been cluttered with models of every description, and he could discuss with authority the performance characteristics of hundreds of aircraft by the time he entered high school. The day he became eligible, on his fourteenth birthday, he joined the school Air Cadet squadron and was soon selected for the summer camp gliding school, followed by a sponsored scholarship to obtain his pilot's licence on powered aircraft. Throughout this early training, he demonstrated exceptional practical skill which matched his enthusiasm and unquenching thirst for knowledge. There was never a doubt that he would pursue his first love as a life-long vocation.

Upon graduation from high school, Bill's parents naturally assumed he would continue his formal education through university, but he was impatient to embark on a full-time career of flying. Many heated family discussions ensued, but Bill could not be deterred from his chosen goal, and his parents reluctantly acceded when he arrived home on his eighteenth birthday with the application forms for entry to the Air Force. His parents did, however, win a major point when they convinced him to apply for the Regular Officer Training Plan which would provide him with a university education concurrent with pilot training.

Bill's driving ambition, coupled with his native intelligence, consistently placed him out in front of his fellow students, and he easily graduated first in his class, both in academic subjects and the practical application of his flying skills. Even so, he still found time to devote to sports and an active social life, both of which he pursued with the same zest he applied to his flying activities. He had developed into a tall, athletic young man with dark, handsome features that made him the envy of his classmates and the object of many of the female students' attention. In fact, it was during his second year at university that he met Jennifer at a post-football game celebration and immediately recognized a kindred spirit who seemed destined to become his wife.

* * *

Bill was consuming his usual hearty breakfast of hot, steaming pancakes with fragrant maple syrup. He caught Jennifer's waist as she passed by the big hand-hewn table.

"I'll bet you never expected to end up this way when I asked you for that date after the football game."

"I must admit that never in my wildest dreams did I imagine that I'd be living in the bush with three kids and a wild-eyed bush pilot. I should have known to stay clear of pilots after having one for a father but I guess we women never learn," she added with a feigned look of resignation.

Jennifer's father had been an air force pilot himself, and she had been enthralled by his stories of flying exploits ever since she learned to talk. On many occasions her father had taken her flying with him when she was a child too small to see out of the cockpit.

As a young adult her characteristic shyness and wholesome fair good looks were the antithesis of Bill, who was ebullient and outgoing. Her looks and demeanour belied an underlying strength of character that enabled her to cope with the transition in her life from urban wife and mother into a pioneer in the remoteness of Buffalo Narrows. Despite their obvious differences, Jennifer and Bill made an ideal couple to undertake such a challenge.

Jennifer was shorter than Bill with short-cropped blonde hair that framed her pretty oval face. Although she was popular and had many friends of both sexes, after she met Bill she devoted most of her time to him and their mutual interests and pursuits. She retained her strong family ties and was delighted when she introduced Bill to her parents and they took an immediate liking to him and approved of their close relationship in college.

During Bill's third and fourth years, he and Jennifer were inseparable, and a deep emotional relationship developed. Marriage was never discussed, but on graduation it just evolved as the natural culmination of their relationship. Typically, they spent their honeymoon in the wilds on a two week canoeing expedition down the Paradis River. Their bridal suite was a two-man nylon tent and their nuptial bed fresh-cut spruce boughs. To Jennifer and Bill, no suite in the finest hotel could have provided as marvellous a setting for the start of their married lives. In fact it was during their honeymoon that their ultimate destiny was decided.

There was little doubt their firstborn, Keith, had been conceived on their honeymoon trip, probably during one of their frequent stops on one of the sandy beaches that punctuated the densely-forested river banks. Without a spoken word, they would beach the canoe on a sandy shore and spontaneously shed all their clothes and plunge into the crystal clear pools followed by tender but passionate lovemaking. Exhausted, they would lie on a sleeping bag with the sun bathing their lithe bodies, observed only by a raucous jay or chattering squirrel. Although not constrained by religious beliefs, the use of contraceptives was never considered as part of their wholesome, uninhibited love-making whenever the urge overwhelmed them. Almost nine months to the day from their marriage, the husky, robust Keith appeared on the scene without complication and prompted spontaneous celebrations in both parental families as the first-born of the new union and first grandchild on both sides. The succeeding two children, Dianne and Dave, were more carefully planned and arrived after three year intervals. The strong bond that deepened between Bill and Jennifer as the years passed was reflected in the close and protective relationship that developed in the three children throughout their formative years.

* * *

Bill's career in the Air Force appeared to be assured of success and his consistently glowing annual assessments earned him accelerated promotion to Captain and appointment as a flight commander in the transport squadron to which he was assigned. Despite accumulation of an impressive number of flying hours in his profession, he continued membership in the local flying club and derived tremendous satisfaction from flying light planes on weekends. Much of this satisfaction came from his ability to share the undiminished thrill of flying with his family.

Slowly, but surely, doubts began to rise in Bill's mind as to whether or not he was destined to spend the rest of his active life in the relatively secure and well-ordered Air Force. There was little doubt that he would progress to a senior rank with its attendant prestige and financial security. Nevertheless, he frequently felt stifled by the rigid guidelines to which he was forced to conform and he was troubled by the lack of roots for his family. But above all, he sensed a compelling urge to mold his own destiny and to own a part of his native land.

By this time Bill was thirty and concluded that if he was to make his move, he could wait no longer. He and Jennifer spent many agonizing hours discussing his plan, many times well into the night as they lay sleepless in bed. Naturally, Jennifer was reluctant to forfeit the security and comradeship of their comfortable life, particularly since they were just achieving a reasonable level of financial security. They had paid off all their furniture and drove two cars. With Bill's flying pay they were also able to enjoy a good social life with the other young couples in the squadron, and the children participated actively in sports and other activities on the base.

After months of agonizing, Bill and Jennifer, somewhat reluctantly, finally decided to make the move and Bill resigned his commission. Having completed ten years of continuous service, he was entitled to a substantial return of pension contributions and other benefits which would provide him with enough cash to launch him in his new career. It was enough to make a down payment on his own aeroplane and to negotiate the purchase of a piece of land in Buffalo Narrows where they had spent part of their honeymoon.

When he announced his intentions, Bill's superiors tried seriously to dissuade him, emphasizing the career potential he had and virtually guaranteeing him accelerated promotion to Major. In fact, his squadron commander summed it up in two words: "You're nuts!" It was further food for thought, but not enough to deter him from his objective. Again, he and Jennifer spent many sleepless nights discussing their plans

before he carefully wrote his letter of resignation and the die
was cast. Now there was no turning back.

*   *   *

During their honeymoon canoe trip down the Paradis River
some ten years before, Bill and Jennifer had fallen in love
with Buffalo Narrows where the river widened in the
flatlands into a small lake. At the head of the lake the rocky
shoreline constricted the flow of the river and created a small,
turbulent waterfall. Jennifer and Bill had portaged the falls
with their canoe and found a large, natural grassy clearing of
about ten acres surrounded by towering spruce. They pitched
their tent on the clearing and after resting and exploring the
area for three days resolved that some day they would own
this place as their personal paradise.

During their exploration of the area they found caves with
petroglyphs covering the walls and many signs of Indian
relics, including arrowheads and shards of pottery. It was a
haven for all kinds of wildlife and they saw deer wandering
and browsing in the long grass, apparently without fear of
human beings. Pursuing their fantasies, they chose a site for
the home they would one day build. They imagined themselves looking out of their front window at a breathtaking
view of the falls and lake, framed by the mountains to the
north. The tall stands of spruce and hemlock made a comforting backdrop, in addition to being the source of the material for their dream home.

When Bill later made enquiries he found that Buffalo Narrows was located on Crown land and could not be purchased.
It was, however, available for long-term lease at a nominal
sum and Bill and Sue dug deeply into their meagre savings to
secure title for an indefinite period. While the children were
young, they would save for many months to rent a small float
plane for a trip into their haven with the children. Eventually, they started laying the foundation for a cabin. Even the

children pitched in with great enthusiasm, hauling stones from the river for the foundation and clearing away brush.

While still in the Air Force, Bill had taken a course in log house building and he and Jennifer spent many pleasant evenings designing the house they would some day build at Buffalo Narrows. It started as a modest, one-room cabin but ultimately expanded on paper into a full-fledged, three-bedroom house. Little did they realize that each additional line they drew on the plan would ultimately entail many hours of backbreaking labour. Moreover, since the closest town, Sioux Falls, was twenty-three miles as the crow flies, every item that could not be obtained or produced on site would have to be flown in. Many days were consumed in compiling detailed lists of every conceivable item they would need in the construction.

In planning their move to Buffalo Narrows, Bill and Jennifer decided to start construction of the house on the first of May, right after spring breakup. For interim accommodation they purchased a large, war-surplus tent which would be their base of operations. The house would have to be closed in before the first snows arrived in October. That left them only five short months to complete the major construction, but finishing the interior would continue through the winter as long as they were protected from the elements. In his usual, methodical way, Bill prepared a detailed flow chart scheduling the various phases of construction to meet the winter deadline since they realized that failure to meet the deadline would delay a permanent move for at least six months. With their financial status marginal, such a delay could even spell the end of their dream.

One real break came that brightened their prospects considerably. Jennifer's father, Mike, called Bill and said, "Could you use an old retired chap for the summer to help build your house? I know which end of a hammer is the business end and I could at least pound the odd nail. It has always been a dream of mine to build a house in the woods, so maybe I can live out my fantasy on yours."

"You're hired," Bill responded without hesitation. He was absolutely thrilled at the prospect, since he looked upon Mike as a second father, his own having died some years earlier. "The pay will be lousy but the grub outstanding thanks to your daughter. I've seen you handle an axe on some of our hunting trips and know you can make the chips fly. Will Sue be all right on her own though?"

Mike's wife, Sue, was less than enthusiastic, however, since she faced five months living alone in the city. She would dearly have loved to participate in the venture but the onset of arthritis constrained her physical activities to the point where she would probably be more burden than helper living in a tent in the wilderness. "She'll probably be delighted to get me out of the house for a while after I retire or I will be reorganising her kitchen. This is definitely the lesser of two evils."

The next, and most vital, step was buying a suitable plane that would be the basis of Bill and Jennifer's livelihood. For many months Bill carefully checked every trade paper and magazine listing used aircraft for sale since a new one was completely beyond reach. After reviewing specifications and performance data on all likely candidates, Bill had concluded that the ideal was a Twin Otter, but prices asked far exceeded budget and he was reluctantly forced to scale down his thinking. After months of frustrating search during which he examined and tested literally dozens of aircraft in various stages of disintegration, he finally heard, through a mutual friend, of a Beaver that was being sold. This particular plane had belonged to the sales manager of the manufacturing company and had been used extensively as a demonstrator. Although the hours flown were high, Bill realized that the Beaver had obviously been well maintained and serviced by company mechanics. Taking along one of his mechanics from the squadron for technical advice, Bill flew down to the plant to inspect the aircraft. He could barely contain his enthusiasm when he saw the immaculate condition of the Beaver, expecially when it was already equipped with floats and northern survival gear. A one hour test flight confirmed his visceral impression that the aircraft was in top condition and he consummated the purchase with palpitating heart and shaking hand. The same day he was on his way home with his — and the bank's — plane.

Bill scarcely slept for days. After his monumental purchase he spent every free minute polishing and maintaining the Beaver. One of his first actions was to christen it 'KEDIDA', a name derived from the first two letters of the three children's names. He carefully lettered the name above his newly formed company name — Buffalo Narrows Airways Ltd. All the family, and a host of friends, vied for rides in 'Kedida' until he finally had to come back down to earth and complete preparations. By then it was March and only two months remained before the move to Buffalo Narrows.

The final two months were a blur of frantic activity, assembling supplies and disposing of non-essential property. Bill and Jennifer had sold their house and moved in with her folks in Edmonton. Many of their prized possessions had to be disposed of because of lack of storage space or the impracticability of moving them to Buffalo Narrows. Jennifer spent a good deal of time arranging correspondence courses for the children and purchasing basic food supplies to last at least two months. When Bill saw the growing mountain of supplies in the garage he began to despair of ever transporting them in the Beaver to Buffalo Narrows.

On the first of May, Mike and Bill flew the Beaver up to check the ice conditions at Buffalo Narrows and were dismayed to find at least two-thirds of the lake still covered in ice. For three frustrating weeks they had to wait for the last floes to disappear over the falls before risking a landing with the heavily loaded Beaver. It was the 23rd of May before they were able to deliver the first load of supplies, a full three weeks behind Bill's schedule.

Transporting the mountain of supplies took almost ten days, but it was finally all stacked inside the big tent, protected from the elements, and work on the house could start in earnest. In short order Bill realized that without Mike's help, he would have faced an impossible task. He felt uneasy at the pace Mike kept up for a man of his age, but he could see that Mike, who was revelling in his first truly physical work in years, would not listen to any suggestions to slow down. Despite his years, Mike still looked surprisingly youthful and carried his six-foot frame erect. His hair and neatly trimmed moustache were turning grey which gave the only clue to his advancing years.

At first progress on the house was agonizingly slow, especially splitting the logs that had to be flattened on one side to form the sill. Once the sill was laid, it went a little faster, round by round, until the walls had grown to a height of seven feet. Days merged into night in a relentless battle against time. Rain didn't stop construction as Bill, Jennifer and Mike laboured, saturated to the skin, hoping that the sun would reappear the next morning. Some nights they were even too tired for the refreshing skinny dip in the sparkling pool at the foot of the falls that had become a daily ritual. At first Mike's innate modesty kept him from shedding all his clothes in the presence of Jennifer and Bill, but even he finally lost all his inhibitions and it became the most natural thing in the world for all three to plunge naked into the pool at the end of a long, hard day.

Work started on the rafters on 17 July, just two days off Bill's schedule. With Mike's unexpected help they had been able to catch up the time lost at the beginning of the project and it began to look hopeful that the house would be closed in by winter. In fact, Bill felt so confident that he decided to take a break from housebuilding for a week so that he and Mike could build a substantial dock projecting well into the lake for tying up the Beaver. They had been beaching the plane up to this point, but Bill knew that Jennifer and he would never be able to push it off the beach alone when Mike left them. Although it still entailed handling big logs and construction, the dock gave them a much-needed break from the monotony of laying round after round of logs on the house.

On completion of the dock, it was unanimously agreed that they could now safely bring in the children who were unhappily left behind with Sue while the major construction work was in progress. Bill and Jennifer had rightly concluded that they could not adequately supervise the children while handling the large logs for the house walls, and he had convinced Jennifer it would be much safer to leave them behind until this phase was completed. The major hazards were now behind them, so they downed tools and piled into the Beaver to go out for the children. Mike was also more than ready for a break and a reunion with Sue.

The three days that Bill had allocated for the break flashed past for the adults and was interminable for the children who were anxious to get to their new home. Jennifer, Mike and Bill luxuriated in their first hot baths in over two months and found the soft beds and clean sheets unbelievable after a steady regime of sleeping bags and spruce boughs. Sue was consumed with curiosity about the Buffalo Narrows project and plied the other three with a never-ending flood of questions in trying to form in her mind's eye a clear vision of the house and environment. Bill had taken a series of photographs of the various stages of construction and of the property. They gave both Sue and the children a much better appreciation of the magnitude of the task and the rugged beauty of Buffalo Narrows.

After a reluctant farewell to Sue, the Beaver once again headed back to Buffalo Narrows at the end of their brief respite, loaded to capacity with provisions. This time Mike had strapped the canoe to the floats, anticipating that they could put it to good use for fishing to augment their food supplies and that Bill could use it in hunting season to bag a moose as the basis of their winter's meat supply.

The first couple of days back in Buffalo Narrows were fairly unproductive as muscles were reconditioned to steady labour. The children were ecstatic and raced around ceaselessly from dawn to dusk, exploring the surroundings and swimming in the pool below the falls. Keith and Dave tried out their new fishing rods while Dianne tried to tame every bird and animal in the area. She carefully saved all the scraps from meal-times, and in no time had the whiskyjacks and squirrels eating out of her hand. She would fly into a rage when the boys came racing around the house and frightened away a bird or squirrel after she had spent hours overcoming its natural fear of humans. "You meanies," she would screech at them as they ran off in search of more adventure.

After their initial burst of curiosity and enthusiasm, they settled into a routine and contributed a great deal of labour by fetching and carrying, cutting firewood, cleaning up and hauling stones for the fireplace. Bill made them a stoneboat and with the three of them in harness they could skid a good load of stones from the river and pile them along the north wall where the fireplace and chimney would rise.

One day when the children were collecting stones they were startled by a strange, plaintive whining noise from the nearby bush. Dianne was terrified and clutched Keith's arm, imploring him to take her back to the cabin. The boys were much more adventurous and could not resist exploring the source of the strange noise. As they crept closer the whining became bleating and they realized it was an animal in dis-tress.Their first thought was that it might be an animal caught in a trap but they proceeded with great caution, Dianne clutching tightly to Keith's shirt. Although trying hard not to show it, Dave's heart was pounding in his throat.

Finally they penetrated the bush far enough to see the source of the cries and were astonished to find a young moose that seemed to be all legs and head. Instead of the usual dark brown colour, its fur was a light golden that accentuated the young animal's big round black eyes with long lashes. There was no evidence of the mother moose and the waif was standing bleating pitifully as if it had been abandoned. When it saw the children it approached them without fear on unsteady legs and started to nuzzle them, obviously looking for food. The children were nonplussed; their father had warned them never to approach a wild animal, especially a young one since its mother could be nearby and could be extremely dangerous when protecting her offspring. Nevertheless, they could not resist fondling the young moose, which was both ugly and cute.

"What are we going to do with it?"whispered Dianne, who was stroking its head lovingly.

"Let's go and get Dad and see what we should do,"answered Keith, also in a whisper, although he didn't know why.

As they reluctantly turned to leave, the young moose shambled along behind them on legs that seemed much too big for its body, all the while emitting small squeaky bleats. Dave decided he would go on ahead, running as fast as his legs would carry him, shouting to his father about their find. He was almost breathless and virtually unintelligible as he babbled out the story.

"Dad, Dad, come quick and see what we've found. Hurry, hurry."

"Whoa, slow down and tell me what's going on."

"It's a young moose and it's following us."

"How many times have I told you not to go near wild animals? Its mother could be right around and could be dangerous." The two of them ran back to the stream with Dave in the lead.

"You guys return to the house and I'll look around to see if its mother is in the area," Bill commanded as he returned to the river bank to see if there was any sign of the cow moose. Although he found one set of large, fresh tracks and one small one, there was no evidence of the cow.

By the time Bill returned to the house, Jennifer and Mike had joined the children and the little moose was nuzzling them in turn, obviously searching for food.

"Oh, the poor little thing is starving," cried Jennifer as instinctive love of animals took charge. "What should we feed it?"

"We shouldn't feed it anything," answered Bill reluctantly. "Wild animals rarely survive after being handled by humans and their mothers will reject them. It looks as if it has been abandoned by its mother. There's a set of large tracks and one small one down by the river. Cow moose will often abandon one of their offspring if they have twins and they leave the weakest of the two to die, so this poor little guy was probably the one selected. It's doubtful if it will survive, but we should try to feed it if we can. We have lots of powdered milk but I doubt if that's rich enough."

"I also have some canned milk which will be richer and have more nutrients," interjected Jennifer. "I'll cut the finger out of a rubber glove and put it on one of those big plastic bottles," she added as she ran into the house. Almost as if understanding what she had said, the young moose ambled after her into the house while the children roared with laughter.

"What're we going to call it?" asked Dianne. "Is it a boy or a girl, Daddy?"

"It's a little cow," answered Bill, "so it will have to be a girl's name."

"How about Molly?" interjected Mike. "Molly the Moose."

"Yeah!" the children all responded in unison. "Will you make her a little house, Daddy?" added Dianne.

"We'll bang a little shelter together for her but first we had better see how your mother is doing with Molly's dinner."

"Get this beast out of my kitchen," shouted Jennifer, laughing and frustrated at the same time. She was trying to prepare the warm milk but Molly sensed a meal in the offing and kept butting Jennifer with her head, to the delight of the children. When the milk was finally ready, Jennifer ran outside, pursued by the moose trying to get at the makeshift teat. She had to hold the bottle with both hands as Molly sucked it dry in seconds and started bleating for more.

"This beast will eat us out of house and home," Jennifer said in exasperation. "Why couldn't you have have found something like a rabbit for a pet?" She turned to Bill. "You'll have to fly out to Sioux Falls for more milk. My stock won't last long at this rate."

"I read somewhere that goat's milk and crushed bananas is what they feed moose waifs when they're brought to the game farm so I'll see if I can get any in Sioux Falls. I would doubt if the Game Department will help because they discourage attempting to raise wild animals. Now that we have adopted Molly we'll have to do everything we can to keep her alive. You kids can get busy making her a shelter while Mike and I take a trip into Sioux Falls. There's a couple of extra bales of insulation that you can use for a bed for her." Secretly Bill was just as enthralled as the children since when he was a boy he was always bringing home stray animals. On one occasion he even found a little fox and raised it until it nipped his mother's ankle one day and had to go to a zoo. Although they were reluctant to expend any money on non-essential things, Molly seemed to present an exception. As if sensing his dilemma, Mike spoke up. "I'd like to pay for the food for this little guy, 'cause I know you can ill afford it right now."

Despite the dire predictions of everyone in Sioux Falls, Molly thrived and became the family pet. She played with the children like a dog but Jennifer chased her with a broom when Molly got into the small garden Jennifer had painstakingly planted behind the house. Molly followed the children wherever they went and even allowed Dianne to ride on her back when she had gained enough strength. She grew rapidly and her golden coat turned dark brown as the summer passed and she developed the typical moose hump on her shoulders. Although she consumed considerable valuable rations, she proved her worth as a constant companion for the children and soon began to graze on her own on the lush grass in the clearing. She was providing another unforgettable episode in the saga of Buffalo Narrows.

Installing the rafters was slow and painstaking work for Bill and Mike because each rafter had to be fitted meticulously to the plate. Meanwhile, Jennifer spent day after day splitting a growing mountain of cedar shakes with a froe. Cedar was not very abundant in the area and Bill and Mike had scouted for three days to find enough good-sized cedars to produce shingles for the roof and outhouses. With the cross-pieces nailed in place, work on the roof went quickly and Bill felt that once this phase was complete they would at least be well protected from the elements in the event of an early fall. Cutting the openings and installing doors and windows proved to be refreshing labour after the backbreaking routine of fitting logs and nailing shingles. The door was a work of art as Bill and Mike fashioned hinges out of hardwood and split the door through the middle to provide a dutch door effect. Then came more tedium as the opening for the fireplace was cut and the chimney started to rise stone by stone. Once again the children did yeoman service by hauling sand for the cement and mixing batch after batch of mortar. Finally, on the 14th day of September, Mike's birthday, the chimney was capped and in celebration a fire was started in the open hearth.

"All right, since it's Mike's birthday, we'll give him the honour of lighting the first fire in the fireplace," announced Bill. "We'll make an appropriate plaque to mount on the house to commemorate the auspicious occasion."

Everyone waited with baited breath and a cheer broke out as Mike touched the birch bark with a match to christen the fireplace. The cheers quickly turned to coughs and yells as smoke billowed back into the room instead of curling up the chimney as it did in the movies. They were forced to evacuate the house and leave all doors and windows open overnight to dispell the choking odour. Next day Mike and Bill had heated discussions on the cause of failure but finally agreed that the throat of the chimney was too wide to create a proper draft, so they started adding more stones and cement to close up the aperture. Each time they added a few stones they lit a small test fire until finally, as if by magic, the billowing smoke reversed its direction and disappeared up the chimney. This time the cheers were long and sustained as the smoke curled lazily out of the chimney and drifted off into the spruce trees. Nothing had given them more satisfaction or more a feeling of seeing the end of their monumental project than the sight of big birch logs blazing in the stone fireplace.

* * *

The opening of hunting season was only two weeks away, and Bill decided that the house was now sufficiently advanced that he could leave Mike and Jennifer to start work on the interior while he tried to earn some much-needed cash with the Beaver. He flew out to Vermilion Bay, which was the railhead terminal for access to the rugged hinterland, and did the rounds of all the outfitters and guides who were feverishly stocking remote camps and preparing for the influx of hunters. Fortunately, his call on Jerry Fortin, who ran the Northern Outfitters, really paid off.

"Holy mackerel!" exclaimed Jerry. "Did you ever turn up at the right time. One of my planes broke off a float on a submerged log yesterday and I was going to have to cancel out some trips that've been booked for months. You're hired on the spot, Buddy. Let's get to work. I'll pay you by the trip 'cause they're all pretty near the same distance, so the more trips you do the more dough you make."

"Thanks, Jerry. Just tell me where to go and I'm on my way. My old bird is as reliable as they come so you'll get your money's worth."

From dawn to dusk Bill kept the Beaver and himself working to the limit, ferrying supplies and hunters into the main and subsidiary camps run by Northern Outfitters. Since Jerry Fortin was paying him by the trip rather than on flat contract, he was determined to squeeze as much revenue as possible from the unexpected bonanza to carry them through the winter and to provide much needed capital to buy the finishing touches for the house. Only darkness and refuelling kept him out of the air for any protracted period, although when one of his trips took him fairly close to Buffalo Narrows he dropped in for a quick visit with the family. He was reassured to find them surviving admirably and Mike happily starting to build furnishings for the house.

Once the hunters were delivered to the camps, business dropped off to zero for ten days until they started their exodus with their trophies and meat. Bill took advantage of this respite to fly back into Buffalo Narrows and see if he too could bag his winter's meat supply.

As Bill taxied up to the dock and shut off the engine, the three children, with Keith in the lead, came racing down the dock, obviously with a serious mission in mind. No sooner had he set foot on the dock than Keith blurted out, "Dad, Dad, Molly has gone. We've looked all over for her and shouted but she has disappeared."

"Yeah, Dad, Molly has taken off," added Dave breathlessly.

Dianne brought up the rear with tears in her eyes as she looked pleadingly at Bill as if he could perform a miracle and produce Molly out of the air.

"Whoa, you guys. How about saying hello first and giving me a hug?"

They all gave him a token hug and resumed their tale about Molly disappearing. By this time Mike and Jennifer had joined them on the dock. They confirmed the story that Molly had disappeared during the night and they wondered if wolves could have taken her.

"No, Molly's too big and smart to let wolves get near her around here. Did you hear any wolves?"

"Not a sound," responded Mike. "But she was here last night and had her dinner."

"Well, I think I've got the answer for you guys. This is the rutting season for moose and their hormones get all messed up. Even though Molly was raised by us and she's too young to be bred, she still has the wild instinct and no doubt got the call of nature to go back and join her own kind for the mating ritual. Have you heard any moose calling in the last few days?"

"As a matter of fact I heard a cow calling just last night when I went out for a walk after dinner," answered Mike. "In

51

fact it may even have been Molly's mother if she's still in the area."

"Will she come back, Daddy?" asked Dianne with tears in her eyes.

"Probably not, once she rejoins her own kind," answered Bill reluctantly. "But you can feel good that we saved her life and maybe one day she'll be having babies of her own."

Bill put his arm around Jennifer as they all strolled back to the house. "How long will you be home?" enquired Jennifer.

"Just long enough to get my laundry done and a little loving," he answered with a smile as he put his arm around her waist.

"You bush pilots are all the same," said Jennifer with mock indignation as she gave him a punch.

"I thought Mike and I would see if we can get in the winter's meat supply while I'm here. What do you say, Mike, could you use a few days break?"

"You betcha," Mike answered without hesitation. "When do we leave?"

"As soon as we can get the gear together and I have a quick visit with my wife," Bill responded with a leer.

The next day they packed the canoe with a light, two-man tent, sleeping bags and supplies for five days which was about all the time Bill could spare before heading back to Vermilion Bay for the second phase of the hunter airlift. At this point a great family crisis developed.

"Dad, can I go with you?" Keith begged. "I'm old enough and you promised you'd take me when I was ten."

"If he goes, I go too," declared David firmly. "You promised me you'd take me one day too."

"Hey, hold on, guys. I've just got a very short time before I have to get back to pick up the hunters, so Grandad and I have to try and get our winter's meat supply in a hurry. Tell you what, this year I'd like you to see if you can get us some nice fat birch partridge around here. The only thing is that you've got to go with your Mum, and she is the boss. What she says goes and she will tell you if you can shoot or not. The other thing is that you are not to leave the clearing 'cause the moose are rutting and they can be dangerous."

Jennifer rolled her eyes in silent protest as Bill knew she disliked guns but she realized they were essential in this environment.

"Aw, Dad, Mum doesn't know anything about hunting so she'd just be in the way," complained Keith in a petulant tone.

"Those are the terms guys, take it or leave it," Bill added with a note of finality.

Keith and David went off to their room in a sulking mood while Dianne smiled smugly. She knew that her mother was afraid of guns and doubted if she would let them shoot any birds around the clearing, some of which she had cultivated as friends.

Bill was sorely tempted to succumb to Keith's pleadings, despite the unspoken, but obvious, opposition of Jennifer, who had previously expressed her reservations about the boys handling firearms until they were mature. On the other hand, Bill felt that the earlier the boys were exposed to guns the greater the respect they would have for them. Accordingly, he had started both Keith and David shooting with an air rifle in the basement of their former home and they were now both remarkably proficient and showed promise of becoming excellent marksmen. Again over the opposition of Jennifer, Bill had bought Keith a new .22 rifle with a four-power scope for his tenth birthday, the only restriction being that he could only use it under supervision and had to account for all ammunition whenever he took it out for target practice.

Bill and Mike left at dawn with the heavily laden canoe, Mike paddling in front and Bill in the rear. Even though they had never paddled before as a team, they quickly fell into a rhythm, with the paddles slicing the glassy surface of the water in perfect unison and the canoe creating a wedge of ripples that spread out to reach both banks of the Paradis River in their wake. There was no conversation, both absorbed in their private thoughts and engrossed by the beauty and tranquility of the river valley. It was a magnificent day with the deep azure sky of Indian Summer. The sun beat on their backs as they paddled north. It was so unseasonably warm that they both soon stripped to the waist. Bill was amazed to see how Mike's body rippled with muscles, developed from a summer of manual labour building the house. Bill thought to himself that he had never seen Mike in such good shape and concluded that the summer in the wilderness had probably added years to his life; he also realized that they had formed an exceptionally close bond between them. Mike had completely filled the void left by the death of Bill's father ten years earlier. They had always got along well but any reserve that had existed between them had now completely evaporated.

Bill and Mike kept up a steady, but not exhausting pace, penetrating deeper into the hinterland. Bill intentionally wanted to hunt well away from the Buffalo Narrows homesite in order to preserve the wildlife intact in that area as an emergency source of food in the event of a particularly severe winter or late spring break-up.He was also purposely staying away from the area where Molly had disappeared. His destination was a swampy area about ten miles up river, where he frequently saw moose browsing in the lily pads and swamp hay as he overflew the area. At the rate they were paddling they should comfortably make the area in late afternoon, in time to establish their camp before nightfall.

It was just a little after three when they paddled into the neck of a lazy shallows where the river almost doubled back on itself in a large S. On the point of the second curve there was a small, sandy beach and immediately above it a grassy shelf, protected in the rear by heavy timber. Bill steered the canoe to shore and beached, while Mike hopped out and tied the securing line to a root projecting from the sandy bank.

"This looks like home sweet home for a while," said Bill, as he dragged the canoe higher on the beach and started unloading the gear.

Mike was already tramping down a grassy area to pitch the tent and collecting stones for a fireplace, while Bill started packing up the supplies to the campsite. They pitched the tent and got their sleeping bags and spare clothes inside before the evening dew began to descend with the sunset.

"We'll probably have a white frost by morning," observed Mike. "There's a full rutting moon and the frost'll sure be on the pumpkin, especially with that clear sky. We'd better stock up on firewood and keep some under the canoe for morning."

When the sun sank below the horizon in a huge crimson ball, the temperature dropped rapidly, and the hunters put on their down jackets to ward off the evening chill. They built a large fire with a reflector of green logs to throw the heat towards the tent and prepared a meal of macaroni and dehydrated beef jerky that exceeded in taste satisfaction the finest steak in an expensive city restaurant. Washed down with coffee brewed in a fire-blackened tin it created a mellow mood that soon had the pair of them nodding off by the fire. Even though it was only seven o'clock, they decided to crawl into their sleeping bags and in short order were snoring in unison in a deep, drug-like sleep.

Mike was the first awake. Looking out of the tent flap, he saw that the sky was still a canopy of twinkling stars from horizon to horizon. The full moon was low on the western horizon and every detail of the forest stood out in stark relief.

Glancing at the luminous face of his watch, Mike saw that it was almost 5 a.m. and couldn't believe that he had slept undisturbed for nearly ten hours. Even his kidneys had co-operated and the urge to relieve himself of the last two cups of coffee from the night before was not strong enough to overcome the delicious warmth of his down sleeping bag. For a few more moments he lay luxuriating and then reluctantly poked Bill to interrupt his even, deep breathing and bring him back to reality. In response he got a few protesting groans, but Bill gradually returned to consciousness.

"Time to get up, old timer, if we're going to fill the larder," Mike offered. "I think I heard a moose splashing in the swamp a short while ago and we should see if we can get his attention."

Wordlessly, Bill sat up and pulled his pants on inside the sleeping bag. It was a trick he had learned long ago and he always undressed and dressed in the sleeping bag. He kept his clothes inside the sleeping bag to ward off the dampness during the night and it really paid handsome dividends in comfort for the first sortie into the bitter cold outside the tent.

They decided not to build a fire in case they spooked any moose in the area, so they silently munched on a cold breakfast of sourdough biscuits and canned meat. Both would have given anything for a cup of hot, steaming coffee but decided the hunt took greater priority at that point and reluctantly fought off the urge.

Bill took his flashlight and looked for a good birch tree to fashion a horn for calling the moose. He cut a strip about three feet long and rolled it into a megaphone shape, pegging it in place with splinters of wood. His old friend, Johnny Crowtree, the Indian trapper, had taught him how to call a bull moose when he was a youngster and he had since practised on many occasions, even when not hunting. In fact it became a standard part of the entertainment whenever his folks were having a party and Bill would have to demonstrate his prowess. Bill's father frequently observed that he hoped it sounded sexy to a moose because it sounded like hell to him.

Bill had also learned from Johnny Crowtree that patience was the essence of moose hunting and that too frequent calling would repel a bull rather than attract it. Even though it was still dark, he started to make the melancholy, eerie call of a cow moose precisely at half-hour intervals and then kept strict silence. He had also learned that he should move around a little but stay in the same general area, so he and Mike silently launched the canoe and wrapped cloth around the paddles to muffle any sound when they touched the canoe. They paddled quietly around the edges of the swamp stopping every half hour to send the plaintive call echoing through the valley. They communicated only in muted whispers and by hand signal.

By four in the afternoon Bill concluded they were not going to have any success that day, so they turned the canoe for the campsite. They had almost reached the point where they could beach the canoe when the two of them were given an unexpected shot of adrenalin. A heart-stopping bellow, followed by a series of short, staccato grunts, reverberated down the valley. Bill knew in an instant that it was a big bull moose, having heard them call before during rutting season, but for Mike it was an unbelievable first experience. It was difficult to tell where the bellow originated from, since it echoed for what sounded like several minutes, but Bill finally concluded it came from the top of a ridge about a mile away.

Bill stopped paddling, reached for the birch bark horn and gave a very quiet call back, realizing that the most difficult part of the hunt was just beginning. Johnny had often told him that it wasn't too hard to get a bull to answer a call, but it was considerably more difficult to overcome its innate caution and get the animal to show itself. But Bill was not prepared for the violent reaction to his quiet call when the bull let out another deafening roar and started down the mountainside on the full run, breaking trees and snorting as it rapidly approached their location.

Mike, sitting in the front of the canoe, held the rifle, while Bill concentrated on keeping the canoe pointed towards the sound of the approaching bull, now crashing through the bush. It stopped just inside the edge of the forest. They could clearly hear the beast snorting and pawing at the ground, but couldn't see a sign of it to get a shot. Mike also remembered that moose have extremely poor eyesight, which is more than compensated for by their acute hearing and sense of smell.

"Get ready Mike," whispered Bill. "Make sure your rifle is ready. We'll only get one chance so don't blow it."

Mike nodded his head in acknowledgment and reaffirmed by gestures that the rifle was ready.

While just a few minutes passed, it seemed like an eternity as the bull continued to pace and snort just inside the tree line where Mike could not get a shot at it. Bill began to despair of ever enticing it out when he remembered one more trick that Johnny Crowtree had taught him. Carefully he picked up the small bailing can from the bottom of the canoe and filled it with water. He slowly poured it back into the river from a height of about three feet. The result was electric. The bull misinterpreted it as a cow urinating, as they frequently do during the rut. It came crashing out of the bush with its enormous rack thrown back against its shoulders. The bull was not more than seventy-five yards away, heading at full speed for the source of the alluring sounds in anticipation of doing its bit for the perpetuation of the moose herd. For an instant Mike was transfixed, the rifle at his shoulder, but apparently incapable of pulling the trigger. He thought he had overcome his buck fever years ago but the sight of that magnificent animal filled him with awe and temporary paralysis.

"If you don't pull that damned trigger he's going to seduce us any minute," whispered Bill as the distance between the men and the raging bull narrowed rapidly.

That snapped Mike out of his trance and he pulled the trigger four times in rapid succession, the explosions echoing throughout the valley in an incredible crescendo. The bull continued its headlong rush for about ten more paces, then suddenly stumbled and crashed in a tangle of flying hooves and antlers to disappear into the tall grass. The silence was awesome after the preceding seconds of thunderous turmoil. Mike, shaking visibly, the rifle still at his shoulder, was totally overwhelmed by the experience.

"Mike, we did it," yelled Bill. He paddled furiously for the bank as he shouted "Reload your rifle just in case it's not dead."

By now Mike had regained his composure to a degree but didn't wait for Bill to beach the canoe before jumping out into knee-deep water. He ignored the shock of the icy water and

Bill's yell that he had almost turned the canoe over. "Wait until I secure the canoe before you approach it, Mike," Bill cautioned in a shaky voice.

Cautiously they approached the inert carcass, lying on its side in the tall grass. Not willing to take a chance on the huge animal coming to life again at close quarters, Mike took careful aim behind the animal's ear and fired one more shot.

As soon as they were sure the moose was dead, the two hunters whooped and danced around like two uninhibited youngsters. The size of the animal was completely staggering from close quarters and they stared in awe at the massive antlers. Nevertheless, they realized that time had passed quickly and darkness was starting to descend and a light snow falling. They had to snap out of their hyped-up mood and start on the long and arduous task of cleaning the beast and cutting it up to transport back to the Narrows.

"Well, the fun's over, Mike. Now comes the hard work," Bill said, bringing them back to reality.

Since there were no trees nearby to hang it up, they had to gut the moose where it lay on the ground, which made the task doubly difficult. Darkness fell and they continued working by the feeble light of a small flashlight that Bill always carried in his survival kit. Finally, they concluded that they would have to suspend operations for the night, although they were reluctant to leave the carcass, in case there were any wolves or coyotes in the vicinity that could strip it overnight. As a measure of protection, they dragged the offal as far as possible from the carcass and lit a good big bonfire, fuelled by the biggest logs they could drag from the bush. They stumbled their way back to the tent, both so utterly exhausted they didn't even stop to wash before crawling into their sleeping bags and lapsing into a fitful sleep.

Mike was awake at dawn, and no longer being concerned about the smoke spooking a moose, he built a roaring fire. The smell of the brewing coffee awoke Bill more effectively than his trusty old alarm clock. He emerged from the cocoon of his sleeping bag fully dressed except for his down jacket which he shrugged on immediately to ward off the penetrating dawn cold.

The ground was white with a fresh blanket of snow and a skin of crystal clear ice covered the bay. Bill was anxious to get the moose skinned and quartered, so after gulping down two mugs of steaming black coffee he took a paddle and broke a path through the ice so that they could get the canoe as close as possible to the carcass to minimize the distance to carry the meat.

By now the carcass was stiff and covered with layer of snow which had probably protected it from marauding animals by killing the scent. The two men were still overwhelmed by the size of the animal and the magnitude of the task facing them.

"Well, as I said last night, the fun is over," observed Bill. "Now comes the tough part."

"This should be nothing compared to some of the construction we've handled this summer," Mike said reassuringly. "For a team like us it'll be a piece of cake."

Between them they managed to roll the moose on its side and both worked on removing the tough, heavily-haired hide. Bill estimated the moose would dress out at about 500 kilos and anticipated the prime meat would last them the entire winter.

It took most of the morning to skin and quarter the animal and struggling to transport the huge and awkward quarters to the canoe. When it was all loaded there was little freeboard remaining. As a final triumphant gesture they tied the antlers to the bow of the canoe resolving to mount them on the front of the cabin as an everlasting souvenir of their first successful hunting trip in search of their winter's meat supply.

It was well past noon by the time the moose and all the gear were loaded and secure, but they started back for Buffalo Narrows at a steady pace, helped by the meandering current.

✝ Chapter Three

Life was settling into a routine for the trappers. All the traps had been strategically distributed along the trapline ready to set when the animal population had been established by their individual tracks. The trappers felt good about having their winter meat supply already in the cache and there was an unusually light-hearted atmosphere around the cabin. At night they regaled each other with tales of hunting prowess, which had been embellished as the years went past and the telling repeated. Suzanne's good cooking also added to the sense of well-being.

One night, in his usual taciturn manner, Willie Bearpaw said, "We'll build shelters for a few days." In anticipation of the vicious winter storms that were in the offing, they took precautions each year to build shelters along the trapline at about two-mile intervals where they could take refuge until the storms abated and they could return to the cabin. "You stay here Suzanne." Although Suzanne had helped to lay out the traps, he did not feel that she could contribute too much to the building of the shelters. Although he did not disclose it he had an ulterior motive in mind when he thought of the fine meal she would have ready for them each evening.

Even though she had known the trappers since she was a little girl, she knew little about them having been away from the reserve for so many years. Although she could remember most of her childhood, there were many gaps in her memory that she was desperate to fill in. She plied them with questions every night about her parents and heritage. Being a blood relative and her favourite, she addressed most of her questions to Willie Bearpaw.

Suzanne's fondest memories of her childhood were of her maternal grandmother who had taken her into her house when her parents had forsaken her. Although she was a big moose of a woman weighing well over two hundred pounds, she was the epitome of maternal instinct and made up for the loss of Suzanne's own parents. She had a cure for everything and as a little girl Suzanne did not dare to disclose any ailments as she knew she would receive doses of foul tasting remedies. Willie and Paul laughed heartily when Suzanne recounted some of the remedies although they were still held in great esteem by the tribe. "Grandma thought she could cure anything and only took me to the reserve nurse as a last resort. I remember she used to give me warm goose grease and oolichan oil for coughs, rancid bear grease rubbed on my chest and back for colds, weak tea or mother's milk for snow blindness, black bear bile for liniment, beaver castors for poultices, and all kinds of plants and brews for aches and pains. For a headache she used to tie a bandana tight around my head and sometimes even stuck an eagle's feather in it. If I got any sores she would tie a beaver or muskrat fur around it until it itched so badly I had to tell her it was cured."

"I gotta tell you something about your grandma when you were a baby and your mother was sick," interjected Willie. "She always used to gather dry moss to line your diaper, and you started howling night and day. One day when she took off the diaper to change the moss, your little bum was all covered in red spots and she figured you had got something. When she looked close she found an ants' nest. They were asleep but when your bum warmed them up and they came back to life they started chewing on you."

They all howled with laughter at the thought but Suzanne followed up with a traumatic experience she had had as a little girl. "One day I looked in my grandma's bible and figured there was a hunk of parchment in there and started to open it up. My grandma came in and started screaming at me and cuffed my ear. When she calmed down a bit she explained that it was the amniotic sac from my birth that she had saved to protect me against the evil spirits. I dropped it on the floor and ran outside to be sick and before I knew it she was chasing me around the cabin trying to get some medicine into me."

Amongst her meagre possessions in the cabin Suzanne had a dog-eared and tattered book that was even burned on the edges after her husband had thrown it in the fire one night in a fit of anger. It was a copy of Chief Dan George's book *'My Heart Soars'*. It had been smuggled into the convent school by a parent who was allowed to make infrequent visits to her daughter, who was also Suzanne's best friend. When she left the convent, she passed the book along to Suzanne who guarded it as one of her most prized possessions. Every spare moment she would read it and carefully conceal it in her clothing for fear of discovery by the nuns. It seemed to provide her with her only link with her past and the words comforted her in her darkest hours and lifted her out of the severe depressions that would envelop her from time to time. Now that she had returned to her own people the words of the book lived and it was a daily ritual that she read parts of it. None of the trappers could read, but they got Suzanne to read aloud to them every night after supper. They sat spellbound as the beautiful words flowed from the pages and they each found themselves transported and communing with their ancestors.

After all the reminiscing and levity followed by Suzanne's reading, Willie led the way and they all retired for the night ready for an early start the next morning.

Since the first morning when she had slept in, Suzanne had made a point of being the first up every day. By the time the men rolled out of their bunks she had a good fire going, the kettle boiling for tea, and the big cast-iron frying pan heated up to cook breakfast. Each day she tried to have a variety of food and took great satisfaction in watching the men wolf it down to sustain them on the trail. She also packed them a lunch to take with them. This was a new experience since normally a handful of pemmican would have to suffice until they got back to the cabin at night.

Although they were stuffed with one of Suzanne's breakfasts, the trappers started out at a brisk pace down the trail, armed with axes to construct the shelters. Willie looked up at what seemed a steady stream of bush planes passing overhead in both directions. "Some more white guys helping us with animal preservation," observed Willie sarcastically. "I guess they can't see us pagan savages down here or they would be down to do us some more favours." Even Mye-Ook had a glimmer of a smile on his face at the thought.

"Those guys are so dumb they call us Indians 'cause some white guy got lost heading for India and figured he had got there when he landed here and saw our ancestors," added Paul with a smile.

As soon as the trappers were out of sight, Suzanne cleared up the cabin and put some fresh bannock on the stove to cook. The smell of the flour and bear grease as it cooked brought back floods of memories of her childhood, when her grandmother used to wrap the dough around sticks and they cooked it over the fire. The only trouble was that despite her warnings they never waited for it to cool properly and ate it while it was still hot, with treacle dripping from it, which invariably resulted in stomach cramps. They dared not complain to their grandmother or they would have been dosed with some foul-tasting potion that would destroy the delicious taste.

When the chores were done she went down the trail towards the river. She had chosen this spot as her own private temple. The black water murmuring between the banks white with snow had an almost mystical attraction for Suzanne. She could feel her soul being cleansed of the evil things that had happened to her in her past life. There was total silence except for the sounds of the river and the occasional drone of planes passing over. As she sat on a large rock protruding into the river Suzanne allowed herself to be soothed by the gentle sound of the water until she was drifting into a trance-like state. Here, by the river, the pain of her life drained away and left her feeling whole and peaceful again. It was for this reason that she came to this special place and she felt that little by little, her wounds were healing.

She lost all sense of time as she was transported out of her body and felt the presence of her beloved grandmother who seemed to talk to her in soothing words. Although she was filled with bitter memories of her youthful years she was reaching a stage of forgiveness for those who had taken her away from her people and subjected her to such indignities.

She emerged from her trance to find that it was getting dusk and she had no idea how long she had been there. She hurried back up the trail, so intent that she almost missed the insistent chattering from a tree branch above her head. It was the squirrel that she had befriended on the first day in the camp. Patiently she had lured the animal closer until finally it would eat the snacks she gave it from her hand. As she emulated its chatter with her lips, the squirrel ran down the tree trunk, looking for the treat Suzanne always brought him every day. She reached into her pocket for the piece of bannock she had saved from breakfast. When she squatted down and held out the morsel, the squirrel took the tidbit from her fingers and dashed back up into the sanctuary of the big spruce tree where he had stashed his winter store of food. At times like these Suzanne felt a pang of nostalgia for her grandfather who had taught her to communicate with wild animals.

Suzanne hurried to get the stove burning brightly and had a big pot of stew and fresh bannock ready when the trappers returned just as darkness fell. Without ceremony they all sat down at the table and waited to be fed.

"How did you make out with the shelters?" Suzanne asked.

"Good," answered Willie with a mouthful of food.

"We got two built," elaborated Paul.

"What kind of shelters do you build out there? I guess I should know 'cause I might have to spend the night in one of them."

"Sure ain't no palaces," Willie explained. "Just enough to keep the snow out if we got to spend the night. Mostly spruce boughs."

Willie belched loudly and headed for his bunk to signal the end of the discussion. Paul was unusually talkative and sensed a change in Suzanne. "What did you do today?" he asked.

"Mostly spent it by the river. I feel better because I feel like I talked to my grandma," she added shyly.

Paul looked at her sympathetically, then slowly continued, "The murmuring you hear from the river is our ancestors talking to us and if you listen you can hear anybody you want. It starts on the big mountain where all the spirits of our people go when they die. Sometimes they get mad at those white guys flying their planes over the mountain, and that's when you hear thunder and see lightning. That's why we call it the Jisah-Seebee, the mighty spirit river." As usual, Paul had a spiritual explanation for everything.

When Paul and Mye-Ook also rolled into their bunks, Suzanne lingered for a few moments and reflected on the day. She felt a renewed link with her native heritage and an unaccustomed peace descended on her as she disappeared into her bunk, but she was careful to also say her prayers to the white God that she had come to respect in her years in the convent. She fell into a peaceful sleep immediately.

Chapter Four

It was more than three days since Bill and Mike had returned from their successful hunting trip. With able assistance from Jennifer, they had cut the moose into manageable portions and packed it up into the meat cache Bill had constructed in the forks of a big spruce tree thirty yards from the house. The meat would be safe from predators and the onset of winter guaranteed power-free refrigeration until the spring thaw.

The second day back at Buffalow Narrows, Bill's trained ear detected the unmistakeable sound of a Cessna 185 heading their way. After a few minutes his aural early warning system was confirmed by the sight of a dot above the treeline which quickly materialized into a red and yellow 185 on an approach into their bay. Bill immediately recognized it as CF-BGS which belonged to Ross Stuart, an old friend. Ross was also a former air force pilot who had now been freelancing in the north for five years. Bill had encountered Ross a few times during the frantic days of the hunter fly-in, just long enough to tell him briefly about his house at Buffalo Narrows and to show off his Beaver.

Ross set the 185 down on the glassy waters of the bay so skillfully that it was virtually impossible to detect the transition from flight to float, except for the wake left by the floats. He was heading right for the dock at what appeared to be excessive speed when he chopped the throttle and glided to a dead stop on the other side of the dock from Bill's Beaver.

Bill caught the trailing rope on the 185's floats and secured it to a cleat just as the door opened and Ross leaped out with his usual ebullient greeting.

Ross seemed to virtually unwind as he climbed out of the 185 and stretched to his full height of six feet three inches. He was the epitome of the typical bush pilot, with a battered ball cap on his head, a badly worn leather jacket with fur collar, and tight-fitting jeans stuck in the tops of his high-laced leather boots. He was tanned almost to a leather appearance, and moved with the lithe ease of good physical condition, without a spare pound on his frame. His face, although angular, was ruggedly good looking and his clear brown eyes were direct and open.

"How're you doing old buddy?" bellowed Ross.

"Super, thanks, Ross. Welcome to Buffalo Narrows," responded Bill. "What brings you to our private paradise?"

"If you're interested I can put some great business your way. I have a friend who works for a mining outfit and they're starting exploration in the Sustut Lake area. They've hired me to fly in most of their people but I can't handle some of the bigger gear. If you're interested you should be able to get about 60 hours out of it. They pay $190 an hour, cash on the barrelhead, so it's good business."

"If you weren't so ugly, you big galoot, I'd kiss you. The only thing I have lined up at the moment is that hunter pickup early next week but I could tie that in with the trips into Sustut and eliminate the dead-heading. It couldn't come at a better time 'cause I have to take my Beaver out to convert to skis for the winter and didn't know how I was going to pay for it. How soon would we start?" asked Bill.

"Right away," replied Ross. "They want to get all their gear into camp and set up before freeze-up."

Bill turned to Mike and said, "I'd planned to fly you out after the hunter pick-up, Mike, but this job will keep me going for at least two weeks. So, either you stay until I finish or I can take you to the railhead on my first pick-up."

"I think you're in pretty good shape for the winter now," said Mike, "and Sue will be anxious to get me back after her lonely summer, so I'll come out with you and hop on a train home."

Ross, anxious to get back before dark, was already on the floats of his 185.

"OK, I'll meet you at the Government Dock at Sioux Falls at nine o'clock tomorrow morning and we'll get you a contract and the gear moving as soon as possible."

Bill untied the floats of the 185 and gave it a shove away from the dock. Instantly the engine burst into life and Ross opened the throttle fully, almost blasting Bill and Mike into the water.

With a huge boyish grin, Ross waved as he got the 185 up on the step and into the air in minimum distance, leaving behind a trail of spray and vapour. In no time he was out of sight over the treetops heading southeast for Sioux Falls. Ross flew as he lived — always at full throttle.

As soon as Ross was out of sight, Bill and Mike hurried back to the house to get Mike's gear all packed and ready to depart at dawn the next morning. When they heard the news, Jennifer and the children were somewhat dismayed. They had come to accept Mike as a full-time member of the family and had not anticipated the hurried departure. Nevertheless, they appreciated how important it was for Bill to get some income before winter and they all pitched in with the packing and transport of bags and equipment down to the Beaver.

"We're sure going to miss you, old timer," said Bill with a catch in his voice.

Mike could not restrain the tears welling up in his eyes as he impulsively hugged Bill when they had finished loading the Beaver. "This is the most unforgettable summer of my life and I never dreamed I would have to retire to do all the things I've always wanted to do." They walked back to the house, each buried in his own thoughts.

That night they celebrated with moose tenderloin steaks grilled over the fire and topped with some of Jennifer's precious dehydrated mushrooms that she had hidden for just such a special occasion. But Mike capped the occasion by producing a bottle of champagne from his duffle bag.

"I was saving this for our first homecoming with Sue here as well, but we'll do it again when she comes up later. Meanwhile, let's toast the success of Buffalo Narrows Airways and your happy home. In fact I'd like to propose a name for your house. It is 'TOHTOHLAH', which is an Indian word meaning 'This is our place, and we are entitled to live here.'"

"I'll certainly drink to that," responded Bill. "That's a great idea and I like the name. What do you think, gang?"

Jennifer and the children agreed in unison and 'Tohtohlah' was adopted unanimously as their home title.

Mike beamed since he felt he had a real stake in the house. "That's great," he said. "Now I know what my winter project will be — I'll get a nice piece of yellow cedar and carve a nameplate for over your door. We'll mount it next year when Sue and I come up in the spring." With that they clinked glasses and raised them in a heartfelt toast.

Everyone retired early in preparation for the next day's activities and it seemed like minutes before the alarm clock exploded at 4.30 a.m..

After collecting his thoughts for a few more minutes, Bill fired up the wood stove with the kindling stored in the oven overnight and put the coffee water on to boil. He left Jennifer snuggled under the down comforter and gently shook Mike awake. Unlike Bill, Mike was the type who was instantly awake and hopped right out of bed in his long johns to help Bill with breakfast. Breakfast was Mike's favourite meal and

70

KITCHENER PUBLIC LIBRARY

he had established a reputation as a great pancake maker which the children loved.

They had made him promise the night before that he would waken them for one last pancake breakfast with Grandad. When the griddle was hot and the batter mixed, he went in to waken all three children to share his pancakes, even though it was still only 5 a.m. and totally dark.

Jennifer joined the family for breakfast, wrapped in her warm housecoat. She felt a strong bond with the two most important men in her life and was unusually subdued at the prospect of them both leaving at once. Mike had carved his niche in the family during the summer construction of the house and she had almost reverted to the same dependance on his solid support that she had had when she was a little girl. She knew that his departure would leave a tremendous void with the children, who loved to sit on his lap and read books or to listen to his never-ending store of tales. He provided a great mental stimulus for them, particularly with their correspondence courses in school. He was always patient and Jennifer often wondered why she had not inherited more of this quality when she became frustrated with the children. She was, however, glad that she had inherited his inner strength that fortified her against the thought of staying alone with the children in this wilderness.

Bill finished his second cup of coffee and said, "Okay, guys. Time to say goodbye to Grandpa. Let's all tell him how we have appreciated his help and presence all summer and how much we'll miss him. He has a place in Tohtohlah whenever he wants to come back. But don't make your goodbyes too long 'cause we have to get going. I'm so stuffed with Grandpa's pancakes I don't know if we'll be able to get the Beaver in the air."

With tears in his eyes, Mike embraced everyone in turn and huskily added, "I feel great knowing you've got a fine house and a good supply of food. It'll take me days to tell Grandma about everything. The last thing I want you young guys to do is promise you'll all keep up with your school work and write

71

to us. You must also obey and help your Mum as much as possible when you are alone."

"We promise, Grandpa." The boys looked uncomfortable but Dianne clung to Mike's neck, reluctant to let him leave.

Bill was anxious to be in the air at first light. He had difficulty containing his excitement about the first solid contract he had arranged and the prospect of establishing a good financial base for the winter, even though it meant leaving Jennifer and the children alone for the first time. He also anticipated that this job could establish his reputation and more work would follow. His long-term goal was to have the Beaver completely paid off within five years, but this would require a lot of hustling and a minimum of unproductive time for the aircraft. Now that the family was securely housed and established he could concentrate all his efforts on the business.

There was a tearful farewell as Bill and Mike donned their outdoor clothes and packed the rest of the baggage down to the dock. Looking back they could see Jennifer and the children clustered around the front window with the warm glow of the oil lamps silhouetting them. The white smoke from the chimney against the still dark sky completed the scene of tranquility.

Since it was still dark, Bill carried out his external inspection of the Beaver with the aid of a flashlight. The plane was covered with a light coating of snow, so Bill and Mike used long-handled brooms to clear it off the control surfaces. They untied the floats and pushed away from the dock just as the first glimmer of light was appearing on the eastern horizon.

By this time Bill had completed the engine run-up and internal checks. There was sufficient light to discern the shoreline of Buffalo Narrows, so Bill pointed the Beaver towards the breaking dawn and opened the throttle with a deafening roar. For a moment the Beaver seemed glued to the water but gradually picked up speed as it came up on the step of the floats. In the cold morning air the propeller bit hard and pulled them into the air without any sensation of becoming airborne. To Bill this was always one of the highlights of flying, and invariably brought to mind the words of the poem *'High Flight'* by John Gillespie Magee Jr., a young pilot who had been killed during the war. He had memorized the poem when he was just a small boy and suddenly started to recite it, much to Mike's delight:

> *"Oh, I have slipped the surly bonds*
>   *of earth,*
> *And danced the skies on laughter -*
>   *silvered wings;*
> *Sunward I've climbed, and joined*
>   *the tumbling mirth*
> *Of sun-split clouds, and done a*
>   *hundred things*
> *You have not dreamed of, wheeled*
>   *and soared and swung,*
> *High in the sunlit silence, Hovering*
>   *there,*
> *I've chased the shouting wind along,*
>   *and flung*
> *My eager craft through footless halls*
>   *of air,*
> *Up, up the long, delirious, burning*
>   *blue,*
> *I've topped the windswept heights with*
>   *easy grace,*
> *Where never lark, or even eagle flew,*
> *And, while with silent, lifting mind*
>   *I've trod,*
> *The high untrespassed sanctity of space*
> *Put out my hand, and touched the*
>   *face of God."*

Mike gave him a thumbs up sign as Bill handed control over to him as soon as they were airborne. He still loved to fly even after all these years, although he no longer kept up a current licence nor would he trust himself with takeoffs and landings on floats. But once airborne he did a good job of flying while Bill did the navigation. Mike always maintained that flying was akin to riding a bicycle — once learned it was never forgotten.

The half-hour trip to Sioux Falls was uneventful and at that hour the air was calm and still, making for smooth flying. Bill took over the controls again as they approached the large, sheltered bay with the government wharf projecting well into the lake. Bill flew the Beaver on to the water and taxied up to the wharf where Mike jumped out on the float and secured the lines. They unloaded Mike's gear on the dock and packed it to the end where they could phone for a taxi to transport them to the railroad depot. Since there was no train until late evening, Mike checked his baggage and returned with Bill to the Big Horn Hotel where the mining company had established a temporary office.

After coffee, Bill left Mike to phone Sue and warn her of his imminent return while he went off to a room on the second floor to sign the contract for the transport of the mining gear.

A hand-painted sign pinned to the outside of the door announced the presence of the Double Eagle Mining Co. Exploration Division, and invited visitors to walk right in. Accepting the invitation, Bill rapped twice on the door and walked into a room cluttered with maps and miscellaneous gear in boxes and crates.

There were four occupants, picking their way gingerly through the obstacle course of crates and equipment, checking it against lists pinned to clipboards. There were three men, two Bill judged to be in their late twenties and one in his mid-thirties. All were bearded and wearing the traditional check shirts and the jeans of the mining fraternity. The fourth was a young woman, also in her late twenties, with short-cropped blonde hair. Bill could tell at a glance she had spent most of her life in the outdoors, judging by her fresh complexion and suntanned arms.

Bill could not help looking at her. She exuded confidence and competence in a world dominated by males. He was sure that she could hold her own amongst the often chauvinistic geologists and miners. He sensed that she and Jennifer would have an instant empathy for each other and resolved to extend an invitation to visit them in Buffalo Narrows when the opportunity arose.

One of the men stepped forward and extended a greeting hand to Bill.

"Hi, I'm Jesse Mathew, chief geologist for Double Eagle. Pardon the mess, but we're checking off the load of gear that came in on the train last night to make sure we got it all. This is Mark Douglas and Brent Sherwood. The one without the beard is Christie Richardson."

Bill shook hands all around and introduced himself, confirming that he had been contacted by Ross Stuart to fly their gear into Sustut.

"Ross told me you'd be in this morning. In fact he took off out of here at dawn to fly in the advance party to set up base camp and a shelter for our gear. Most of our gear's too bulky to fit in his 185, so it felt real good to hear he'd lined up a Beaver. I have the contract all ready here if you'd like to read it through and then sign at the bottom. How soon could you start, Bill?"

"How about today?" Bill replied. "You couldn't have got me at a better time since I'm free until the hunter fly-out next week. Even then I can tie the two things in together and pick up a load of hunters each trip back from Sustut. Forgive me if I sound a little eager, but I can also use the money having just finished my house at Buffalo Narrows and a payment coming up on the Beaver next month."

"That would be great!" exclaimed Jesse. "We can't start until we get our instruments and equipment into Sustut. We'd like to get a rough survey of the claim completed before the heavy snows arrive and the lake freezes over."

"I should have added that we're doing a detailed evaluation of a claim staked by a Czech immigrant. The samples he brought out are really promising, and we'll be deciding the commercial potential of the claim."

"Not only that, but I intend to do my personal evaluation of the fishing in Sustut," added Christie. "I hear it's one of the best steelhead areas in the country."

"I've never personally fished it but I've heard some spectacular tales about it," observed Bill. "You're obviously a keen fisherman. Or is it fisherperson?"

"Love it," laughed Christie. "My Dad got me started when I was barely walking. He used to pack me miles on his back through the bush to reach his favourite fishing holes. That's probably why I became a mining geologist — so I could indulge my passion for fishing while earning a living."

"She's much better with a fishing rod than a surveyor's rod," laughed Mark.

"And she's also become an expert at reeling in unsuspecting bachelors, poor fish," added Brent.

Christie playfully swatted at the pair of them with a roll of maps she was holding until Jesse halted the horseplay with a sharp whistle.

"OK, you guys. Save your energy for getting this gear sorted and establish priorities for what goes first. You think you'll do a trip today, Bill?" Jesse asked.

"If I can be in the air by noon I should be able to get in one round trip by dark. It's 135 air miles to Sustut, so it'll be roughly an hour's flying time each way plus unloading at the far end."

"We have a crew of four in at the lake now so that should speed up the unloading. If you plan to go today we already have a good load in a warehouse on the dock, all of which we'll need early in our operations," Mark interjected. "We can help you load for this first trip."

Always the cautious type, Bill scanned the contract confirming the rates and liabilities to be assumed by him as the carrier. The first thing he had done when he bought the Beaver was to make sure he had complete insurance coverage, both for the plane and liability for passengers and baggage.

"Looks good to me," confirmed Bill. "The sooner I get started the better." The formalities out of the way, the five of them headed down the dock to where the Beaver was tied up, making small talk on the way.

As they passed through the hotel lobby they ran into Mike who was just emerging from the phone booth. Bill introduced his new associates and excitedly confirmed the consummation of the contract. Mike was delighted and advised Bill that he had contacted Sue and she would meet him off the train the following afternoon. "Since I've got to wait until 8:30 p.m. for the train I'll volunteer to help you with the first load."

Bill was grateful for the offer as Mike had gained a lot of experience packing the Beaver to the limit when they were flying house materials into Buffalo Narrows. With the six of them working, he should comfortably meet his noon departure time. The weather also looked pretty good with a low overcast but excellent visibility towards the north, the general heading towards Sustut. They all piled into Jesse's company station wagon and headed for the warehouse on the wharf.

Bill had carefully calculated the weight and balance figures for the aircraft and filled the fuel tanks to provide enough range for the round trip to Sustut plus thirty minutes reserve in case he encountered any bad weather en route. The altitude at Sustut required a long take off run so he wanted to minimize fuel load remaining at the lake.

The load was comprised of a wide variety of sizes and shapes which Bill sorted according to weight and cubic content before starting to load. Some of the longer items like drill rods and core boxes were set aside to be tied externally on the struts and floats. With Mike's help he removed the passenger door and co-pilot's and rear seats to maximize available space for the boxes of instruments that were to be carried inside the cabin. Bill stowed the boxes as they were handed in to him, filling every available nook and cranny. He carefully noted the weight of each item to make sure he stayed within his cargo limit since he had to climb to 9,000 feet en route to clear the pass through the White Goat Mountains into Sustut.

When the cabin was packed to capacity, there was just room for Bill to climb over the load into the left hand pilot's seat. He felt a sudden empathy for Charles Lindbergh having seen the Spirit of St. Louis in the Smithsonian Institute during a visit to Washington. The prime difference was that Bill had minimized his fuel load while Lindbergh had filled every spare nook and cranny with gasoline for the trip across the Atlantic. Bill couldn't even conceive of sitting in that cramped little space for thirty-three and a half hours. His backside protested after three hours in the Beaver without standing up to stretch.

It was just 11:00 a.m. when Bill expressed himself satisfied with the load so he climbed out on the wharf for a final farewell with Mike. Mike had even suggested to Bill that he accompany him on the trip but Bill diplomatically refused his offer by pointing out that if they were delayed in any way, Mike would miss his train and reunion with Sue. Moreover, he delicately added that Mike's weight was almost worth the equivalent of gold in instruments for the mining crews.

The tears welled up in Mike's eyes as he squeezed Bill's hand and in an uncharacteristic physical show of affection put his arms around Bill and with a voice choked with emotion added, "Damnit lad, if I'd had a son of my own I would have wanted him to be just like you. Thanks for letting me share an unforgettable experience with you this summer. It's going to be a very mundane existence in the city this winter, so be prepared for us to be back in the spring. Now that the house is livable, maybe you could tolerate both Sue and me for a while."

Bill was overwhelmed by Mike's unbridled affection and found that he too had difficulty choking back the tears.

"I can never thank you enough for the physical and moral support you've given us this summer. We simply couldn't have done it without you. And that's not to mention the help with getting the winter's meat supply in. Needless to say,

'Tohtohlah' is just as much home for you and Sue as it is to us, so we'll look forward to your return with the robins in the spring."

The mining geologists were engaged in idle chatter a few feet away trying to appear totally disinterested in the emotional scene, but Bill noticed that Christie also had tears in her eyes as she unwittingly became drawn into the feeling of the moment. It reminded her of the close family ties that she enjoyed and the emotion of her farewells when she had left to go to college and later on her protracted mining evaluation trips.

Bill turned away trying to re-assume his businesslike air as he hopped on to the floats of the Beaver and untied the securing lines before struggling into the cockpit.

The engine burst into shuddering life, and as he taxied away from the wharf he waved at the small group watching his departure. As he taxied he performed the engine and pre-flight checks. Finally he turned into wind and opened the throttle to full power.

With the full load, his take-off run was unusually long but once he had the Beaver up on the step he hauled it off the water and started milking up flaps to increase speed and start his climb. The group on the wharf watched until the Beaver was just a dot above the horizon as it climbed on course for Sustut.

Once airborne Bill turned on to a heading of 340 degrees on a direct track to the pass through White Goat Mountain range. He throttled back to an economical 300 feet per minute cruise climb which would get him to the required 9,000 feet altitude to transit the pass in 30 minutes, leaving him 15 minutes leeway before entering the mountains. With his heavy load he wanted to minimize the time he could encounter turbulence on the lee side of the mountains.

The sky was overcast but forward visibility was excellent so that Bill had no difficulty picking out the salient landmarks along his route. There was evidence of fresh snow on the ground, particularly at higher altitude, heralding the onset of winter. Looking down as he flew over one of the myriad of lakes en route he saw a large vee of Canada geese in ragged formation heading for their wintering grounds. Bill admired the instinct that had regulated their evolution by taking advantage of the best of seasons in their annual migration. Despite their claimed mental superiority, he mused, human beings had only recently started to emulate their feathered friends' migration habits with their annual flights south to escape the hardships of winter in the northern hemisphere.

The Beaver was running beautifully and Bill's trained eye scanned the instruments in a methodical sequence, noting temperatures, pressures and performance figures. He felt grateful for finding such an excellent and reliable aircraft, particularly when he looked down at the solid green carpet of timber punctuated only by the sparkling lakes and rivers. Bill never lost his sense of wonder at the grandeur and magnitude of this country and the courage and endurance of the early explorers and trappers who had first penetrated this wilderness on foot and by canoe. The development of the aircraft had caused a virtual explosion of travel into the wilderness in relative comfort. With this easy access had come the inevitable abuse of nature, and Bill was appalled when he flew into what appeared to be a pristine lake, only to find evidence of man's desecrations in the form of tin cans and miscellaneous garbage strewn along the shorelines. The ugly scars of mining operations were becoming more prevalent and Bill suddenly felt a twinge of guilt that he was contributing to the destruction of this wilderness paradise by supporting mining exploration.

On reaching 9,000 feet, Bill levelled off the Beaver and headed directly for the pass through the White Goat Mountains which were now clearly visible, although the peaks were shrouded in clouds. Snow extended well down the sides of the mountains and the freezing level was clearly distinguishable as the white snow abruptly turned into the dark green of the forest. This too would shortly turn to a blanket of white when the freezing level started its inexorable move down into the valleys and lakes. In fact a number of the lakes at higher levels were already showing evidence of ice creeping out from the shorelines, which ultimately would form a solid cap for the winter.

As the Beaver approached the pass, the expected turbulence started to build as the downslope wind effect increased. With the heavy load Bill worked hard to maintain straight and level flight, but he had no qualms about the ability of the Beaver to take a lot of punishment. It was a great old workhorse with an incomparable safety and reliability record around the world. It was the bush pilot's Cadillac and the epitome of rugged and reliable transportation in the wilderness areas of the world.

As he entered the pass Bill noted a herd of white mountain goats disturbed by the engine noise and leaping from rocky ledges to the slide area running down into the valley. He marvelled at their incredible agility and sure-footedness, and often wondered what they could find to sustain themselves in this apparently barren area well above the timber line. There appeared to be about thirty goats in the herd, ranging from the magnificent billys with their black horns and white coats reaching to the ground, to the current year kids leaping and frolicking along behind their mothers.

As expected, the turbulence increased as the Beaver flew further into the pass with the mountain peaks closing in on both sides. Bill expertly used the controls to maintain level flight about five hundred feet above the canyon floor. Frequently he changed the throttle setting to counter the downdrafts created by the surface wind being buffeted off the rock-strewn canyon floor.

Without warning the Beaver was caught in a vicious downdraft that turned it virtually upside-down and started it plunging towards the canyon floor. Bill immediately applied full power and opposite rudder and aileron to regain level flight. The aircraft responded in a slow rolling motion but continued descending at an alarming rate as if being drawn by a giant hand. Bill struggled desperately to avoid the aircraft going into a stall, which would force him to lower the nose to regain flying speed, thereby increasing the rate of descent. Although working furiously to overcome gravity and keep the Beaver flying, Bill was mesmerized by the rock-strewn canyon floor that was coming up to meet him in what appeared to be slow motion. His heart was pounding and perspiration started to run down his face. For the first time in his flying career he felt nauseous, and for a fleeting second he had an overwhelming urge to give up the struggle and let the Beaver carry him to certain destruction.

In the midst of this desperate struggle for survival, Bill suddenly had a flashback to his days as a young student. His flying instructor, although only a few years older than Bill, appeared to be endowed with infinite wisdom and consummate flying skill. On one of their early flights together the instructor turned to Bill and said, "You know, I've concluded that flying is comprised of hours of sheer boredom punctuated by moments of stark terror." Bill, with a few thousand hours of relatively routine flying and few emergency situations, was now living those words. Never before had he physically experienced the moments of stark terror that now confronted him.

Somewhere in his inner person Bill suddenly found a reserve that was triggered by an innate instinct for survival. He snapped out of his feeling of resignation and despair with a renewed anger that this was actually happening to him. He had lost many good friends in flying accidents but he had never even considered that one day he would be placed in a position that could have lethal results.

The Beaver was still sinking at an alarming rate even though Bill had applied full power and he could see that he would crash into the canyon floor in seconds. In a last desperate attempt to keep the aircraft flying he dropped the flaps to the fully down position. The effect was dramatic as it changed the attitude of the aircraft immediately and created a ballooning effect, halting the rapid descent momentarily. Simultaneously the aircraft lurched violently as the right float struck a large rock protruding from the side of the canyon and bounced back into the air. Bill fought to regain control as the aircraft began a slow turn away from the canyon wall, but it was immediately evident that the Beaver had sustained serious damage and it was all Bill could do to try and hold up the wing on the damaged side. Although he was unable to see it Bill correctly surmised that some of the equipment that had been tied to the float had torn loose and damaged the tailplane.

The glancing blow had turned the aircraft through 180 degrees and Bill was relieved to see that he was now reversing his path into the canyon and heading back towards the entrance, just feet above the canyon floor. Even with full opposite rudder and aileron, Bill was unable to control a slow turn to the right, but the floor of the canyon began to fall away giving him more airspace to maneuver out of the canyon. It was like suspended animation as Bill realized he was still flying despite what was obviously a mortal wound to the aircraft.

Slowly and cautiously Bill began experimenting to determine the residual capability of the Beaver. First he tried to reduce the drag by raising the flaps a little at a time while maintaining full throttle. He was relieved to note the airspeed starting to build away from the stalling speed. He knew that he would be incapable of recovering from a stall with the limited control available to him, so it was crucial that he maintain a safety margin. At the same time he did not want to increase the airspeed too much as it could aggravate the damage to the control surfaces which were just giving him marginal stability.

Although only seconds had elapsed Bill was mentally and physically drained; only the adrenalin released by his peril allowed him to cope with the situation. He appreciated how a drowning man could reach a state of euphoria and give up the struggle. He was almost at that point but that last vestige of survival instinct kept him fighting, determined that he still wanted survival more than permanent peace.

Despite applying full opposite rudder and aileron, the Beaver continued in a slow turn to the right which, for the time being, was creating a path away from the mountain. However, Bill also realized that the aircraft would ultimately turn back towards the mountain and the possibility of crashing into the deep side of the canyon. Cautiously he eased back on the throttle, which caused the Beaver to go into a slow, descending turn towards a long valley that intersected the canyon from the west and away from his original intended path. By easing off pressure on the rudder the turn was accelerated so that he was able to exercise some measure of control over the radius of the turn. He therefore found that by accelerating the turn towards the mountain he could reduce the distance to the steep slopes. When turning away from the mountain he applied rudder and aileron with all his strength which flattened the turn and moved him progressively further away from the mountainside.

Already he had lost three thousand feet of altitude, but as he increased the distance from the mountain he could afford to go lower in the hope that he would increase stability of the aircraft. His left leg and both arms ached from the constant pressure since the trim tabs had obviously been damaged and were totally ineffective. He wondered how much longer he could endure this excruciating pain before he had to relieve his aching leg and arms. Doing so would almost certainly put the Beaver into an uncontrollable turn, or even worse, a spin from which he knew he could not recover.

His wide arc carried him over a small lake with a river flowing from the south end. The lake was big enough to accommodate the Beaver, but he couldn't conceive how he could carry out a successful landing even if he could control the direction of the aircraft. He also was aware that his right float was seriously damaged which would make a landing on water extremely hazardous. Nevertheless, he decided that the lake offered more chance of survival than crashing into the heavy timber, so he manipulated throttle and rudder alternately to try to position the aircraft on or close to the lake.

Cautiously he reduced power and started a slow, spiral descent trying to estimate where his arc would intercept the lake. His left leg was virtually numb from the pressure he exerted on the rudder pedal but the moment he eased off pressure the turning momentum accelerated alarmingly. The boxes of freight that cluttered the cockpit further complicated his efforts.

The altimeter showed him passing through 3,000 feet above sea level, which he estimated was about 1,000 feet above the lake. By applying bursts of power he was able to better control the rate of turn in addition to speed of descent to the lake which appeared to be about a mile long and surrounded by tall spruce trees, except where the river exited, leaving a sharp cleavage. Bill decided that if he could control his approach on the final arc through the clearing in the trees over the river, he might be able to complete the turn into the lake without striking the trees on the shoreline.

Looking back over his shoulder Bill could still see the river, so he reduced power and pressure on the rudder to accelerate the turn and reduce the radius. His heart was thumping in his chest and he desperately needed a drink to ease his parched throat. The pain in his left leg and arms was almost unbearable and he realized he had to make one last desperate gamble to get down before he totally lost control.

The Beaver was in a forty five degree bank as it spiralled down towards the lake and Bill planned to kick the rudder with all his remaining strength to try and raise the wing before hitting the lake. Glancing at the instruments he noted that his airspeed was over one hundred and twenty miles per hour so he dropped the flaps to increase drag and reduce speed. This pitched the aircraft into a nose-down attitude but did reduce his speed to less than one hundred miles per hour.

The Beaver was now less than one hundred feet above the treetops which were coming up at an alarming rate. Bill applied maximum pressure on the rudder pedal to raise the wing and reduce the rate of turn. Almost mechanically he cut the engine switches and turned off the fuel selectors to minimize the possibility of fire.

The sudden loss of power made the Beaver drop rapidly and Bill could see that he was not going to make it to the lake. For a fleeting moment he considered trying to restart the engine but immediately realized it was futile and resigned himself to the inevitable. In a flash the lower wing caught the upper branches of a tall spruce tree, cartwheeling the aircraft in a rending, crashing mass into the surrounding forest. Bill was violently thrown forward by the impact, momentarily aware of the horrendous sound of tearing metal and objects flying in the cockpit. Relief was instant as he plunged into unconsciousness.

Chapter Five

The smell of fresh bannock and moose nose frying in bear grease filled the small cabin and elicited groans and creaks from the men's bunks. Willie Bearpaw was the first to emerge in his long johns, scratching his ample belly and ruffling his hair. The other two were hard on his heels as the lure of the delicious aroma was stronger than the desire to stay in bed for a while longer. Without dressing they sat at the trestle table and were ready to eat without any more formalities.

"Holy smokes, Suzanne, what're you cookin'?" enquired Willie.

"Just something to get you started for the day on the trapline," she answered as she brought the big cast-iron frying pan to the table and served up ample portions on each plate. "That bear grease is some good for cooking," she added.

The previous day, Paul was setting traps when he noticed steam rising from a hole at the bottom of a tree. When he pulled back the snow and leaves covering the hole he found a large den with a hibernating black bear occupying it. Without disturbing the sleeping bear, he carefully took his rifle off his back and shot the bear once through the head. It didn't move and looked as if it was still sleeping.

Paul tried to extricate it himself but it was too heavy for one man, so he fired three more shots in rapid succession to alert the other trappers who were also setting out traps nearby. The first one on the scene was Mye-Ook, who beamed with pleasure when he saw the prize. He and Paul were just trying to pull the bear out of the hole by its front paws when Willie came trotting up to join them. It took the three of them all their strength and when they finally got it out of the hole, they found it was a big boar weighing about two hundred kilos.

It took them more than two hours to clean and skin the bear, which had a thick, jet black coat. They cut the meat into manageable portions and started the long pack back to the cabin. Once again, since Mye-Ook was the strongest, he carried the skin on top of his pack while the other two carried the prime pieces of meat. They had left Suzanne in the camp because she could not help much setting out the traps, which was a skilled task. When they arrived back at the cabin she was elated with the prize.

The men were consuming the feast with little conversation and when they had finished their meal Paul belched loudly in appreciation and observed, "The Spirits are sure being good to us this year, and it's a good omen for our trapping. Like the moose, that bear was left there for us as a gift from Schetxwen, the God of bears. He and the Indians are related and he looks after us in the forest when we need food and clothing."

Willie nodded in agreement, not wanting to question something he did not really understand. All he knew was that he was grateful to the Spirits for their help. He couldn't help but feel that having Suzanne along also had something to do with it — he thought she was a good omen that had come into his life.

"Okay, guys, we'd better hit the trail. We gotta get back to the trapline and get our traps out before any more snow comes. There was sure lots of tracks around yesterday in that new snow, so we can see the best places to put the traps."

"Want me to come with you and help?" enquired Suzanne as she started to clean up the table.

"No, you stay here and scrape the bear skin. Then it has to be nailed on the side of the cabin to dry. I'm going to give that one to the chief for a new ceremonial robe. You know how to tan it when it's dry, Suzanne?"

"My grandmother always used to do it but she never showed me how."

"Well, we're lucky we got you along 'cause only a woman can do it. When it's dry you have to pee on it and rub it into the skin every day. Man's pee don't work so you'll have to do it."

Suzanne laughed, not knowing whether to believe Willie, but Paul backed him up. "No foolin'. The bear gets his skin from his mother when he's born so you gotta use the same stuff that was inside her or it don't work." Suzanne, anxious to regain some of her lost Indian heritage, reluctantly accepted the instructions.

At last she was starting to realize that she had to accept some things without question.

The men put on their mocassins and light jackets and started back down the trail towards White Goat Mountain, where they had left off the day before. The days were getting shorter so they had to start as soon as there was enough light to see the trail. Once they got all the traps set they would divide up the line and follow a set pattern every day, starting from each end and meeting in the middle.

They stopped for a lunch of bannock and cold sliced moose tongue beside a hot fire where they brewed their tea in the smoke-blackened tin. As they were relaxing after lunch they heard a plane going overhead in the direction of the mountain and spotted him just under the low clouds. "Must be some-thing' doin' in Sustut," observed Paul. "They seem to be flyin' in there regular. They'll sure be messin' up the huntin' and trappin' in there too. That used to be part of our territory 'til they stuck us on the reserve. The Kwakwalas used to have a summer camp in there and fish and hunt. Now Indians never go in there. Only damn white men."

Willie grunted in agreement as he watched the plane disappear towards the notch. "Well, let's go guys, we still got a lotta traps to lay."

After a few minutes they heard the plane again but could not see it. It sounded as if it was going in circles with the engine roaring more than normal. At one point Willie caught a glimpse of it turning into the valley ahead of them and then lost it again below the tree line. He decided to ignore it and get on with his trap setting when it suddenly caught his attention again as the engine stopped. He judged that it was somewhere near No Name Lake, a small lake where he sometimes trapped beaver, but he had never seen planes go in there before. It was surrounded by high trees and did not seem long enough for a plane to land.

Consumed with curiosity, he blew on his whistle to summon the other two, who had not travelled far since their lunch break. They appeared on the trail very shortly and Willie shouted, "Did you hear that plane near No Name Lake?"

"Sure did," replied Paul. "Sounded like his engine quit. Sure wouldn't be trying to land on that lake. I figured I heard trees breaking right after. Maybe we should go take a look."

"That's a good walk in there and we're really behind getting our traps out. It's already afternoon and it'll get dark early with those low clouds. Looks like snow too," observed Willie. "But I guess we'd better go see what happened. There's been some funny things happen on this trip, so maybe this is another. Mye-Ook, you run on ahead and see what you find, then maybe we won't have to come all the way if there ain't nothin' to it."

Mye-Ook loped off down the trail ahead of them towards No Name Lake while the other two walked at a more leisurely pace. "Trouble is we're gettin' farther away from the cabin all the time and pretty soon we'll have to stay out for the night. Sure would hate to miss one of Suzanne's dinners," added Willie.

They had walked about half a mile when they heard Mye-Ook shouting in the distance, but they were unable to understand what he was saying. Spurred by the urgency in his voice, they quickened their pace to catch up to him. As they approached, they heard his calls off to the side of the trail and followed his path through the snow into the high trees, breaking into a run when they saw what he had found. It was a scene of total devastation, with wreckage just barely recognizable as parts of an aeroplane. The wings had been sheared off and the cockpit was hanging from the branches of a tree that had been broken off in the impact.

"Holy smokes," exclaimed Willie. "Some mess. There can't be nobody alive in that wreck but I guess we'd better take a look. Mye-Ook, climb up and take a gander."

Mye-Ook scrambled up through the broken branches until he could reach the remnants of the shattered cockpit and could peer into the side window. As if he had been struck he suddenly recoiled and shouted down, "White guy."

"Is he alive?" shouted back Willie.

"Can't tell," grunted Mye-Ook. "I'm not touching him, dead or alive."

"Come on down Mye-Ook, and let me look," said Paul in exasperation. Sometimes Mye-Ook infuriated him, but he tried to temper his anger with pity.

Paul clambered up the branches and called back down, "It's a white guy sure enough and he's really bleeding on his face. Hard to tell but I think he's breathing, but he's more dead than alive. It's going to be tough to get him out though 'cause he's trapped in the wreck. Mye-Ook get back up here and help me. I don't care what colour he is," ordered Paul.

Reluctantly Mye-Ook clambered back alongside and started tearing at the wreckage of the cockpit with his bare hands, as Paul tried to keep the debris clear of the pilot's face.

"Holy smokes," shouted Paul. "The guy's really alive. He just groaned and moved a bit. This is gonna take a while, Willie. There's no way we can get him out much before dark so we'd better figure to spend the night. Why don't you get a fire going and build us a shelter while we work on getting the guy out."

Without responding, Willie started to clear an area for a camp and a fire with the axe he always carried in his pack. He was careful to stay far enough away from the wreckage in case there was any gasoline leaking from it. He cut a good supply of dry wood from a deadfall nearby and got a fire going to brew some tea. Then he looked around for two small trees that would serve as the uprights for the shelter, and one for a crossbar. Once these were in place he selected good, bushy boughs and wove them into a roof that would be virtually waterproof, as he had done dozens of times before when he had to spend the night in the forest. Finally, he piled spruce boughs on the floor of the shelter until there was enough resilience to keep them away from the cold ground.

By this time the blackened tin can was bubbling over the hot fire and he threw in a handful of tea to brew for a while before calling Paul and Mye-Ook down for a break from their strenuous labour.

"My God, that guy's really jammed in there and I think we'll have to use your axe to cut him out," reported Paul.

"Holy Jeez," grumbled Willie. "That's my good axe. It's gonna get wrecked, but I guess we can't just leave the guy in there, even if he is a white guy. The Spirits are sure givin' us some attention this year."

"He's gonna need some medicine if we can ever get him out so I'll brew up some Indian tea."

As the other two resumed their labours, Willie got down on his hands and knees and carefully brushed away the snow, looking for a tiny plant that resembled a small fern. It was a powerful herbal drug known and used by the Indians for centuries to induce sleep and reduce pain. Willie searched for half an hour before he found enough to brew a tin full. It would have been a much simpler task in the summertime when there was a profusion of the tiny plants.

It was already late in the afternoon and Paul and Mye-Ook were working feverishly to release the pilot before dark, as they were convinced that he would not survive until morning trapped in the plane. They were too far away from the fire to feel any effects from it and the temperature was beginning to drop dramatically as the sun descended over Goat Mountain. Paul was almost exhausted so when Willie had the Indian tea brewing, he relieved him, prying loose pieces of the cockpit.

They cut away as much of the tree as they could without fear of it falling on them, to make room for the three of them to extract the pilot and move him into the shelter for the night.

While Paul and Mye-Ook worked, Willie shot three big snowshoe rabbits with his .22 and got them roasting on a spit over the fire. The aroma of the roasting meat drifted to where they were working, spurring them on to more Herculean efforts. Finally they were ready to free the pilot. "Okay, Willie I figure we got him. Come on up and give us a hand for the last lift," called Paul.

* * *

At the cabin, Suzanne was preparing a huge moose stew. She knew the men would be ravenous after spending the day laying traps up near Goat Mountain. It was already getting dusk and she had lit the oil lamp as she looked expectantly up the trail for the trappers to appear. As the sun disappeared behind Goat Mountain and darkness arrived, Suzanne felt the first twinges of apprehension. She knew that they had shelters made on the trapline in case they were caught in a blizzard, but the weather was fairly good and she couldn't imagine the circumstances that would keep them out overnight. They had enough meat for the winter and she was sure they would not be involved with another big game animal. As the evening wore on she set the stew to the back of the stove and rolled into her bed with all her clothes on, dropping into a fitful sleep, punctuated by nightmares of having to spend the winter alone in the cabin.

When she awoke it was daylight, but there was no sign of the trappers. Without restarting the fire, she put a handful of jerky in her pocket and laced up her high mocassins. Then she donned her parka and headed up the trail towards Goat Mountain. She had absolutely no idea where the men would be and was full of trepidation as she started to walk, without even a rifle to protect herself. She did at least still have the whistle that Willie had given her and intended to blow it at the slightest sign of danger. As an afterthought she tucked the small kindling axe into her belt and took a stout willow stave that stood on the porch to use as a walking cane and to defend herself if necessary.

As she walked along the well-known trail towards Goat Mountain she was disturbed to find that overnight snow had obliterated the trappers' tracks. However, the myriad of animal tracks crisscrossing the trail were small, relieving her of the worry of encountering a large animal. Every few minutes she stopped and blew her whistle but elicited no response. When she estimated that she had walked about five miles from the cabin, she became concerned about getting too far away to return to the sanctuary of the cabin at night. Finally, she resolved that she would only walk another half hour before turning back.

Just as she was about to turn back, she was sure she heard a faint response to her whistle call and hurried along the trail towards the source of the sound. Every so often she stopped and blew three short blasts and strained to hear an answer. Finally it was unmistakable and her heart leapt. The most puzzling aspect was that the answering whistle seemed to come from off to the side of the trail and there was no obvious sign of tracks leading to the source. She was reluctant to leave the main trail in case she became lost, and had no desire to spend the night in the bush by herself. Finally, she could make out Willie's shout telling her to come towards them through the bush and they would guide her as she approached. She stumbled through the tangle of fallen trees and underbrush and finally broke out into the small clearing.

*   *   *

Bill Headingly drifted in and out of consciousness for an indeterminate length of time. Each time he became semi-aware of his circumstances, he experienced extreme pain in his right leg and a warm, sticky sensation on his face. He shook violently from a combination of cold and shock that added to his extreme pain. After a short period he would mercifully lapse into unconsciousness punctuated by wild dreams.

During one of his semi-conscious periods he imagined he heard strange voices, speaking in a gutteral tongue that he could not understand. He cried out both in pain and fear of what he was experiencing, but gradually realized that the voices he heard were real. Eventually one of the voices spoke to him in English.

"Who are you?" Bill managed to gasp.

"We're Indian trappers," one of them replied in heavily-accented English. "We were about two miles away when we heard your plane crash, so we headed right over here to see what had happened. We can't believe that anybody could still be alive in this mess, but it's goin' to be tough gettin' you out."

Bill groaned in agony. "Could you give me something for my pain?"

"We've been tryin' to find a first aid kit but the wreck's so bad we can't get to it. Meantime, one of our guys is brewing some Indian tea and that'll help."

Bill continued to shake violently but the thought that someone had found him was in itself reassuring. He could hear them tearing at the fuselage as they worked, speaking in a dialect totally unfamiliar to him, but he sensed the urgency with which they worked. He tried to maintain consciousness but frequently he slipped into welcome blackness. As he awoke from one of these episodes he felt a hot liquid being forced between his lips. At first he coughed violently. The scalding liquid seared his throat as it went down but it had quite a pleasant taste and provided some much-needed warmth to his body. He eagerly gulped the rest down.

In a short while, Bill could feel a pleasantly relaxed feeling swimming over his body and the pain seemed to subside. When he tried to talk his words were thick and slurred, but he was able to remain conscious while the Indians worked to free him.

"Wow, I don't know what that is but it sure feels good," slurred Bill.

"It's an old Indian remedy that we've used for centuries," replied the one who spoke English. "When we're out in the bush like this there's no place for the white man's medicine, so we've got to make our own. We've pretty near got you out but it looks like your right leg is broke so we'll have to brace it before we can move you. We're getting some birch bark to wrap around it. You also got some bad cuts on your face but we've stopped the bleeding with snow."

By this time Bill was in a pleasant state of euphoria, but still shook violently from cold and shock. He could hear the Indians conversing in their native dialect so was unable to discern what they were discussing. Out of the corner of his eye he could see a fire burning and suddenly panicked thinking that the plane was on fire. The one who could speak English identified himself as Willie Bearpaw said, "Don't worry, Buddy, the fire's well away from the plane." At that point Bill felt himself being lifted bodily from the plane, and even through his drug-induced euphoria he cried out in agony as he was lowered to the ground and carried to the campfire.

Bill was laid on some skins near the fire and wrapped up. Willie Bearpaw confirmed that his right leg was broken and added, "We'll have to make a travois to move you back to our camp. It's about five miles away. We've made a shelter for the night 'cause it's gettin' dark." Bill was grateful when they forced some more scalding Indian tea between his lips. Finally, he lapsed into a fitful sleep that was punctuated by wild nightmares and wakeful periods of great pain.

As Bill slowly returned to semi-consciousness, he was only partly lucid. He started convulsive shaking that he was unable to control. It was partly from the cold and partly from shock. He was aware of activity around him and voices speaking in their native tongue, which gave the whole scene a surrealistic aura in which he was not sure if he was a part or just an outside observer. There was little doubt that the extreme pain he felt in his right leg was real and he involuntarily cried out.

A face that looked vaguely familar came close, and in a heavy accent said, "You sure had some good sleep for a guy that lived through that mess. Case you don't remember, I'm Willie Bearpaw and we're goin' to try to move you back to our camp. We're Indian trappers and were out on our trapline when we heard you crash. It was too late to move you last night but there's a bad storm coming so we'll have to get moving. We've fixed up your leg as good as we can and we've built a travois to carry you on. At least you're alive and we can take better care of you back at the camp."

As the Indians lifted him on to the travois, Bill gasped in pain as his broken leg was jostled. "We don't have nothing better," said Willie, "but I'm goin' to give you a chunk of moose jerky to chew on. It'll give you something to concentrate on and some food at the same time."

Although it nauseated him to put anything into his mouth, Bill fought back the urge to throw up and concentrated on chewing on the salty, hard meat. He was surprised to find that it really did seem to help the pain as the travois bounced along the trail. He was barely aware of the tree branches overhead and the snowflakes that were falling on his face. The Indians pushed on wordlessly but Bill was aware from time to time that they would switch places, pulling the travois without stopping, but he had no idea of time as he drifted in and out of consciousness. Whenever he became semi-lucid, he shook uncontrollably, even though he was well wrapped in skins, which had a distinct wild animal odour.

At one point he was sure he heard a woman's voice having an animated discussion with the Indians, but he was too drugged to make any sense out of it. All he knew was that there could not be any women in this wilderness and he must be hallucinating.

After an indeterminate length of time Bill felt himself being lifted off the travois and carried into a cabin. He again detected a female voice amongst the others but was unable to understand any of the discussion. Suddenly, he realized that the female voice was speaking to him in unaccented English. He opened his eyes and saw a young woman with raven black hair bending over him, holding a lamp that smelled of coal oil close to his face.

"Hi, I'm Suzanne. You really made a mess of yourself, didn't you. This isn't exactly a big city hospital and we don't have any wonder drugs, but we've got our own medicine. First we'll get you into bed and see what we can do with you. You're in shock and have a badly broken leg that we'll have to try and fix up. Now we'll give you a shot of strong medicine that tastes terrible but sure works. It's Oolichan Oil and it's made from a little fish. Open your mouth and we'll see how it works on a white man."

"Bill obediently opened his mouth and Suzanne poured a large potion of the oil down his throat. He gagged at the strong, fishy taste and struggled valiantly to keep it down without success. He threw up on the floor beside the bed.

"So that's all you think of our medicine," exclaimed Suzanne. "There's no white man's drug store out here so you'd better get used to it. It'll really help if you can keep it down so I'm going to try it once more."

Bill steeled himself for the pungent liquid, and this time managed to keep most of it down, probably out of pride more than desire. He still shook uncontrollably even though Suzanne piled on more covers. "We've got to try and ward off you getting pneumonia if we can, that's why the oolichan oil will help. If any of our people fall in the water or get chilled that's our first treatment. I'm also going to give you some more Indian tea and see if you can get to sleep. Do you figure you could eat anything?" added Suzanne.

"No, I'm afraid I couldn't cope with anything," gasped Bill.

"That's too bad. I've got a big pot of moose stew on the stove for the guys who brought you in, and it'll nourish you. Never mind right now, we'll give you some more Indian tea to warm you up and ease the pain."

Suzanne held the steaming tea to his mouth and his teeth rattled against the tin mug as he eagerly gulped the hot liquid. In a short time Bill started to feel drowsy and the voices in the cabin became an unintelligible drone. He was aware of a hand gently stroking his head as he drifted off into a deep sleep induced by the drug in the tea.

✝ Chapter Six

Ross Stuart arrived back at Sioux Falls in mid-afternoon. With his usual flair, he kept his 185 airborne a few inches above the water until the last minute. When he closed the throttle, the plane dropped gently on to the floats and the deceleration was rapid, the drag of the water acting as an invisible brake. Cutting the switches and turning off the fuel, he opened the door and stepped out on to the floats as the plane ran smoothly alongside the dock.

The four geologists were still on the dock sorting equipment for Bill to take when he returned for the next load. They had decided that if they loaded the Beaver that night Bill could leave at daylight the next morning and probably do two trips to Sustut in one day, which would give them enough equipment to start the survey operation. On the second day two of them would fly into Sustut with Ross Stuart and start setting up and calibrating instruments.

Christie stepped forward and caught the moving rope that Ross tossed to her, wordlessly slipping it expertly through a mooring ring and tying a bowline knot.

"Who taught you to tie knots like that?" Ross asked.

"My father. I was supposed to be a boy, but when I turned out to be a girl he set out to make me the most practical one in the north country. Instead of playing with dolls in the house he had me helping to build a log playhouse in the bush."

"He also taught her how to use her fists, so don't try to get fresh with her," interjected Mark with his usual mischievous grin.

Christie gave him a playful cuff and turned back to Ross.

"Did you see Bill Headingly on the trip back?" she asked.

"No, I didn't. It was pretty rough through the pass so when I was coming back empty I climbed up and came through the saddle notch about ten miles east of the pass. What time did he leave?"

"Just before noon and he had a good load aboard," Jesse responded. "No doubt with that load he'd take it easy. He'd planned to make it back here tonight and we were going to load the plane so that he could be in the air at dawn tomorrow."

"Good. It's too late to start back in tonight so I'll fire up at daybreak too. What've you got for my next load?" asked Ross.

"There's two more men and their gear that I'd like to get in as soon as possible. One of them is the cook and it would be nice to get him set up before we come in," replied Jesse.

"Then we won't have to eat any of Christie's terrible cooking," laughed Brent. "Any man that marries her will need a cast-iron constitution. She cooked one summer at her dad's hunting and fishing lodge and the food was so bad, they used it for bear bait!"

"All right you jokers, leave Christie alone and let's get this gear sorted ready for Bill's next load," interjected Jesse. "But talking of food, why don't you join us for dinner at the hotel, Ross? We usually eat about seven thirty and the food isn't too bad."

"Sounds good to an old bachelor like me. Christie's cooking must be gourmet compared to some of the things I turn out in my cabin."

"Actually, we were joking. Christie's a superb cook," Mark added to bring the conversation back to an even keel. "Just wait until you taste some of the fresh trout she catches and prepares while they're still twitching."

"I'll look forward to that. I'm a keen fisherman myself but don't do justice to my catch in the kitchen. If you're interested, I've got a couple of secret lakes I fish and I'll take you in there when we get some free time," said Ross.

"Super," replied Christie. "I'm looking forward to some good steelhead fishing in the Sustut area. I hear it's outstanding."

"Well, I'm going to get cleaned up so I'll see you at the hotel at about seven-thirty. Tell your two men to be on the dock here at five-thirty a.m. with their gear so that we can be airborne at first light. I want to do two trips tomorrow and the weather looks as if it will be good." Ross checked the mooring ropes once more on the 185 and ambled off along the dock. Christie furtively stole a glance at his retreating back as he disappeared down the dock. In their brief acquaintance Christie had found herself strongly attracted to this easygoing character who seemed to be the typical bush pilot. She was careful not to give any outward sign of her feelings as it would have triggered another round of good-natured ribbing by her fellow geologists.

It was getting dusk when the geologists headed back to the hotel after sorting another good load ready for the Beaver when it returned. Since Bill was not yet back they assumed he would probably not return until morning now, but at least everything was ready.

In her room, Christie looked through her meagre wardrobe and decided for a change she would wear a skirt, a luxury she missed when out in remote camps for extended periods. Her favourite denim skirt and checkered blouse packed easily and complemented her blonde hair and tanned face and arms. Although she was endowed with a clear skin and fresh complexion, the result of a lifetime in the outdoors, she added a touch of rouge and a judicious application of lipstick. She gave her hair a few extra strokes with the brush and studied the result for a minute in the bathroom mirror.

The four men were already seated in the dining room when Christie entered, but all eyes turned in her direction. It was a rare treat for her fellow geologists to see her dressed in a skirt and Ross could ill-conceal his spontaneous admiration. He immediately rose and pulled in an empty chair alongside his own place. Gallantly he held the chair while Christie sat, to the amused stares of the other three who had long ago come to accept her as "one of the guys."

"How about a drink before dinner?" offered Ross.

"I'll have a glass of white wine, please," Christie responded, looking very demure and flattered by all the attention. Although she was very self-sufficient and independent she nevertheless enjoyed being treated with old-fashioned courtesies on special occasions.

Throughout the dinner, the conversation was animated and relaxed. Others in the dining room frequently turned their heads to this good-looking and carefree group of four men and one woman. Ross and Jesse were about the same age and showed the maturity that seems to emerge in the mid-thirties. The other two men and Christie ranged in age from twenty-five to twenty-nine and frequently joked about the two 'senior citizens' who were obviously past their prime, having crossed the great thirty-year threshold to middle age.

After dinner, Ross and Christie walked into the lobby of the hotel together. They were about to part when, on an impulse, Ross said, "How would you like a breath of fresh air before you turn in?"

"Glad to. I always take a walk before bed," responded Christie, trying to sound nonchalant. "Give me a minute to get a jacket."

She returned in a few minutes wearing a blue eskimo parka with a white fur hood that framed her face.

"What a beautiful parka. Did you get it in the Arctic?"

"Yes. Well, my father did. He often travelled in the north as a consultant on wildlife management and on one of his trips he had it made for me in Cambridge Bay. He got one for my mother too, so we were a matching pair."

"If your mother looked as good in hers as you do you must have made a stunning pair."

Christie hurried through the door into the crisp night, surprised at the hot flush Ross's words brought to her face. She thought that during her university years she had completely overcome her girlhood tendency to blush, even with the good-natured teasing of the other geologists and miners with whom she worked. But something about Ross made her feel younger and more vulnerable.

Ross and Christie turned and walked towards the dock where the 185 was moored. The night was clear and crisp with a canopy of twinkling stars and a sliver of new moon suspended above the western horizon. The lights of the aurora borealis flashed and faded, bathing the northern sky in a cascade of changing colour.

"Have you got a quarter in your pocket?" Christie asked.

"Sure. Why, are you going to make a phone call?" Ross said with a smile.

"No. I'm going to make a wish on the new moon. When I was little my grandmother always told me that any wish you make on a new moon always comes true. She was a wealth of folklore and she had a saying to fit any circumstance. Oh, by the way, one of the rules is that you must not look at the new moon through glass or your wish won't come true."

"She sounds like quite a character. Is she still alive?"

"No, she passed away last year. I still miss her terribly. We were very close and I can still feel her presence when I go home," Christie paused. Her mood became serious. "She spent her last years with my folks and I still can't go into her room."

Ross was touched by Christie's emotion and he said gently, "Well, in memory of your grandmother let's both make a wish on the new moon." He took two quarters from his pocket and offered one to Christie.

104

As their hands touched Christie was very aware of a strong current of attraction between herself and Ross. She had had her share of suitors and a couple of college romances had flared into extended relationships. But as time wore on she always found more flaws, with a corresponding cooling of ardour. Certainly she had never succumbed to some of their pleadings of undying love that could only be requited in bed. Although some of her friends had wholeheartedly joined the bed-hopping crowd at university, her wholesome upbringing and somewhat straight-laced father's influence had ingrained in her a sense of propriety that she could not cast aside. As a result she had earned a reputation as somewhat of a prude, but she found that after a while even some of her high-flying fellow students started to treat her with a grudging respect.

They stood side-by-side, silently holding their quarters and looking at the moon.

"Can I tell you my wish?" Ross broke the spell as he turned towards Christie. She could just make out a faint smile on his face.

"Absolutely not. My grandmother was very specific on that point. If you tell anyone it will not come true."

"Well, I'm going to chance it. I wished I could kiss you." He turned towards her, taking her two hands in his and drawing her closer. Wordlessly she responded and allowed herself to move against his body. For the first time she really appreciated how much taller Ross was, at least a head taller, as he bent to kiss her.

The kiss was almost a total disaster and certainly nothing like the fireworks-producing passionate kiss of the romantic novels. Their cold noses seemed to get in the way and Ross' moustache tickled Christie's lip. Instead of the heart-stopping, swooning effect they were supposed to experience they both burst into laughter that totally shattered the spell. Fortunately, they were totally alone at the end of the dock or a casual observer would have thought they had partaken of something much stronger that white wine.

"My God, your grandmother was right," said Ross. "She's probably looking down on us now and taking perverse pleasure in observing that performance."

Christie had laughed so hard that her cheeks were damp and she had to squeeze her legs tight to avoid dampening her pants. Ross' unexpected invitation to the walk had interrupted her planned visit to the bathroom and now the combination of the laughter and cold night air were almost too much for her distended bladder.

"Ross, I really must get back and wash my hair," she suddenly interjected with undue haste. "And you need a good night's sleep for tomorrow's flying."

Ross did not attempt to discourage Christie's hurried departure but had to almost break into a run to keep up with her. Silently he took her hand in his and felt the warmth of her surprisingly smooth fingers. He had thought she might be hardened by her outdoor life. He responded to the pressure of her hand by kissing her lightly on the cheek as they walked.

When they reached the hotel, Christie barely broke her stride as she pecked him quickly on the lips, wished him goodnight and bounded up the stairs two at a time.

Meanwhile, Ross made his way to his jeep in the parking lot completely baffled by Christie's reaction. Resignedly he shrugged his shoulders and attributed his failure to one more aspect of the female mind that had kept him a bachelor for his thirty-five years. He started up the jeep and headed for his trailer home on the outskirts of the town. Try as he might he could not eliminate the image of Christie as he undressed and got into bed. He lay awake for an uncharacteristically long time before sinking into a deep sleep that was shattered in what seemed like minutes when the alarm clock rang at four-thirty a.m.

After a good breakfast washed down by three cups of strong coffee, Ross hopped into the jeep and drove down to the dock where the 185 was tied up. There was hoar frost on the dock and he knew that he would have to de-ice the wings before he could take off.

He was standing on one of the struts using a long-handled stiff broom to dislodge the frost when he heard footsteps on the dock and saw three figures emerging from the predawn darkness. Two were carrying heavy packs but the third, somewhat shorter, was bundled in a parka against the chill air. Ross looked twice before he realized that the third person was Christie.

"Well, good morning," Ross called from the strut, looking at Christie and ignoring the two men. "What gets you out at this ungodly hour?"

"When I went back last night I called Jesse to see if he would mind if I flew into Sustut with you on this trip. I could start getting some of the gear set up and come back out with you on your second trip today. Do you mind?"

"I'll be delighted to have the company. It'll be a little crowded, but if these fellows don't mind nursing their packs on their knees, I'll put the extra seat back in the cargo space."

"Okay with us," one of the men responded. Judging by his portly figure he must be the cook, Ross surmised.

"As soon as I get rid of the rest of this frost we'll load up and be in the air by daybreak," Ross said, noting the first light streaks on the eastern horizon.

When he was satisfied that no ice remained Ross started to load the 185.

Trying to sound very casual he said, "Why don't you sit up front with me, Christie, to balance the load? The two fellows can sit in the back with their packs on their knees. The odds and ends I can stow in the luggage compartment."

He asked each person's weight and hefted the baggage, checking the total against his weight and balance chart in the cockpit. Turning on the master switch in the cockpit he waited for the fuel gauges to creep up to a reliable reading before calculating the fuel weight and adding it to the weight of people and baggage. The all-up weight was checked against the maximum for the altitude and temperature and Ross found that he had one hundred and fifty pounds to spare. He decided that he would use up the extra capacity in fuel, so he instructed one of the miners how to operate the wobble pump on the fuel tank on the dock while he clambered up on the strut with the nozzle.

"Watch the gauge and let me know when I hit ten gallons," he called down from the strut.

Christie held a flashlight and watched the gauge, calling out when the ten gallon marker came up.

Ross switched the nozzle to the other tanks and added the same amount to maintain stability.

"Okay, that should do it. That twenty gallons can come in handy sometimes. All aboard. You first, Christie, climb into the front right seat. You fellows next into the back seat and I'll pass in your packs."

Ross noted the lecherous leer on the cook's face as he ogled Christie's well-shaped and firm bottom as she stretched her jeans to the limit climbing into the seat. He was surprised to experience a fleeting moment of jealousy and an urge to knock the leer off the cook's pudgy countenance. Ross wondered how Christie warded off advances in remote camps but he found reassurance in thinking that her father had undoubtedly included a short course in good old 'knee-to-the-crotch' tactics in her upbringing.

With the two miners and their packs loaded, Ross untied the 185 and pushed it away from the dock, climbing into the front seat alongside Christie. With practiced skill he primed the engine, turned on the master switch, cracked the throttle and pushed the starter switch. The engine protested as the cold battery produced minimum power to turn the propellor but it suddenly speeded up after two revolutions and burst into life, sending a spray of water up onto the windshield. The red glow of the instrument lights provided an eerie effect in the cockpit as Ross' hands flicked over switches and instruments. While the engine was coming up to operating temperature, Ross checked all the control and trim movements for freedom and lowered 15 degrees of flaps for the take-off. When the cylinder head temperature reached the green zone he did a full engine run up and checked magnetos, finally throttling back to idling.

"Okay. Everyone strapped in?" Ross checked that doors and windows were closed and pointed the nose towards the breaking sun.

Despite the many hours she had flown in bush planes during her two years with the mining company, Christie always got a nervous knot in the pit of her stomach on takeoff. But she felt more relaxed with Ross than she ever had before. Despite his casual attitude, he was obviously a professional and instilled total confidence in his passengers. He was virtually part of the plane and there was no doubt that he was completely in control.

As soon as they were airborne and settled on a climbing course for Sustut, Ross turned to Christie and said, "Like flying?"

"So, so. I guess I've been afraid of flying since my father almost died in a plane crash when I was a little girl. He and this bush pilot were checking a pack of wolves on a frozen lake when they caught a wingtip on a snowdrift and cartwheeled into an island. The plane was totally demolished but they managed to walk away from it. I still have a picture of my dad standing beside the wreckage."

"That does tend to make you a little gun-shy, but really it's one of the safest modes of transportation if it's done properly. We have a saying that there are old pilots, and there are bold pilots, but there are no old, bold pilots."

"That's a good philosophy. You are not old, but I'm not too sure you aren't bold, either!" Christie retorted.

In order to make herself heard over the engine noise, Christie found it necessary to put her lips close to Ross's ear. Ross found this highly erotic and kept thinking of ways to prolong the conversation. He wondered what on earth was happening to him when a woman's warm breath in his ear in the cockpit in the presence of two strange men could turn him on. He had come to regard himself as a confirmed bachelor and totally noncommittal in dealing with women. It was obvious that this one was unlike any he had ever met before and he was totally nonplussed by her reaction the night before.

As if reading his thoughts, Christie leaned over and spoke into his ear, trying to avoid the possibility of the two men in the back overhearing her words.

"I owe you an explanation about last night. My sudden departure had nothing to do with the kiss. We had that wine with dinner and a couple of cups of coffee. Then you surprised me with the invitation to take a walk. I failed to take the Queen's advice and go to the bathroom whenever the opportunity arises whether you need to or not. It was fine until we hit the cold air and suddenly I had a desperate urge to go. If I hadn't made a run for it back to the hotel I'm afraid that I would have made a large puddle on the dock."

Ross couldn't contain himself as he threw back his head and guffawed with amusement.

"I must admit that I wondered what I'd done and spent a few waking hours after I went to bed. I'd never had that effect on women before and had decided I should change my aftershave lotion."

"Believe me, I enjoyed every minute of it, but felt I owed you an explanation. If those guys weren't sitting in the back I would suggest we try it again, even at eight thousand feet."

A beam of pleasure came over Ross's face as he levelled off and headed through the pass into Sustut Lake.

It was now full daylight, with the making of a spectacular Indian summer day. The mountains were capped with fresh snow and framed against deep blue sky. The air through the pass was calm and still, making the transit into the valley beyond smooth. As soon as they passed the crest, the mountains fell away in an almost vertical descent to a cascading river that flowed into Sustut Lake on the western end of the valley. The lake was now clearly visible as Ross closed the throttle and pushed down the nose to lose altitude. He advised his passengers to pinch their noses and blow to equalize the pressure in their ears during the rapid descent into the lake. Wanting to conserve fuel, he decided on the straight-in rapid descent rather than doing a 360 degree turn to lose altitude. Glancing sideways at the mountain he saw a large herd of mountain goats scampering down the mountain at the sound of the plane. He pointed them out to his passengers as a diversion during the somewhat frightening descent.

Christie was speechless as they crested the mountain and began their descent into Sustut Lake. She had travelled extensively, both in Europe and North America, but she was not prepared for the breathtaking view that now unfolded before them. Ross looked over to see if she was having problems with his rapid descent but he could see that she was simply responding to the work of nature that lay before them. The sparkling lake was like an emerald surrounded by the grandeur of the mountains as if it had been hidden from casual view when God created the earth. The massive old-growth trees that grew right at the water's edge were punctuated with green grassy areas, a haven for wild animals. Unconsciously, Christie concluded that this must be the most beautiful place on earth and she felt a twinge of guilt that she might contribute to the desecration of the area by prospecting for a potential mine site.

Sustut Lake was calm as glass with the reflections of the surrounding mountain peaks forming a perfect mirror-image on the surface. Beautiful as it was, Ross respected these conditions as the most hazardous for landing with a float plane. Since there was no wind he lined up for a landing along the path giving himself the longest possible landing run, and for the final 2000 feet put the aircraft into a very gentle descent, just above the stalling speed, until he felt the floats touch the glassy surface and cut the throttle to drop the plane smoothly onto the water. Like most float-plane pilots he treated glassy water surfaces with utmost respect as it was virtually impossible to judge height above water without ripples.

Ross taxied the plane back down the lake to where the advance party had set up a temporary camp at the edge of a sandy beach. He had previously inspected the beach and approaches and knew there were no hidden hazards so he ran the floats up onto the sand beach before shutting down the engine.

The two members of the advance party came down to greet the party. Since Ross's last trip they had set up two large tents with wooden floors. A black chimney pipe protruded through one of them with smoke lazily drifting off into the bush.

Ross opened the cabin door and passed down the packs of the rear-seat passengers, allowing them to escape from their cramped quarters as they mumbled obscenities about being treated like bloody cattle. Christie wore a benign smile as she knew the remarks were indirectly aimed at her for coming along on the trip and forcing them to nurse their baggage. Ross smiled outright and winked at her as he helped her down on to the float.

"I sure hope that smoke means hot coffee," Ross observed to one of the men helping to carry the packs and other equipment. "We were up before breakfast this morning."

"We just happen to have a fresh pot on the stove," the husky bearded one responded. "Guaranteed to get your heart pumping again."

As they walked up to the mess tent, Ross casually asked what time Bill Headingly had left the previous day.

With unfeigned surprise one of the men responded, "Who's Bill Headingly?"

"The Beaver pilot who flew in the instruments yesterday," said Ross with a sudden twinge of apprehension.

"We haven't seen a soul since you left yesterday. We heard one plane overflying here late yesterday afternoon but he was high and certainly didn't land."

"That's odd. What time did he leave Sioux Falls, Christie?"

"About noon, as soon as we helped him load the Beaver. He expected to be back late in the afternoon to take out a load this morning. When he didn't get back we just assumed he'd been delayed unloading and decided not to come back until this morning," Christie replied.

"Oh well, Bill's a big boy and I'm sure he'll be okay. Maybe he had a little engine trouble and dropped into a lake to fix it before coming over the pass. Bill's a real professional and does everything by the numbers, so I'm not the least bit worried. Let's have some of the coffee and then I'll head back for another load."

As they sipped the steaming brew, Christie said, "With no equipment or instruments here there's little point in me staying until your second trip, so I may as well come back with you now."

"Glad to have the company," Ross answered, trying hard to suppress his enthusiasm about having Christie as a passenger on the return trip.

"Finish your coffee and we'll be on our way. And remembering last night you'd better take the Queen's advice and take a trip into the bush before we leave. The facilities on my plane are quite limited."

While Christie disappeared into the bush Ross did a quick inspection of the 185 and with the help of the four men pushed it off the beach, turning it facing out onto the lake. As soon as Christie reappeared they climbed into the cockpit which now seemed spacious without the other two passengers and their packs and the load. Without delay Ross started the engine and taxied out into the lake, flushing a large flock of Canada geese that had been hidden in the reeds at the southern end.

The lake was still glassy smooth, so Ross taxied in circles until he had the surface broken into small swells that radiated from the floats and started lapping on the shore.

"Look what you've done to the beautiful picture in the lake," Christie laughed. "Why did you do that?"

"To help to get my floats on the step. On a glassy surface they stick like glue and make your take-off run twice as long. Believe it or not, we float pilots despise glassy water, beautiful as it may look. There are many float planes at the bottom of nice, glassy lakes."

By now the surface of the lake was marred by ripples so Ross turned down the lake and opened the throttle fully for the take-off run. As they became airborne Christie looked back and saw a stream of water droplets leaving the back of the floats and the four miners standing on the beach waving. She automatically waved back, not thinking that they probably couldn't see her in the cockpit.

With just under half the fuel load gone, and the passengers and baggage left behind, the 185 climbed rapidly and Ross headed straight for the pass. The air was still calm and smooth through the pass so Ross allowed minimum clearance from the floor of the canyon. Christie was absorbed in the spectacle of the mountains towering on either side of them and felt little of her customary apprehension. This tall, easy-going bush pilot had managed to put her at her ease, allowing her to experience the beauty and excitement of flying for the first time.

As they exited from the pass, Ross reached into the map case and selected a large scale topographical map which he spread over the controls. Turning to Christie he casually said, "How would you like to fly for a while while I do a few calculations?"

"I've never flown a plane in my life and I wouldn't know how to start," she protested.

"Nothing to it. Just keep the nose on the horizon and pointed at that puffy little cloud."

He showed Christie how to put her feet on the rudder pedals and hold the control column, giving her a quick demonstration of the effects of each control. Glancing over he saw the whites of her knuckles showing as she grasped the wheel in a death grip.

"Relax. An aeroplane must be handled with delicate respect. It's like a pretty lady. The delicate touch brings the best results."

For the first few minutes the aircraft made some wild maneuvers as Christie over-corrected each motion. Then Ross had her take her hands off the rudder and control column and she was amazed that it resumed almost perfect straight and level flight without any intervention on her behalf.

114

"See, treated gently, she will do most of the work for you. The trim tabs are set so that all you have to do is keep track and make sure the bird continues doing that. Now, just rest your hands and feet on the controls and make only minor corrections."

Christie quickly grasped the basics and in a few minutes was doing a passable job of keeping the aircraft level. Her face reflected the tremendous thrill she was experiencing from being allowed to unveil some of the mysticism of flying. Ross regarded her face with amusement as she grimaced and frowned whenever she made a wrong move, but the sparkle in her eyes revealed the thrill she was experiencing. He knew she was hooked on what he had always considered to be the ultimate high, and could almost predict she would want to take lessons in the future.

Although he kept glancing up to make sure they were maintaining a fairly constant course and altitude, Ross concentrated on the map and made measurements with a protractor, and using his small pocket calculator, he made a few entries and pensively looked at the results.

"You know, I have a feeling that if Bill had any problems he may have headed back into Buffalo Narrows where he could spend the night and work on the Beaver. I know Jennifer has a single side-band radio that she monitors at set hours but unfortunately I don't carry the frequency band they operate in. I just did a quick calculation and I have enough fuel with twenty minutes to spare. If Bill is having any trouble I could help him out, and if necessary fly out for parts."

Christie was so engrossed in trying to keep the plane level that she only absorbed part of Ross' plan, but enough to detect a worried note in his voice. She nodded mutely in assent and felt a great physical and mental relief when Ross took over the controls again and changed course directly to Buffalo Narrows. He advised her that it would be about thirty-five minutes flying time from their present position so Christie relaxed in her seat and enjoyed the spectacular view beneath.

Ross was obviously preoccupied with his thoughts so she did not interrupt with casual conversation.

It was a clear day and Buffalo Narrows was visible from twenty miles distance. Once again Christie marvelled that there were so many beautiful places in this land as she looked down on the pretty little lake that drained into a cascading waterfall. Nestled against the trees she could see the cabin with smoke curling out of the chimney. She could clearly see a woman and three children emerge from the cabin at the sound of the plane's motor and head for the dock that protruded into the lake about fifty yards from the cabin. The children were waving vigorously and Christie responded, although she doubted if they could see her. There was no sign of Bill's Beaver tied up to the dock and she suddenly had a sinking feeling in the pit of her stomach.

As they landed and taxied towards the dock they saw Jennifer and the three children come running down to meet them. When Ross shut down the engine, Keith and David grabbed the rope on the front of the floats and strained to pull the aircraft closer. Christie was sure for a moment that they would both end up in the water, but with Jennifer's help they managed to secure the rope to a cleat on the dock.

"Come out and meet Jennifer and the kids," Ross invited Christie.

Ross warmly embraced Jennifer and gave her a resounding kiss. Dianne was hanging back, but Ross playfully dashed at her and said, "You're next, young lady. My gosh you've grown so much you're almost ready to get married." Dianne feigned annoyance but did not resist as Ross was a great favourite and she always looked forward to his visits. Next he tousled the boys' hair and made a few jesting swings with his fists at their bobbing heads.

"Jennifer, this is Christie Richardson. She's a geologist with the mining outfit that is setting up in Sustut Lake. She's also an expert co-pilot and flew us most of the way here."

"Hi, Christie. Welcome to Buffalo Narrows. What brings you two over here? I thought you were going full blast on the airlift into Sustut?"

Trying to sound casual and unconcerned Ross replied, "Well, we already went in there this morning so we thought we'd drop by to say hello."

Jennifer had a quizzical look on her face and blurted out, "Where's Bill?"

"That's really the prime reason we dropped in. Please don't be alarmed, Jennifer, but Bill didn't turn up at Sustut yesterday. When we found that out this morning we thought he might have come back over here to get parts or do repairs."

Jennifer's quizzical look suddenly turned to one of total shock. "I was concerned when he didn't check in with me on the radio at our regular times but I just assumed that if he was in Sustut the mountains would block his transmissions. Where do you think he could be?"

The children detected the concern in Jennifer's voice and Keith looked grave. The tears welled up in David's eyes. Dianne couldn't contain her feelings and buried her head against Jennifer, starting to sob.

"Hey, look guys, Bill's an outstanding professional and that old Beaver is almost indestructible. I'm sure he may have had a small problem and dropped into any one of the dozens of lakes along the route. By the way Jennifer, do you know if Bill had his ELT — electronic locator transmitter — aboard when he left?"

"I know he had it installed, but he'd been having trouble with the battery leaking acid, so he took it out and cleaned it all up last week. Hopefully it was working again, although he didn't mention it."

"Good. Well, if it's working we'll find him in no time." Ross hesitated, then said, "If you're okay Jennifer, I'd better get back to Sioux Falls and get a search started. I'll be back in a few hours so I'll leave Christie here so that you can have some girl talk while I'm away. If anything comes up in the mean-

117

time, I'll contact you on the single side-band radio, so monitor it on the hour every hour. Are there any suplies you need?"

"No thanks, Ross. Bill brought in a good load just before he left in anticipation of being away for a while. It'll be nice to have some girl talk and get caught up on what's happening in the outside world — and the children will be delighted to have someone around who's not crabbing at them all the time."

"Thanks Jennifer. I'd love to see your house. My dad was a log house builder and he built me a log playhouse when I was just two. It's still standing behind the house, and I'm sure he's waiting for me to provide a granddaughter to play in it now. Actually, I think he's given up on me ever even getting married."

Jennifer caught the glance that passed between Christie and Ross and she immediately sensed more than a professional rapport between these two independent souls. They had known Ross for many years and on a few occasions when he had visited them, Jennifer had introduced him to some of her single friends. Nothing had ever materialized though, and she had concluded that Ross would remain a confirmed bachelor. But this wholesome, blonde, self-sufficient woman had obviously made a great impact on Ross, even though he was a few years her senior.

As Ross started his take-off run, Christie, Jennifer and the children stood forlornly on the end of the dock. In one painful flashback, Jennifer recalled that her last glimpse of Bill and her father was as they disappeared over the horizon in the same direction the day before. Silently she put her arms around the three children and they walked slowly back up to the house, unable to fight back the tears of apprehension. She wanted desperately to avoid any outward show of alarm, but she also sensed that the children were experiencing the same inner gnawing fear about the fate of their loved one. Arriving back at the house she made tea for herself and Christie and assigned chores to each of the children to keep them occupied. She even broke a cardinal rule and allowed the children to miss their mandatory two-hour study period in the afternoon.

118

Chapter Seven

As Ross taxied up to the dock at Sioux Falls he could see the other three geologists working on a pile of equipment, readying it for another trip to Sustut.

Mark stepped forward and caught the float strut, pulling the plane alongside the dock and securing the lines.

"What took you guys so long?" he smirked as Ross climbed out of the cockpit. "Been off joyriding into some secluded lake, I'll bet."

He immediately stopped his mocking greeting when he noted the serious expression on Ross's face.

"What's the problem?"

By this time Jesse and Brent had joined them at the plane.

"Bill Headingly didn't arrive at Sustut yesterday," Ross said heavily. "When we found out, we flew into Buffalo Narrows to see if he'd stopped off to see his family, but no luck. Normally he'd check in with Jennifer by radio but yesterday he didn't call in."

Ross checked the moorings on the 185 and started up the dock. "We'd better get a search started. Would you mind driving me up to the hotel so that I can do some telephoning? First I thought I'd check with Jerry Fortin over at Vermilion Bay. Bill has been flying hunters for him and he just may have stopped in there to coordinate the fly-out."

On the way to the hotel Ross was uncharacteristically quiet. He was concerned about Bill and even felt a twinge of responsibility for involving him in this operation, which he quickly dismissed as being just one of the hazards of this occupation.

"Why don't you use the phone in our office," Jesse suggested.

Ross was grateful for the opportunity to make the calls in privacy, otherwise rumours would be flying in no time.

Jerry Fortin's wife answered the phone and advised Ross that Jerry was out on a trip with hunters. When Ross told her the purpose of the call she added, "But I've been around the depot all weekend and I definitely haven't seen Bill with his Beaver. Anything we can do for you?"

"Don't raise any alarm yet Christina, but Bill hasn't been seen since he took a load into Sustut. Would you get Jerry to give me a call when he comes back. I might be back in Sustut but he could give me a call on the radio. Talk to you later," he added as he hung up.

Taking out his pilot's handbook he looked up the toll-free number for the Rescue Coordination Centre and dialed the number.

A cheery voice answered immediately.

"Good morning. Rescue Coordination Centre. Captain Robinson speaking."

"Good morning. This is Ross Stuart calling from Sioux Falls. We have an aircraft overdue on a trip from here to Sustut Lake. He left about noon yesterday and had planned to return here last night but failed to do so. I did a trip into Sustut this morning and the aircraft had not been in there. On the way back I checked his home base without success. Since I arrived back here I've made a telephone check at Vermilion Bay where he was involved in flying hunters but he hasn't been seen there either."

The voice on the other end was all business as it rattled off a series of questions from a prepared checklist. Type of aircraft? Colour? Registration number? Pilot's name? Route to be flown? And most important, was the aircraft equipped with an ELT?

Ross gave succinct replies to the questions but added, "I know that the plane was equipped with an ELT, but like the rest of us, Bill had been experiencing problems with the battery leaking. His wife advised me that he took it out to clean it last week but she wasn't sure if it was working again."

"All right, sir. If he has a working ELT there will be no problem. The satellite is due to come over the horizon in another twenty minutes, so we'll have it do a scan of the route for ELT signals. Can I reach you there for a while?"

Ross covered the mouthpiece of the telephone with his hand as he turned to Jesse and asked, "Do you mind if I leave this number for the SAR people to call me back?"

"Absolutely, Ross. Use any of our facilities you like and we will all be glad to do anything we can to help."

Ross gave Captain Robinson the number and hung up. Mark offered to stay in the office and listen for the phone while Jesse and Ross went down to the coffee shop.

"What do you think are the chances of finding Bill in a hurry?" Jesse asked.

"If his ELT is working, probably in a very short time. This new SARSAT satellite system is fantastic and it can pin down an emergency transmitter in minutes. This is one time the Soviets have cooperated fully in a joint programme and they're giving us excellent data. It's very comforting to know the system is working when you're flying over this country. My only concern is that Bill's transmitter is not working. That would be the bottom line and it would be like searching for a needle in a haystack."

They finished their coffee and went back up to the office.

"Jerry Fortin called back while you were out. He hasn't seen or heard from Bill but asked that you call him if you hear anything. Meanwhile, he said he will get his pilots to monitor 121.5 on their radios for ELT signals, whatever that means."

"Thanks, Mark. I was just giving Jesse a rundown on how the system works. If Bill's ELT is working we'll find him in no time."

"And if it isn't?" Brent queried.

"That's a totally different story and could involve hundreds of hours of flying. You saw how rugged the terrain is between here and Sustut so you can appreciate the magnitude of the problem."

It was almost two hours before the phone rang. "Sorry for the delay, but we've been experiencing communication problems with the Russians and Americans. Unfortunately we've come up with nothing anyway. We had the satellite scan the entire area without success, so it doesn't look like we have an ELT signal to work with. Meanwhile, I've put in a request for a Hercules to do a track crawl and we'll assign a Buffalo and a Labrador helicopter as soon as possible. But that probably won't be before tomorrow."

"Tomorrow!" exploded Ross. "It could be a matter of life and death!"

"I'm sorry, Mr. Stuart, but we're stretched pretty thin. Meanwhile, can we get any local planes to start a search along the route? We'll send in a searchmaster along with the Labrador as soon as it's free. By the way, can we appoint you as our on-site expert?"

"Gladly! The Double Eagle Mining Company has offered their office and services so they can man the phones. Meanwhile I'll ask Jerry Fortin to assign as many planes as he can and as soon as I refuel, I'm going to start searching the route."

"Great! We'll keep in close touch and get a Buffalo and Labrador up there as soon as possible. The Hercules has a full range of communications equipment so I would suggest that you call them on 121.5 and they'll give you a frequency to operate on. Their call sign is Wild Bill."

Ross hung up the phone and outlined the plan to Jesse, who agreed they would keep someone in the office at all times.

Ross also requested one or more people to fly with him as observers.

"I left Christie with Jennifer in Buffalo Narrows, so I'll pick her up on the way out again. She can act as the observer on the first trip. She doesn't seem to mind flying with me; in fact I even had her at the controls for a while on the way back from Sustut," boasted Ross. "I'll take her the first trip and then we'll rotate for the rest of the time."

"Okay. Mark, Brent and I will spell you off in between office work and manning the phone here."

"Could you pick up some sandwiches in the coffee shop? Christie and I will probably stay out until dark. If you don't mind doing that, I'll go and start refuelling the bird. Maybe they'll also loan us a thermos," Ross added over his shoulder as he walked out of the door. "See you at the plane."

Despite the mission, Ross felt a surge of excitement at the thought of Christie joining him on the search. He couldn't help but feel flattered at the haste with which she had volunteered to fly with him and her unsolicited comment about his flying ability filling her with confidence. She was extraordinary, totally unlike anyone he had ever met before, and he felt completely at ease in her presence.

As Ross was just finishing topping off the fuel tanks which would give him an endurance of about four and a half hours, Brent was making his way down the dock with a couple of brown bags and a large, commercial-type thermos. He was also carrying Christie's Eskimo parka and mukluks, and Ross immediately knew he did not have to worry about this crew since he had forgotten to tell Christie to wear warm clothing.

"Okay, I think we're ready to go," said Ross. "If I get into the air right away we should be able to get to Sustut with light remaining. We'll stay in the camp over there for the night and then be out again at first light in the morning. I have a feeling that our most productive search area will be closer to Sustut, in or near the pass through the mountains, so we won't waste any time on this end of Bill's route."

Suddenly Ross excused himself and hurried up the dock, explaining that he still had one more important mission to fulfill. They could hear the tires on his jeep squealing as he headed off.

Ross pulled up in a cloud of dust on the outskirts of town and ran into a dilapidated tarpaper shack, opening the door without knocking. "Are you home Tommy?" he shouted as he entered the dim interior which smelled of urine.

A figure was lying on the bed with an empty bottle beside him on the floor. There was no response so Ross shook the inert figure until he got a mumbled growl indicating that he was still alive. "Have you still got that litter of pups, Tommy?"

It took a few minutes for the decrepit hulk to answer but he managed to mumble through his stupor that there was only one left as he had sold the rest at the pub the night before. In reponse to Ross's insistent shaking, he pointed to the back door, which led to a fenced backyard littered with junk. As Ross entered the yard an undernourished dog slunk up to him followed by a perky little ball of fur that bounced around and rubbed against Ross's legs. After patting the mother, Ross picked up the puppy and examined it, finding that it was a little male that licked his face enthusiastically.

Ross went back into the house and looked around until he found part of a loaf of bread and a carton of milk that smelled old but still edible. Taking it into the backyard he found a battered old dish into which he broke the bread and poured the milk. The dog ravenously gulped it down and looked up at Ross, wagging her tail and licking her lips. At one time she had been a purebred golden retriever but neglect had left her hair matted and dull. She was a good mother, though, and the pup looked fat and healthy. Ross patted her again as he made his way back into the shack with the pup snuggled against him and licking his face.

"You old drunk, you don't deserve to have dogs," Ross said with disgust. "I'm taking the pup and leaving ten bucks on the table for it. Don't spend it on booze and feed that poor animal in the back or I'll turn you in to the cops."

All Ross received in return was a grunt as the hulk rolled over and went back to sleep. Ross jumped back into his jeep and roared back into town, making a quick stop at the store to pick up a bag of puppy food and a box of dried milk, before he parked his vehicle at the hotel and went off down the dock at a lope with the puppy zipped into his flying jacket.

Ross landed at Buffalo Narrows and taxied full speed right up to the dock where Jennifer, Christie and the children were waiting. He cut the engine at the last moment and glided alongside the dock where the women caught the strut and held the plane while he clambered out. The children were fascinated by his flying jacket which seemed so bulky and appeared to be wriggling.

"Come over here you guys and give your Uncle Ross a hug before I go."

They approached him hesitantly; he was known for his pranks and they were not sure what to expect. "Dianne, would you help me with this zipper on my jacket? It's stuck and I can't get it open," he called. Reluctantly she came close as he squatted down and she slowly pulled down the zipper. Instantly the puppy stuck out its little black nose and yelped as it squirmed to get out of the hole.

"A puppy!" all exclaimed as they tried to release him from his shelter. Dianne, admonishing the boys for trying to grab the pup, tenderly lifted it out and it licked her face enthusiastically. It was a case of love at first sight. Turning to the boys, Ross asked them to get the food from the plane.

Tears welled up in Jennifer's eyes. Ross knew that she and Bill had discussed getting the children a dog next time they took a trip out. It was intended to take the place of Molly the Moose who was still missing. Silently she walked over to Ross and gave him a hug of unbridled affection and a kiss. Christie, observing the scene, thought that Ross seemed to spread good will wherever he went. She had no doubt that she was falling in love with him.

"Okay, you guys. You look after your Mummy and that puppy while Christie and I go and find your Dad. What are you going to call him?"

"Buck!" David responded without a moment's hesitation, which indicated that he had been anticipating this moment for a long time.

"Great name," Ross said. He helped Christie into the plane and pushed off from the dock before climbing into the left seat. The engine was still warm and burst into life instantly as Ross turned for the takeoff run. Looking back over his shoulder he waved to the group on the dock and saw that Dianne was still hugging the puppy while the boys were trying to remove it from her arms.

"That was a nice thing to do, Ross," Christie said, with a catch in her voice.

As he taxied away from the dock Ross performed an engine check, lowered flap because of the heavy fuel load and turned the 185 towards the setting sun which was turning into a huge crimson ball as it neared the horizon. Both of them were so engulfed by the spectacular beauty that they did not say a word as the plane gathered speed and almost imperceptibly broke contact with the water as it started a slow climb towards the west.

Levelling off at 3000 feet, Ross tried to visualize the route that Bill would have taken with a heavily loaded plane en route to Sustut. Bill's Beaver would not have climbed as quickly or attained the same airspeed as the 185 so Ross throttled back both to conserve fuel and to permit better visibility of the flight path.

There was no conversation between Ross and Christie as they both concentrated all their attention on the carpet of green forest and emerald lakes passing beneath them at an apparent snail's pace. It was difficult to conceive that they were actually travelling at 180 miles per hour, but from 3000 feet there was virtually no sensation of speed.

As they approached the saddle notch through the mountains for the descent into Sustut, dusk was just beginning to fall, making objects on the ground difficult to discern. Ross turned to Christie and said, "I'm afraid that we'll have to give it up for tonight and start up again at dawn. Maybe there will still be enough light left for you to catch us a few trout for dinner. Did you bring a rod?"

"Never without one," replied Christie with a smile, and reaching inside her parka, she withdrew a canvas pouch about eighteen inches long, flipping back the cover to reveal a split cane rod broken down into six sections. "This was my Dad's. He had it made by Hardy in England during the war and gave it to me on my twenty-first birthday. I carry it on all my trips, along with this fly reel and a box of flies. You would not believe the size of the fish I've landed with it."

"How about big suckers?" Ross laughed.

"Even some of those!" Christie replied with a straight face.

"Well, we'll try it out in Sustut tonight and see what that fat, greasy cook can do with them. Sustut used to be one of the most famous steelhead spawning lakes until the railroad construction caused a massive landslide that blocked most of the inlet channel. Now there's just a fraction of the fish there used to be."

"That sad story is just too true in too many places now," sighed Christie. "Civilization is pushing the frontier back every year. You know," she added, "people like us are just as responsible as anyone. My father loved to reminisce about the good old days when he could feed the entire family out of the local stream. Now there's not a fish left."

Ross pointed the nose of the 185 through the crotch and the twinkling lights of the camp were immediately visible on the western end of the lake. Since the sun had already set behind the mountains Ross wasted no time and made a rapid descent down to the water. The rapid change in pressure made Christie's ears hurt so Ross showed her how to hold her nose and blow until the pressure equalized and her ears popped. Without delay Ross landed and he used his landing lights to illuminate the route to the camp. He knew there were a couple of deadhead logs in the lake that could make an unpleasant hole in his floats.

The 185 glided towards the sandy beach, where three figures had congregated to meet them. They instantly recognized the portly cook, who stood back while the other two caught the struts and beached the plane.

As Ross and Christie climbed out on to the struts one of the young engineers called to say that someone had been trying to contact Ross on the HF radio, a Jerry Fortin. Ross's heart skipped a beat as he immediately assumed that Bill had been found and they were calling off the search. As soon as the plane was secure he ran up the beach to the tent that doubled as an office and started calling Jerry Fortin's home base HF radio. There was no response for a few minutes but finally Jerry's voice responded through the static. That, coupled with Jerry's French Canadian accent, made it difficult to carry on an intelligible conversation.

"Jerry, this is Ross Stuart calling from Sustut."

"Roger Ross. Any luck?"

"Negative. We came directly to Sustut but it was getting dusk so we didn't do much searching. How about you?"

"You're hard to understand, but we haven't heard from Bill. What are your plans now?"

"I'll be out of here at dawn and we'll do a thorough search of all the lakes back to Sioux Falls."

"Listen, Ross, I have a bunch of hunters sitting in the bush that Bill was going to pick up for me. Can you fly over and get them for me first thing in the morning?"

"No way, Jerry. The priority now is the search for Bill. This is the second day now and I'm putting all my effort into finding him."

"Yeah, but my hunters are going to be mad as hell if I don't get them out as we promised. It'll only take you two days to pick them all up and I'll pay you one and a half contract rate. Okay, Ross?"

"Go to hell, Jerry. Your damned hunters can wait. We know where they are but we sure as hell don't know where Bill

Headingly is. Besides, there's a storm moving in from the west so we don't have time to spare. Even the pass is getting tough with lots of snow on the peaks and moving lower. Did you hear anything from the Search and Rescue guys?"

"I hear they're sending a chopper up to Sioux Falls but will have no Buffaloes or Hercules for at least three days."

"That makes it all the more important that we keep searching. Sorry, Jerry, but your hunters are low priority until we find Bill. Over and out."

Ross slammed down the microphone in disgust and said, "It would be different if that SOB was missing. He'd expect us to drop everything and come looking for him."

Stepping outside the tent he met Christie walking up from the beach with four nice trout on a forked stick. "My gosh," exclaimed Ross. "You really can catch fish. Now, if you'll just get them cleaned we'll get the cook to fry them for supper."

"No way," responded Christie. "I catch them, you clean them, or no dinner."

"Boy, your old man really did train you right! Or was it your mother?"

"Definitely my mother! My father was the world's champion chauvinist, but my mother was a crafty lady who could wrap him around her little finger without him knowing. She let him think he ran the show, but it was secretly her pulling the strings that brought it all together."

"They sound like a great pair; I'd like to meet them sometime."

"Hopefully you will," answered Christie, trying to suppress a blush.

They strolled together up to the camp where Ross niftily evaded his fish cleaning chore by handing them intact to the cook and patronizingly said, "How'd you like to clean these and give us your gourmet version of fresh caught trout for supper. I hear you're an expert."

Ross winked at Christie who stood in mock frustration, with hands on hips, as the cook swallowed the bait and went off to clean the fish while the skillet heated.

Meanwhile, Ross and the two geologists gathered wood and they soon had a roaring fire going with showers of sparks flying heavenward to mingle with the bright canopy of stars. It looked so inviting that they all brought seats and gathered around the fire, moving only to pick up the food the cook had prepared and returning to the fire to consume it. The temperature had dropped well below freezing after sunset and the warmth of the fire was most welcome.

"My only wish is that Bill, wherever he is, is sitting by a fire like this," said Ross, breaking the silence induced by the hypnotic effect of the fire, now becoming a large bed of glowing embers. "Bill's a pretty woods-wise guy and could survive a long time in the bush. In fact, we took the survival course together when we were still in the Air Force. He built the shelter and provided most of the food, and of course I was happy to let him do it!"

Christie gave him a mock punch of disapproval, but realized that Ross was trying to reassure himself of the ability of his best friend to survive in any conditions.

The cook finished his chores and grunted a goodnight to the group. This prompted the two geologists to agree that it had been a long day and they were both going to turn in early. Ross and Christie bade them goodnight but remained by the fire silent, transfixed by the dying embers.

Wordlessly, Ross reached over and took Christie's hand in his which made her involuntarily move closer on the log they shared in the flickering shadows. No longer impeded by the onlookers, the two came together in a passionate, uninhibited embrace. Their lips met in a lingering kiss that expressed their pent-up emotions and threatened to turn into a total loss of their normal reserve.

Struggling to regain her composure, Christie gently pushed Ross away and said, "No, Ross, this is neither the time or the place, not that I wouldn't love to carry on. But we have a serious mission to perform that takes priority right now. So, I think we should both go our separate ways to our tents and get as much rest as we can for an early departure tomorrow morning."

"You're absolutely right, darling. I knew from the first moment I met you that you were the practical, sensible type. Just the thing a hairy, wild guy like me needs to make him fly right. Okay, let's turn in and see what tomorrow brings. But I certainly make no apologies for what I did; I've been dying to do it ever since we met."

Christie realized that she was trembling, not from the cold night air, but from the suddenly released emotions that had occurred so naturally. It was the first time since she was in college that someone had had such an effect on her and she had responded without hesitation. Ross calling her 'darling' was another surprise that sent a surging thrill through her body.

They walked silently back to the tents, hand in hand, and Ross gently kissed her as she prepared to enter her quarters.

"Goodnight, darling. I'm afraid that I've fallen for a pretty lady geologist. I never thought I would meet the right lady and was resigned to a life of bachelorhood. You have certainly put a serious dent in my armour."

"Goodnight, Ross," Christie responded as she kissed him on the cheek and turned to enter the tent. She was struggling hard to control her emotions and appear cool and indifferent, but inside her emotions were in turmoil and she didn't expect she would sleep tonight.

Christie had finally lapsed into a deep sleep after a fitful night when she suddenly sat bolt upright and let out a stifled cry. Something was grasping her big toe with a firm grip.

"Relax, it's only me," whispered Ross. "I'm sorry if I startled you but it's less than an hour to daylight. The cook is making inviting smells from the kitchen so we'd better grab a good breakfast before we leave."

"Ugh! I couldn't think of anything I would want less at this hour. I'll be satisfied with a glass of juice and a piece of toast which will carry me a long way."

131

"Okay, as you wish. Meanwhile I'll go down and break the ice loose around the floats."

As Christie was dressing inside her sleeping bag, a trick she had learned as a little girl when she had gone off on fishing trips with her father, she could see Ross with the bobbing beam of his flashlight as he broke loose the ice that had formed overnight around the floats. He had predicted the previous evening that such would be the case and this would probably be his last trip in on floats until Spring. As winter deepened the ice would become progressively thicker and would take three to four weeks to become strong enough to support the 185 on skis. Meanwhile, the crew who were left behind had sufficient supplies to last for a couple of months. As Christie emerged fully dressed in her wool slacks and parka she felt a twinge of conscience that she too should be remaining behind to start the geological survey; however, she reasoned that she could be of more immediate help in the search and moral support of Jennifer Headingly who badly needed another woman around at this time. With another twinge of guilt she also realized that she would rather be in close proximity to Ross. She hardly dared reflect on the events of the past two days and there was little doubt that she was falling for this free spirit. Her every waking thought seemed to be preoccupied with thoughts of him and she experienced a little thrill as she saw him make his way back up to the camp and lead her by the hand into the overpowering heat and light of the kitchen.

"How about a half dozen sausage and three eggs over easy, Chef?" Ross ordered as he entered the door. "I'll make the toast. How many Christie?"

"One piece of brown, please," she replied.

"Good grief, you'll fade away eating like that," Ross laughed. "And I like you just the way you are."

Christie blushed as she removed her parka and noted the offensive leer on the cook's face. "I never have been able to eat when I first get up. It was a constant battle with my folks when I was going to school, particularly when my father and brothers could eat like horses as soon as their feet hit the floor."

"There are people like that, but I'm afraid that I can consume great quantities of food at any time. It's surprising that I don't weigh three hundred pounds."

"Nervous energy," observed Christie who noted that Ross ate at the same rate he did everything else — on the full gallop.

They ate in silence, thanked the cook, and made their way to the plane. The first streaks of daylight were just appearing in the east and Ross wanted to be airborne as soon as the light was good enough to see objects clearly on the ground.

When Christie was ensconced in the cockpit, Ross pushed the plane clear of the sand and swung it around to point it down the lake. He could see that the center of the lake was still clear water and he just had to break the ice with a paddle for another thirty feet before breaking loose. He stood on the front of the floats breaking the ice ahead to open up a pathway that would not damage the floats. Climbing into the cockpit he gave Christie's knee a friendly squeeze before starting his pre-start check. The engine protested and turned over slowly for a few revolutions before suddenly bursting into life that echoed through the valley.

Taxiing slowly with his landing lights on until the engine reached operating temperature, Ross pointed to a big bull moose leaving a grassy area in great, high-stepping bounds heading for the safety of the bush.

"They're not the brightest creatures on earth, but they're certainly one of the most magnificent," observed Ross.

"I was practically raised on moose meat," said Christie. "It was like the Holy Grail each year when Dad went off on his annual moose hunt. Then, when my two brothers were old enough they joined the loyal order of the moose hunters. I put all my energies into fishing and couldn't bring myself to hurt one of those magnificent creatures. However, I must admit that the meat tasted good in mid-winter when we could get no other supplies. My mother had sixty-four different ways of presenting moose meat, but surprisingly I still maintain my taste for it."

"Well-prepared, there's no meat to compare to it," agreed Ross. "I'll still fly miles out of my way for a good moose roast and the trimmings. By the way, I hope that your mother taught you those sixty-four varieties!"

The cockpit was bathed in the eerie glow of the instrument lights, creating the aura of being totally detached from the surroundings. As soon as the engine was up to operating temperature, Ross eased the throttle up to 1000 RPM and checked the magnetos. He then ran the engine up to full throttle while still taxiing and performed his pre-takeoff check. At the roar of the engine, the moose ran at full speed for the safety of the surrounding bush, its gangly legs sending spray flying in all directions. Ross never failed to marvel how such an ungainly-looking beast, hampered by an enormous rack on its head, could navigate the bush at such speed without getting hopelessly tangled. As it ran it laid its antlers back on its shoulders, which effectively streamlined its body and the antlers were no longer an impediment.

When Ross was satisfied that all was ready for takeoff, he smiled and winked at Christie, jokingly adding that he hoped he hadn't forgotten how to get it into the air. He taxied to the edge of the ice in order to get the maximum takeoff run and opened the throttle fully.

For ages the floats appeared to be glued to the water and Christie unconsciously dug her fingernails into the palms of her hand. Suddenly the plane broke free of the water and went into a steep climb over the trees at the end of the lake. As soon as he had sufficient airspeed Ross turned 180 degrees and headed toward the notch in the mountains. Being cold and the air still, Christie got the feeling of suspended animation as the plane climbed toward the mountains. She suddenly realized why people like Ross were totally enamoured of flying and recalled her father's unbridled pleasure when he flew. She now felt for the first time the spirit that inhabited all aviators even though she had flown many times before.

The 185 climbed well in the cold morning air and with only half of the fuel load remaining. Ross pointed the nose at the notch in the mountains instead of performing the usual climbing turns to reach altitude. To Christie it appeared as if they would crash into the mountain well below the summit but she had developed great faith in Ross's ability as a pilot and was relieved to see daylight through the notch as the far horizon became visible. Again she spotted the herd of mountain goats fleeing at the sound of the approaching plane and she marvelled at the nimbleness and sure-footed way they leaped from rocky ledge to rock ridge barely big enough to hold their four feet. The young kids were particularly fascinating as they followed their mothers in flight down the ridge to safety.

Ross guided the 185 through the notch and followed the terrain of the east side of the mountain which fell away abruptly into the valley below. There was no conversation as they carefully scanned the sides and bottom of the valley for any unusual objects.

"We just got out of there in time," shouted Ross, pointing to a black cloud moving quickly over the mountain top. A few flakes of snow were already visible in the air and the 185 started to be buffeted by the building wind. "We may have had to spend the winter in there together without the benefit of a clergyman," he joked as Christie punched him playfully on the shoulder.

"I just caught a glimpse of something down there," exclaimed Christie. "It looked like a long metal tube of some kind but I couldn't be sure. It may just have been a fallen tree but it was an unusual colour."

"I don't have much room to manoeuver in here," responded Ross, "but we'll try one more pass over the area. I have to watch my fuel too, particularly if we want to divert into Buffalo Narrows on the way home. I'm sure that Jennifer could use some news and company about now."

Ross put the 185 into a steep turn that had Christie hanging on to her seat as he turned back to the area where Christie had spotted the object. The snow was starting to fall quite heavily now, reducing the visibility to less than a mile and the sides of the canyon were barely visible.

"One pass and we have to get out of here or they'll be looking for us too," observed Ross, a serious look on his face for the first time since Christie had met him.

Christie directed him to the area where she thought she had seen the object but visibility had lowered so much that she was unable to be sure of the exact location. She peered intently through the haze but could barely discern objects on the ground.

"That's it, I'm afraid," called Ross as he performed another tight turn to resume his heading out of the pass. "But if you actually did see something down there it will give the Search and Rescue people something to go on and it was certainly in a likely area. As soon as we get within radio range of Sioux Falls I'll report a possible sighting in this area, although the way the weather is closing in it's unlikely that they'll start searching 'til it clears off again."

They flew on in silence, absorbed in their own thoughts. When they got within radio range of Sioux Falls Ross called ahead and reported the sighting that Christie had made. He also reported on the deteriorating weather at the Sustut Lake area and was advised that a large cold front was approaching and that it was unlikely that a search of the area would be initiated before the front had gone through. Armed with this information Ross turned toward Buffalo Narrows to pass along the word to Jennifer Headingly.

He landed the 185 and taxied up to the dock where Jennifer and the children, with the puppy bouncing along behind, had come out to meet them as soon as they heard the engine of the plane. As he cut the engine and glided toward the dock Keith ran forward to catch the rope trailing from the float and secured it to a cleat.

"You're getting pretty good at that young man," called Ross as he emerged from the plane and helped Christie out of the cockpit. "I think I'll hire you for my co-pilot."

136

Keith blushed as Ross tousled his hair and then turned to Dianne and David who were standing back shyly. "Come on you two guys, give me a hug before I dunk you in the lake," he said as he grabbed them both in a bear hug and swung them around the dock. Christie moved wordlessly toward Jennifer and the two embraced, Jennifer bravely fighting back tears.

"How about a cup of tea before I hit the road again?" Ross said to Jennifer who was obviously desperate to ask if they had any news and yet afraid to ask. He put his arm around her and held her close as they walked up the trail to the cabin.

Once inside Ross broached the subject and said, "We might have sighted something in the pass coming out of Sustut, but we weren't able to confirm it because of deteriorating weather. I passed along word to the Search and Rescue detachment who will be going out to investigate the sighting as soon as the weather breaks." Jennifer did not respond but hurried about getting out teacups and homemade cake on to the table. She had busied herself with baking and cleaning to keep occupied while Christie and Ross were away.

"Bill's a tough customer, you know, and well experienced in survival techniques. I'm sure that he's snuggled up comfortably in a shelter and just waiting for a plane to go over his location so that he can contact us," Ross tried to reassure Jennifer. She was on the brink of tears but bravely trying to maintain her composure as she and Christie handed around the tea and cake. The children were also unusually subdued as they listened intently to see if there was any word of their father. Dianne hugged the puppy on her lap for comfort. She had made him a collar out of bright red material that emphasized his cuteness.

"How would you like a little company for a couple of days, Jennifer?" Christie asked. "It would be a pleasant change from the all-male crew I hang around with all the time."

"We'd be delighted," Jennifer responded.

"Please stay," added Dianne pleadingly. The boys nodded mutely in agreement. They had all come to like Christie and looked forward to the many stories she promised she would tell and read them. Dianne had climbed on to her knee and wordlessly gave her a tight hug in a gesture of unspoken affection.

"Well, since this invitation obviously doesn't include me, I'd better get back to Sioux Falls. I'll be back to get you in a couple of days, Christie, unless I'm back sooner with news. Monitor your radio every hour Jennifer and if we have anything to report we'll call you."

Ross walked back to the dock with his arm around Jennifer trying to reassure her that things would work out fine. Before casting off from the dock he kissed her gently on the cheek and then unabashedly kissed Christie firmly on the lips, causing her to blush, a response she thought she had lost.

They watched as Ross climbed out of sight and walked back hand in hand to the cabin, sharing an unspoken affection and love of their respective men.

Chapter Eight

Bill was aware of someone wiping his brow with a damp cloth as he slowly regained consciousness. He felt utterly drained and limp but gradually became aware of his circumstances. He no longer shook uncontrollably and felt comfortably warm. The dull pain in his right leg persisted but was not as excruciating as it had been.

"Welcome back, stranger," said the pleasant female voice. "Remember me? I'm Suzanne, your private nurse. You had us worried for a while there that you were going to leave us and we would've been blamed for getting rid of another white man!"

"How long have I been out of it?" Bill asked with effort.

"Would you believe two days? I've never seen anybody shake so badly, but it was a combination of shock and hypothermia. I was afraid that you were developing pneumonia, but I guess the oolichan oil works even on a white man. Do you remember any of the past two days?"

"Only flashes, and I must have been dreaming because I imagined that I was in bed with a woman who was deliciously warm. I guess I must have been dreaming that I was home in bed with my wife, Jennifer."

"That was no dream, and it wasn't your wife! It was me! It's an old Indian remedy whenever anybody falls into the water or gets hypothermia from exposure. We strip them off and another person climbs into the bed with them to transmit body heat. It saves a lot of lives and it's completely natural for us to share anything we have, even our bodies, to save another human being. Even a white man! I can also believe that you thought you were in bed with your wife 'cause even with your problems you were getting pretty amorous."

"You must be kidding! My apologies, Suzanne! You're a beautiful lady but I really didn't know what I was doing, or at least that's my excuse. Boy, I owe you guys my life. You can be sure that this is one white man who has developed a new respect for our Indian brothers and sisters! I must admit that up to now I've been like most white folks and treated your people with some indifference. Where are the guys who brought me in from the wreck?"

"They're out on the traplines. After this snow the game will be really moving and they can't miss any time. Normally I would be out with them but I had to stay home and nurse you back to life. Who knows, maybe it'll pay off and we'll get a little work out of you when you're fit enough! You can be the camp squaw and keep the home fires burning," Suzanne added with a tinkling laugh.

"Who are you guys and where do you come from, Suzanne?"

"We're members of the Dogrib Nation and live on the Kwakwala reserve near Tatlatui Lake in the summer time. Then in winter some of us move out to our traplines on the Stikine Plateau. You're lucky that we'd just arrived a few days before you crashed or you'd probably never have been heard of again. I'm sure that you've flown over this area enough to know what a wilderness it is and the likelihood of anyone locating the crash site would be one in a millon. Our guys just happened to be setting out traps in the area when they heard you go down and got to you in time."

140

"Boy, if I had to crash I sure picked the time and place to do it. I'll never be able to repay you guys for saving my life but I'll certainly try when I get out of here."

"You know, you white guys are all afraid to die. How come you like to go to sleep every night but you're afraid of the big sleep which is what you call dying? Our tribal laws require us to feed and look after any injured person and take them into our tribe. The reason was in the old days when we had inter-tribal wars there was heavy male mortality and we had to save any male and, if necessary, share him with other wives who had lost their partners. It used to be common practice to lend a visitor one of the wives for the night in the hope that they could produce another kid for the tribe. At one time they used to kill off most of the girl children until they found that the tribe was being destroyed. Incest was strictly taboo but polygamy was widely practiced and accepted, especially with brothers sharing wives. Although we still preserve most of our old tribal practices, we're pretty enlightened now and have got rid of most of the old anti-social rules."

"You seem to be a very well educated woman, Suzanne, and you don't have any trace of an accent."

"You can thank the white man for that but I'm not sure that I do. However, that's another story, and you look like you're getting pooped. Do you figure you could eat some of this soup I have on the stove? It's made from ptarmigan, moose and muskrat so it has all the nutrients you need to get you back on your feet."

"Apart from muskrat it sounds delicious. Sure I'll try some, and judging by the smell it'll have me leaping out of bed and chasing you around the cabin."

"Holy smokes, you're starting to sound like an Indian already, but of course white men are every bit as bad in that department."

Bill eagerly gulped down the soup as it was offered and realized that he had not eaten for almost three days. He could have consumed the whole potful but Suzanne reminded him that he was still pretty weak and that small portions would be better until he started to regain his strength. Reluctantly he followed her advice and lay back on the bed pleasantly relaxed despite the gnawing pain in his leg. His face still felt badly swollen but Suzanne refused to give him a mirror to check his appearance.

It was the first time Bill had been able to look around his haven. He was lying on the bottom of one of three double bunk beds. From his bed he could look out through the only window at the dense forest surrounding the cabin, and even in daylight it barely illuminated the interior. The centre of the cabin was taken up with a rough-hewn table with benches pushed under the edges. Heat and cooking facilities were provided by an old square tin stove that showed the flickering embers through cracks along the sides. Bill immediately thought that it would have been condemned under normal circumstances but it was typical of the austere equipment in the many trappers' cabins he had visited on hunting and fishing trips. The walls were hung with smoky old pots and pans and a couple of grubby towels hung from nails. The door was a work of art, fashioned from split cedar and hung with leather hinges. It was burdened with surplus clothing hung from a wooden peg. There was a fascinating mix of odours in the cabin, ranging from body odour to cooking smells and the wild smell of furs that were piled in the corner ready for Suzanne to scrape.

He was also able for the first time to pay attention to Suzanne who had raven black hair, tanned skin and the typically high cheekbones of the aboriginal people. She wore heavy wool pants and a wool shirt which hid her figure. He estimated that she must be in her early thirties as she moved gracefully around the cabin in her mocassins, unaware of Bill's eyes following her movements. Her woman's touch was obvious as the cabin was surprisingly clean and tidy for a trappers' cabin. Bill had no idea how long this would be his home, but under the circumstances he was most grateful for the shelter it provided him, along with the sustenance and nursing provided by Suzanne. Exhausted by his chat with

Suzanne, and warmed by the food in his stomach, Bill drifted off to sleep again.

He had no idea how long he had slept, but when he awoke he found the trappers back in the cabin and eagerly wolfing down the dinner Suzanne had waiting for them. They were conversing in Kwakwala and Bill had no idea what they were discussing. Suzanne noticed that Bill was stirring again and pointed this out to the trappers. The one whom Bill remembered speaking English paused in his eating and turned to Bill. "How're you doing, white man?" he asked with a mouthful of food.

"Not bad, thanks," Bill responded. "Way better than when you guys found me anyway. That's some nurse you got in this hospital and I think I'll live now, thanks to you guys. Like I said to Suzanne, if I had to crash I sure picked the right place and time to do it."

The short husky one turned back to his meal which obviously signalled the end of the conversation, so Bill lay back on his pillow again. "Feel like more grub?" Suzanne asked him.

"That last was sure good, so if there's lots I wouldn't mind a little more, please."

"I'll just give you another small portion again until your belly gets used to eating again," she responded. "I don't want to clean up any more messes off the floor like I did when I gave you the oolichan oil," she added with a smile.

The trappers let out satisfied belches and the shorter one rubbed his belly and said something to Suzanne in Kwakwala, which was obviously a compliment to her. She looked pleased as the other two nodded in unison. Without much more discussion they went to their bunks and were soon emitting a chorus of snores in unison. Bill lay back after his light meal, but was not sleepy as he watched Suzanne clean up the dinner residue. When it appeared that she too was about to go to bed, Bill whispered, "Do you think I could have some more of that Indian tea to help me sleep, Suzanne?"

"That's pretty good stuff, eh?" she answered. "Sure. The kettle's hot so I'll brew you some before I hit the hay. The days

143

are pretty long and the nights short out here." Suzanne handed him the steaming mug of tea and disappeared behind her curtain. By the time Bill had drained the mug he became drowsy and dropped off to sleep almost immediately. He did not awaken the next morning until the trappers had already left for the trapline and Suzanne was fully dressed and cleaning up the cabin.

"Wow, I've got to get the recipe for that stuff," Bill exclaimed when he found that he had slept through the night. Even the pain from his leg had not disturbed him.

"No way," Suzanne responded. "That's an Indian secret but I'm glad to see it even works on a white man. How about some breakfast?"

"I must admit I'm ravenous, so I must be recovering. That bannock smells delicious."

Suzanne sliced off a couple of rounds of bannock and slipped moose tongue between them. Bill bit into it and exclaimed, "My gosh, that's delicious. What is it?"

"Would you believe moose tongue?"

"Wow! Next time I shoot a moose I'm going to save the tongue instead of throwing it away."

"There's the difference between natives and white men. We use every scrap of an animal while you guys throw away the best parts. Maybe we'll make an Indian of you before you get out of here."

"Now that I've got my stomach full again, I'd love to hear the rest of your story Suzanne. You sound pretty bitter about the white man."

"Like a lot of natives, I've good reason. It's not pretty in places but if you're interested I'll fill you in on the details, and maybe explain why the Indians still have a great mistrust of the white man. I was born on the reserve and, unfortunately, my parents became alcoholics after they guided an American hunting party who supplied them with all the booze they wanted. Before the end of the trip they were both hopelessly hooked, and would go to any lengths to get alcohol of any kind. They took off for the city and I was left with my grandmother who raised me 'til I was ten. Then the Roman Catholic priest from the reserve decided that I should be raised and educated by the white people in Prince George. My grandmother tried to hide me in the bush but they sent in the Mounties to find me and took me away in a police car. To this day, I can still hear my grandmother screaming and moaning as they drove me out of the reserve locked in the back of the police car. My Indian name was Washababino, but that was the last time I heard it, or saw my grandmother, who I loved dearly, 'cause she died before I made it back to the reserve, probably from a broken heart more than any other ailment."

"My God, Suzanne, where did they take you from there?"

"The Mounties took me to the railroad junction at Sioux Falls, where I was held along with another nine kids of various ages 'til a nun arrived on the train and bundled us all aboard. Needless to say, we were absolutely terrified, never even having seen a train before, and being separated from our familes for the first time. Every time we whimpered, or spoke in our native tongue, the nun cracked us across the head and told us to be quiet. We were even too scared to ask to go to the bathroom, and when our kidneys wouldn't hold out any longer we wet our pants right in the seat. Then the nun cracked us again and called us filthy pagan savages."

"Finally, when we arrived in Prince George we were driven in a ramshackle old bus to the convent where we spent the next six years of our lives. We were issued with drab, scratchy uniforms and assigned to a dormitory with about fifty other Indian kids from various reserves. Our beds had straw mattresses, and our night time toilet was a bucket in the corner. We did have a shower room, which was totally unheated, and we all had to shower together with carbolic soap. We ranged in age from about six to sixteen, so it was an overwhelming experience seeing girls who had attained puberty, and endowed with breasts and pubic hair. We didn't have any toothpaste so we had to brush our teeth with the same carbolic soap. To this day if I smell carbolic in any form I get sick. We used to call it cat's pee!"

"My God, it sounds like a Dickensian novel!" said Bill trying to disguise the incredulous tone in his voice.

"We hadn't heard of Dickens in those years, but if we had we would have thought we'd been transported to an old English workhouse. Certainly, the regime we had to follow would have been appropriate to a workhouse. We had to attend classes six days a week from 8 a.m. to 4 p.m., and then had to do all the chores. We were wakened at six in the morning and all had to tramp outside to the outdoor toilet, regardless of the weather, and even if we were sick. We weren't allowed to use the indoor toilets, which were reserved for the nuns, but we had to scrub them and keep them clean. It was a great deterrent from complaining of sickness 'cause we knew that we would be treated with a large dose of castor oil by Sister Pain-in-the-Ass, as we called her. At noon every day we had to go out for our fresh air period, regardless of the weather, or the state of our health. If we were caught speaking our native tongue we were punished by having to stand outside for hours without a coat. One girl, that was subjected to the icebox treatment, became very sick but she wasn't allowed to stay in bed, and was actually carried outside for the fresh air period where she was laid on the stone steps for an hour in freezing weather. Finally, the sisters figured there really was something seriously wrong with her, and called the public health nurse. After she had examined her, we heard great shouting in the hall and they finally came in and carried her away. We never saw her again, but we had to say prayers for her on Sunday so we figured that she must have died. After that, the nuns actually were a bit more sympathetic to anybody pleading sickness."

Suzanne couldn't believe that she was pouring out her story to a total stranger, but it had been bottled up in her for so many years that the floodgates had opened when she had found a sympathetic ear who had no direct involvement in her life. Bill reached over and gently squeezed Suzanne's hand in a silent gesture of sympathy, feeling a strong sense of guilt that his fellow man had treated other human beings in such a manner. "Did you ever have any visitors during the time you were there?"

"Not a one! As I mentioned, my parents became alcoholics and abandoned the family when they went to the city. I've tried to trace them since I grew up, but had no luck. Apparently my grandmother died about six months after I came to the convent."

"As I was growing up, I was told I would become a nun and return to the reserve to help convert the savages. Fortunately, I had a natural ability to nurse people back to health, so when I was sixteen I was sent to the Catholic Hospital in Prince George to train as a practical nurse, and then to return to become a nun. I was allowed to stay in the Nurses' Residence, which was like paradise, with flush toilets and privacy to shower or bathe. The pittance we were paid was to be returned to the church, but I always managed to spirit a little away, which was augmented by tips given by the patients for doing little favours for them. I befriended one girl about my own age who was dying of cancer, and spent many of my meager free hours comforting her. When she died, her mother gave me many of her possessions, including clothes, the like of which I'd never even tried on. After that, I carefully started to work out a plan to go my own way, and finally saved enough to pay for my bus fare, and enough to live on for a while, and disappeared during the night. I headed for Calgary where I didn't think they'd look for me. I was terrified, never having been outside my regimented life, but once safely in Calgary I went to the YWCA and got a room while I looked for work. I was rejected by many because of my obvious native features, but I was finally hired by a lady to be the nanny of her two children. I had my own room, and was treated like one of the family. I stayed with them for five years, until I met a handsome young white boy, and fell madly in love with him. He asked me to marry him, and my adopted family gave us a fine wedding."

"Things went pretty well for a couple of years, until my husband started to get restless. It was almost as if he became reluctant to be seen with me, and would go off for days on end, claiming he was working in the oilfields. Finally, he didn't return, and I was left destitute on my own. Fortunately, we hadn't had any kids. In desperation I decided to return to my roots, and sold enough possessions to get the bus and train back to the reserve."

Bill listened in rapt silence.

"I wasn't prepared for the reception I got there either, 'cause the elders told me I'd lost my Indian status by marrying a white man, and that I couldn't stay on the reserve. Fortunately, I had an uncle who remembered me, and took me into his house. The Indian agent was really a sympathetic guy, and helped me prepare an appeal to the government to have my Indian status reinstated. Finally, the Band reluctantly relented, especially when I could help with some of my acquired nursing skills, and applied to have my wedding annulled. So, here I am, a full-blood native Indian again, and damned proud of my heritage. That's why I've come out with my uncle, to help him on his trapline and spend the winter in here cooking, nursing and preparing skins. I'm very happy here, and I've put my early life behind me. I guess that it's made me a much stronger person and better able to cope with this tough life."

"What an incredible story," Bill observed, unable to mask his feelings. "A lesser person would be bitter and anxious to extract revenge for such treatment. I've heard stories of the treatment of our native people before, but this is the first time I've heard it first hand from someone who's actually experienced it."

Suzanne changed the subject suddenly when she heard the voices of the returning trappers. "I've almost let the fire go out while I've been yakking, and the guys'll be cold and hungry."

"Which is your uncle?" Bill asked.

"Willie Bearpaw. You might remember him pulling you out of the wreckage of the plane. Appropriately, his Indian name is 'Chu-Sup' which means 'Man who helps'. "

148

"I just remember flashes 'cause I was out of it most of the time, but I'll owe all of you an eternal debt of gratitude for saving my life and especially for you being here."

Bill could hear the other three Indians shaking off the snow from their clothes and mocassins before entering the cabin. Although he could not understand what they were saying, they sounded in a jovial mood as they entered. Only Willie Bearpaw acknowledged his presence, and came over to the bunk where he was lying.

"How're you doin', White Man?" he asked in his taciturn way.

"Lots better thanks, Willie. This is some nurse I've got here. I think if it wasn't for her I might not be as good as I am. She even managed to get some oolichan oil into me, and I figure that would cure anything!"

Willie threw back his head and let out a hearty laugh that filled the cabin. Paul also smiled a pleasant smile, but Bill noted that Mye-Ook looked away with a frown on his face. Bill realized that he would have to be most careful what he said in Mye-Ook's presence, particularly when Suzanne was involved. He suspected that Mye-Ook was an admirer of Suzanne, and made no secret of his hatred of the white man, which was understandable given the background story that Suzanne had told.

"That oolichan oil is some good stuff," interjected Paul. "Every year the Kwenis, the Orca Whale, herds all the oolichans into a big bunch, and drives them up Hunae-Chin Inlet, where the natives from all over come and catch them in big nets. There's a place there where the Schetxwen, the big bears, have dug a great big pit and all the Indians dump the oolichans in there 'til it's full to the top. Every night the Schetxwen come back and eat the oolichans off the top, but the oil all runs down to the bottom of the pit, and after all the flesh has gone, there's nothing but oil left, and the natives put it in bottles. Nobody but the Kwenis knows where the oolichan comes from, but every year they come back at the same time, from their secret place in the big ocean."

149

"That's really interesting, Paul, and I promise I won't throw any more up on the floor. How's the trapping?" asked Bill to divert attention away from himself.

"Real good," answered Willie in his flat monotone. "Good quality too. Must've been that wolverine we killed that's bringing us good luck. Sure as hell couldn't be with having a white man around," he added.

Bill's mouth twitched as he suppressed a smile. He had taken an instant liking to Willie, and knew they would become fast friends. Paul was somewhat of an enigma, and a naturally reserved man, who showed flashes of concern and was most courteous to Suzanne. Bill knew that it would be impossible to penetrate Mye-Ook's inscrutable, and even hostile, manner and resolved to avoid anything that would provoke him into possible violence.

Suzanne wordlessly hustled around the cabin, getting dinner for the hungry trappers who sat at the table, as she filled their plates with the stew that had been cooking on the stove all day. As soon as the food was on their plates, they started eating and wiped their plates with pieces of fresh bannock. Paul paid her the ultimate compliment by picking up his plate and licking it.

"How about you, White Man? Would you like some more?"

"No thanks, Suzanne," Bill answered reluctantly, not wanting to take any food away from the hungry trappers. He also did not want to overburden his stomach too much after his enforced fast.

After dinner the men stayed at the table, speaking in their native tongue, while Suzanne cleared away the dishes. Although he could not understand what they were saying, Bill got the impression they were discussing him, as they kept glancing at him. Feeling very uncomfortable, he feigned sleep and was grateful when they finally went to their respective bunks and were soon snoring. Suzanne was the last to bed, as she turned out the light and disappeared behind her curtain into her bunk. Bill laid awake for what seemed hours, as he replayed the events of the last few days and wondered how

Jennifer and the children were faring. He could not restrain the tears that rolled down his cheeks when he tried to antici-pate what would happen to him, and how he would get back to civilization, possibly a number of months away, in spring. Finally, he also lapsed into a fitful sleep that made the night seem unending.

Chapter Nine

As Ross turned and flew toward Sioux Falls he was in an uncharacteristic depressed mood. The events of the past few days had caught up to him, and he fully appreciated the gravity of the situation with Bill Headingly. In the best of conditions, finding a downed plane in that vast expanse of country was an almost forbidding task. He was somewhat baffled by the fact that they had not had any response from the electronic beacon on Bill's aircraft, since Bill was an atypical bush pilot and never took any chances with equipment or weather. It seemed ironic that of all the wild bush pilots Ross knew, himself included, it had to be Bill who was missing while the others were looking for him. He was also concerned about Jennifer, and knew that she could not survive a winter at Buffalo Narrows alone with the children. He concluded that he would bring them out when he went back for Christie. His thoughts then drifted to Christie, and he was again disturbed by the feelings he had developed for her. It seemed that thoughts of her were even intruding into the serious matter at hand. In fact, he was already missing her company in the plane as he flew almost by instinct.

As Sioux Falls came into sight, the leading edge of the storm front was just catching up to him and visibility was rapidly lowering as he landed and taxied straight up to the dock. Snow was starting to fall quite heavily as he shut down the engine and climbed out on the float to tie the plane down.

There was a small crowd on the dock to greet him, including the geologists from the mining company, and an individual in an orange military flying suit with Captain's bars on the shoulder. He was the first to greet Ross, and introduced himself as Doug Stewart, the pilot of the big Labrador Helicopter which was parked at the end of the dock.

"Hi, I'm Ross Stuart."

"That's a coincidence," responded the Captain. "My name is Doug Stewart. S-T-E-W-A-R-T."

"I knew there had to be a difference. No Stuart who spelled his name properly would fly one of those beasts," joked Ross.

"Only way to spell and only way to fly," cracked back the Captain. "However, we're not here to discuss family trees, so down to the serious business. Have you had any luck in your search?"

"Not a sign," responded Ross seriously. Ross took an instant liking to the Captain, despite the exchange about their names, and as they walked back up the dock together Ross gave him all the details about the sighting Christie had made in White Goat Pass.

"It's not much to go on," said the Captain, "but at least it's a start. I don't have to tell you what a big country that is out there, and when we have no beacon to home on it becomes a chance in a million. It's too bad, because the system we have with the Russians now will let us pinpoint a crash site to within a hundred yards. It's one of the first times we have had total cooperation from the Russians, and the joint use of our SAR satellites could point the way to other areas of cooperation, we hope. But even if we knew where the crash was, we couldn't fly in this weather, and it looks as if we'll be playing bridge for a few days until this front passes. This snow will virtually obliterate all signs of wreckage."

"I just got out of Sustut in time, and took a chance going into Buffalo Narrows to see Bill's wife. I also dropped off the female geologist 'cause I thought Jennifer could use a little company for a couple of days. If it clears off, I'll go back and pick them all up. The freeze-up has already started and it'll be a good month before I can get back in on skis."

"That's a good idea," interjected the chief geologist. "I've already lost my best geologist, who's supposed to be in at Sustut right now starting the winter's exploration."

"You may have lost her for good," added Ross with a grin on his face. He didn't elaborate further, and left the geologist with a puzzled look on his face.

As Ross and the Captain strolled back up the dock together, they discussed the likelihood of finding Bill alive and agreed that the prospect was highly remote. It would have been sufficiently difficult if the weather had not closed in, and the heavy snow would soon obliterate all traces of a crash site until spring. Nevertheless, they agreed that they would give it a maximum effort until all hope had passed. The weather outlook was grim, and they could anticipate at least three days before it was flyable again.

"How about joining us for dinner at the hotel, Ross?" the Captain invited.

"Okay, Doug," Ross responded. "But first I have to get cleaned up at my trailer and make some phone calls to Jennifer's and Bill's folks. Bill's Dad is dead, but Jennifer's father thinks of Bill as a son. They've done a lot of flying together and it's a ritual that they go hunting together in the fall. He also spent the summer helping to build the house. I'm sure that Mike will be shattered, and undoubtedly will want to come up here, even though there's nothing he can do at this stage. When the weather clears, I'd like to get back into Buffalo Narrows and pick up Jennifer and the kids, and try to convince them to go to her folks for a while. It'll be tough trying to get her out of there but she couldn't possibly survive the winter alone. Fortunately, there's a good current at Buffalo Narrows, so it won't freeze up as quickly, and I've a little grace getting them out. Besides, there's a young lady in there I have a special interest in, and I don't want her trapped in there for the winter!"

"Sounds serious for an old bachelor like you, but it happens to the best of us," the Captain added with a smile.

Ross left the Captain and picked up his Jeep from behind the Hotel to drive over to his trailer. For the first time he realized what a mess it was, and before taking his shower spent half an hour picking up clothing and miscellaneous junk, after which by his standards it looked remarkably tidy. He had to admit, though, that it probably needed a woman's touch to make it really livable, and indulged in a little fantasy that that woman could be Christie. Already he missed her, and anxiously looked out at the sky for a sign of clearing, but the snow came down like a thick blanket. He resigned himself to the fact that it would be at least a couple of days before they could fly again.

After showering and changing, he drove back over to the Hotel and made phone calls to Jennifer's folks and Bill's mother. It was one of the most difficult things he had ever done and made all the more difficult by having to make the calls from the pay phone in the lobby. As he expected, Mike wanted to leave immediately and come back to Sioux Falls.

"Honestly, Mike, there isn't a thing you can do up here. I left Christie, the young geologist you met, with Jennifer and the kids, and as soon as the weather clears I'll go back and bring them all out here. They can stay in my trailer for a while but I'll try and convince Jennifer that she and the kids should come down to visit you if we don't find Bill right away. It won't be easy, 'cause as you know she's a little bloody minded, and will no doubt want to stick it out here. I promise I'll call you as soon as I have any news, Mike. Meanwhile, be assured we're doing everything humanly possible, and we now have the Search and Rescue boys with us too, so we've got the pros on the job."

"Thanks, Ross. You know what Bill means to me, so you can understand me being a little upset," Ross heard Mike say as he hung up.

The drink that was offered by the Captain was most welcome as they went into the dining room for dinner. There was an immediate rapport between Ross and him, and they started to recount the various experiences they had encountered during their respective careers.

"Interesting," the Captain observed. "I recognised the name Bill Headingly and now I remember we were on a couple of courses together. He always impressed me as a real pro, and it's hard to believe that he's got himself into a jackpot."

"I agree," responded Ross. "Of all the bush pilots up here, Bill was the most atypical, and it must've been unusual circumstances to catch him, 'cause he did everything by the numbers, not like the rest of us seat-of-the-pants flyers."

"I guess there's a law of averages somewhere for us aviators, and when your number comes up, you're next. That's why we're in business to try and save as many mistakes as possible."

The one drink turned into a few, and they soon became the most boisterous group in the Hotel, which was quite a claim to fame in Sioux Falls. However, the Captain suddenly looked at his watch and said, "This is great fun, but just in case the weather breaks, I have to get the requisite hours of sleep. Talk about doing it by the numbers, we're experts at it," he added with a laugh.

The crew of the helicopter spent their imposed non-productive time servicing the aircraft and playing cards for hours on end. After many years of the same routine they had learned to relax when the circumstances permitted, knowing full well that they would put in many long and arduous hours when they could fly again. Ross took the time to do some badly needed service work on his 185, but also enjoyed the fellowship of the Search and Rescue crew, particularly the Captain, who was more his own age and a little more edifying than most of the residents of Sioux Falls.

On the morning of the third day, the sky started to brighten in the west and there was feverish activity as the helicopter crew prepared to begin their search. Ross swept the snow off all the wings and control surfaces of the 185, and pumped fuel into the tanks. He deliberately left the tanks only half full in anticipation that he could bring all the residents of Buffalo Falls out in one trip. He assured Captain Stewart that he would join the search as soon as he had Bill's family and Christie organized. Immediately the ceiling lifted sufficiently to safely fly, he took off and flew directly to Buffalo Narrows where he found the whole family waiting for him on the dock.

After their isolation they were desperate for news and rushed at Ross. "Any news of Bill?" blurted out Jennifer.

"No, I'm sorry, gal. But the weather has been so bad none of us have been able to fly. Even the search and rescue helicopter has been grounded in Sioux Lookout, but they took off out of there at dawn to check out the pipe that Christie saw in the pass. They will be flying from dawn to dusk now. By the way, I called your folks, and of course Mike immediately wanted to come back up here but I assured him that there was absolutely nothing he could do right now. They both sent their love to everybody."

As they walked back towards the cabin, Ross, with his arm around Jennifer and the children, added, "Mike agrees with me that the only sensible thing to do right now is to come back out to Sioux Falls with me before the lake freezes and you're trapped for the winter. You can all live in my trailer and I'll move in with a friend of mine. Another reason is that you would be right there to get any news."

Jennifer shook her head but understood that it was the only sensible thing to do under the circumstances. "All right, Ross, I agree. Come on kids, lets get packing and decide what we want to take with us."

The next hour was consumed by selecting only those items of clothing and personal use that could safely be carried in the 185. Ross went around outside and put shutters on all the windows and closed off the chimney to keep out animals that would be looking for a place to hibernate for the winter.

Jennifer and the children were in tears as they carried their packs and the puppy down to the plane where Ross stowed them and piled the passengers in, being careful to assign Christie the seat next to him. As he glanced at the floats he knew that he was overloaded, but there was a long takeoff run out of Buffalo Narrows so it didn't give great concern. As a precaution, he warmed the engine thoroughly before starting his takeoff run and taxied around in circles a number of times to roughen the surface of the lake for better lift. Finally the floats broke loose from the water surface, and the 185 surged ahead once airborne and climbed to a safe altitude. Jennifer and the children looked back wistfully at Tohtohlah as they headed for Sioux Falls.

Try as he might, Ross could not convince Jennifer that she should take the children and visit her folks while the search was in progress, and she dogmatically insisted that she wanted to stay in Sioux Falls where the search was centered so that she would be immediately apprised of any developments. Ross reluctantly then reaffirmed his offer that they stay in his mobile home, and he would bunk in with a friend. This arrangement completely shattered his plans to ask Christie to move in with him. It was obvious that she had anticipated such a proposal as she sat with an inscrutable smile on her face while the discussion was taking place, and finally agreed that she would move back into her old room at the Hotel, which the mining company was holding for her. Ross looked crestfallen, but resigned himself under the circumstances to waiting for a more opportune time. At least Christie would be in the same town, if he could convince her and her boss that she should stay and run the office in Sioux Falls rather than returning to Sustut for the winter.

158

Chapter Ten

As Searchmaster, Captain Stewart had devised a precise search pattern for the Labrador Helicopter and the volunteer bush pilots who were to take part in the search. It was centered on the White Goat Pass area, where Christie had made the sighting of the suspected pipe. The helicopter would search the central area while the other pilots were assigned specific corridors so that the area was completely blanketed. After the heavy snowfall, the ground was a virtual moonscape punctuated by the massive timber, making the prospects of sighting any wreckage extremely remote. Their greatest hope was that if Bill had survived he would be able to light a fire and the smoke could be detected from some distance.

Both the helicopter and the other search planes flew from dawn to dusk, and the crews were utterly exhausted by nightfall, but ready to go again at first light. Despite the concentrated effort, not a sign was detected. After seven days Captain Stewart called a meeting of all the pilots, and announced, "Well guys, we've given it the royal shot, but given the conditions and lack of a beacon to work from, I'm afraid we'll have to scale down the search. Moreover, the temperature is going well below freezing every night and the ice forming around the rim of the lakes is creating a serious hazard for the aircraft on floats. They would normally have been pulled out of the water for fitting with skis for the winter. So, although it's always rough to call off a search without success, I'm afraid that's the only sensible thing left to us. I would like to thank you all for your cooperation and professionalism, and I know you hate to give up on one of your own kind. If we get even a clue we'll be back."

The other pilots agreed reluctantly, but since that was the time they normally took for vacations after the hectic pace of the hunting season, they were almost relieved. They also agreed that there was little point in risking more lives or equipment in what appeared to be a hopeless situation. It then remained for someone to tell Jennifer that the search was being suspended, which virtually meant that Bill was being given up for lost.

Reluctantly, Ross volunteered to tell Jennifer and the children because he knew them best, even though Captain Stewart offered to carry out the unpleasant duty, which was part of his responsibility as the Searchmaster. A pall of depression hung over the pilots since they were loathe to admit that one of their own had gone, even though they were very much aware of the hazards of their occupation.

Ross picked up Christie at the Hotel on his way to the trailer, as he knew he would need her moral support. As they entered the trailer, they could tell that Jennifer already expected the worst, and Keith, Dianne and David were uncharacteristically subdued. Jennifer had busied herself while the search was going on cleaning up Ross's trailer which now shone and smelled fresh from the disinfectants she had used. She immediately offered them fresh coffee from the sparkling pot which she joked would only hold one cup full before she cleaned out all the old grounds. They made awkward small talk while Ross wrestled with the boys until he said, "Christie, how about staying with the kids while I take Jennifer for some fresh air."

When they were well away from the trailer, Ross turned to Jennifer, and taking her hands in his said, "I'm afraid that we've had to give up the search. It's getting pretty dangerous for us to operate on floats with the ice forming on the lakes. The Search and Rescue people have also concluded that with the present conditions there's little point in continuing or someone else is likely to be lost. We've all given it our very best, but we didn't find a trace of Bill's plane. If he had survived, we would at least have spotted a fire 'cause he was well equipped with survival gear and could last a long time. I'm afraid that we have to face up to the inevitable and be realistic."

Jennifer started to weep silently and sobbed, "Oh, God, no. If you do, you're condemning him to death. You may have given up, but I never will. I just know he's alive somewhere and we'll find him."

"I'm glad to hear you say that, Jennifer. You must never give up hope, and you may be assured that we'll be constantly on the lookout when we can get into the air again. Meanwhile, I think the sensible thing to do would be to go out with the kids and stay with your folks for a while. I can't do much until I can operate the 185 on skis for the winter, so I was going to propose that I accompany you out for a while. I haven't had time to discuss it with her but I wondered if Christie would be interested in joining us."

Christie was taken totally by surprise at the proposal, but after her initial fluster, she agreed, "That might not be a bad idea. I've completely screwed up the plans for me to be in at Sustut and we can't really do much until we get replacement equipment. I haven't taken any vacations this year so maybe this would be a good time to do it. Would your folks have enough room for us Jennifer?"

"They rattle around in a big old house and they would be delighted to have someone to share it for a while, especially the kids. I don't mind admitting that having a little moral support from people who understand the situation would also help."

The surprise announcement by Ross had taken away the pain of the moment as Jennifer and Christie hugged each other silently. The children joined in for a mass hug while Ross stood uncomfortably on the outside.

"Okay everybody, we've all got a lot of work to do to get ready. I still have to put the 185 on skis before we leave and I'm sure that Christie's boss will be just thrilled to lose his top geologist without warning."

Sensing that it would be best to leave Jennifer and the children alone for a while so that she could break the news to them about their father, Ross and Christie left the trailer holding hands, in an uncharacteristic public show of affection, and hopped into Ross' Jeep as they headed for the Hotel to break the news to the rest of the geologists. As they entered the room cluttered with survey maps and instruments, Jesse Mathews looked up from the map he, Mark Douglas, and Brenton Sherwood were studying intently.

"Good grief!" he exploded. "You look as if you'd swallowed the cat, Christie. What's happening?"

"Well, I still have four weeks vacation coming, and I've decided to take them now for a trip to the city, or other warmer climes," she responded with a straight face.

"Absolutely impossible," growled Jesse with mock indignation. "We have to finish that survey this winter in Sustut and we're already way behind schedule with Bill's crash. You're the senior geologist on our crew and we just can't do without you right now."

"Okay then, I quit," Christie responded in a flash of anger. "Now you'll have to get along on your own."

"Whoa, just a minute! What's going on here? You've been with us for twelve years, starting as a student, and you're one of our senior field people. You can't just walk away from a promising career for no reason," Jesse exclaimed while Mark and Brent looked on wide-eyed. They all joshed Christie, but she was highly respected for her technical skill and practical knowledge in the field.

"You can if you're going to accompany Jennifer and the kids to her folks. Until we get our replacement equipment and can fly it in on skis there's not a lot I can do around here. Ross is also coming with us," she added nonchalantly.

"Aha, now we have the truth," smirked Brenton. "You and he are just sneaking off together."

"If she is it's none of your business, so you'd better get started learning what's going on around here, Brent. You're always complaining that we never give you enough responsibility, so now's your chance to prove it. How soon will you be leaving, Christie?"

"It'll take Ross about five days to get his plane on to skis for the winter operation, so that's about how much time we have."

"Okay Brent, we're going to utilize every minute of Christie's time until she leaves, so you'd better get qualified to replace her at Sustut. Christie can help Mark and me in the office when she returns."

Meanwhile, Ross enlisted the help of one of the other pilots who was down at the dock and pulled the 185 along the dock until they reached the ramp at the end. There they laid out planks and Ross backed his Jeep down until he could get a tow rope attached to the struts. In one way the fresh snow was a blessing, as it made a slippery surface for the floats to slide up the ramp, but on the other hand it made the footing for the jeep equally slippery, and he was not able to get enough traction to tow the plane up the ramp to the point where he could work on it and replace the floats with skis for winter operation. Finally, he had to give up and walk off in search of the only tow truck operator in town. It proved to be a lengthy process and dusk was upon him before he finally located the truck parked outside the pub. Without disclosing the reason for his haste, he had a difficult time persuading the operator away from his beer and then only upon agreeing to double time which Ross could ill-afford. With the tow truck hitched

163

to the jeep the 185 slid smoothly up the ramp and on to a clear area where Ross could work on it.

It was already dark when Ross arrived back at his trailer to find Jennifer, Christie and the children all dressed and waiting for him to take them to dinner. Although Jennifer had protested strenuously, she finally agreed that it would be a diversion for the children. He had forgotten about his invitation when he became involved with the 185.

Ross blurted out his excuse as he rushed to get washed and dressed, while the children impatiently stood by the door. Jennifer was trying to convince them that the pup would be fine on its own for a while and would probably sleep the whole time. They had made it a bed in a box lined with one of Ross's old sweaters, and it was curled up sound asleep, the picture of contentment. Ross saw the impact the pup was having on them and was relieved that it was easing the pain of missing their father.

As they entered the hotel dining room, a group of heads turned and a number of people came over to give Jennifer and the children their condolences. Although well-meaning, they made it very difficult for Jennifer and she wished she had not come. On the other hand, it seemed that everyone had heard about Ross and Christie accompanying her out to her folks. It was already common knowledge about the blossoming romance between Christie and Ross and it elicited a few underbreath ribald remarks which Ross tried to ignore. It was a difficult evening for Jennifer and the children. She was fighting back tears and most relieved when it was finally over and they were able to go back to the sanctity of Ross's trailer. Christie and Ross left Jennifer alone there with the children and they were also grateful to be alone for a while to discuss their plans.

"Jesse was just thrilled when I told him I was going out with Jennifer, to accompany her home, but when I offered to quit he changed his tune drastically. He's going to send Brent into Sustut as soon as they can get in, and I'll work in the office for a while when I get back."

"Good. I think it will help Jennifer's morale when she has got someone with a direct link to Bill to go out with her. I had a tough time convincing her she should go to her folks for a while, instead of hanging around Sioux Falls, but I think she's resigned to it now. It's great of you to volunteer to come along since you two seem to have really hit it off."

"I can certainly feel for her, especially not knowing what happened to Bill and leaving it in limbo. She's a brave lady and I admire her for following her man into this country, and the life he was leading."

The next few days were a blur of activity for everyone as they prepared to leave Sioux Falls on the Friday train. Christie worked long hours trying to get Brent checked out as a replacement in Sustut for the winter while Ross worked from dawn to dusk winterizing the 185. Replacing the floats with skis was always a difficult job, but it seemed even more so when he was preoccupied with thoughts of Christie and Bill. The problem was compounded when a group of his friends decided to have a farewell party for him, which left him in questionable health for the next couple of days. Jennifer tried to concentrate on catching up the children on their schoolwork, which had fallen behind during the search and subsequent move to Sioux Falls.

Jennifer's parents offered again to come up and accompany her and the children back to the city, but she was able to dissuade them when she told them of the decision of Ross and Christie to come with her. They had known Ross for many years and Mike had met Christie on his way out from Buffalo Narrows. They were excited about the prospect of having the visitors and immediately started on preparations. Although the circumstances were unfortunate, they could not contain their pleasure at the thought of having Jennifer and the children with them, at least for the winter.

Finally, everything came together and they arrived at the railroad station in time for the Friday train. Virtually the entire town turned out to see them off and it was a tearful farewell. As the conductor loaded them on to the train he

165

looked suspiciously at the cardboard box with the holes cut in it that Keith was carrying very carefully. He correctly surmised that there was an animal in it but decided to turn a blind eye to the violation of the railroad rules prohibiting animals in the passenger compartment. "What you got there, young fellow? School books I'll bet," he said giving Keith a knowing wink as he helped him aboard with his cargo and showed them to their seats. Keith blushed furiously and was tempted to show off Buck but kept his peace. As the train pulled out, Jennifer could not hold back the tears that flowed down her cheeks as she left with heavy heart, not knowing the fate of Bill. Christie and Ross tried to console her and encouraged her to never give up hope.

Jennifer had forgotten that the children had never travelled on a train before, and they were enthralled, for which she was thankful as it took their minds off the reason for the journey. Ross was tremendous with them, playing games and generally keeping them amused. One of their favourites was the horse game where they were allotted sides of the train to watch and each time they saw a horse they scored points according to the colour of the horse. Christie teamed up with Dianne against the boys and there was great rivalry to see which team reached one hundred points. One of the rules was that a team had to bury all their horses if they saw a cemetery on their side. Soon the whole car of passengers was participating, assisting their favourite teams to spot horses. Christie was delighted to see how Ross could keep the children occupied and immediately started fantasizing about having children of her own.

Finally, the children became tired of the game and Ross went off in search of the friendly conductor who had welcomed them aboard and turned a blind eye to the squirming box. Ross explained the circumstances of their trip and, as he suspected, the conductor was most cooperative. He came up to the children and announced in an official voice, "Are you the Headingly children?"

"Yes, sir," answered Keith in his usual polite manner.

"Well, the engineer has requested your presence in the engine compartment." Wide-eyed, they followed in silence as the conductor unlocked the door leading into the engineer's compartment, where they had a spectacular view of the tracks and the scenery ahead. The conductor whispered in the engineer's ear who turned and said, "Who can blow this whistle for me at the next bend?"

The boys fought to see who could be first but finally the engineer said, "Ladies first," and lifted Dianne up on his knee where she could reach the chain. "Alright, now!" he commanded and Dianne's face lit up as the mournful whistle echoed down the track. The boys followed and the conductor had a hard time getting them to leave, but finally they thanked the engineer and returned to the compartment just bubbling and competing to see who could tell Jennifer and Christie about their experience. Wordlessly, Jennifer turned and kissed Ross on the cheek. "You've found yourself a gem here, Christie, once you've taken the raw edges off!" The two women giggled knowingly as they shared their womanly insight to the embarassment of Ross who tried to look occupied with the scenery.

The hours rolled by and it was almost midnight when the train rolled into the station in Edmonton. All the children were sound asleep and could not be aroused so each of the adults picked one up, followed by the conductor with the squirming box and their luggage which he placed on a cart and went off in search of a porter. At that point, Mike came running down the platform to greet them, followed at a slower pace by Sue who was impeded by her arthritis. It was a tearful reunion and Ross and Christie stood back awkwardly while Jennifer was embraced by her parents. Seeing the children were asleep, Mike and Sue resisted the urge to hug them all and led them to their station wagon parked at the entrance. Ross went back to thank the kindly conductor and promised to let him know if they got any news about Bill as he took the pup in the box from him. "With service like this I think I'll take the train all the time instead of flying. Now that I think

167

of it, it was my lifelong ambition when I was a youngster to be a train engineer. Maybe I'll reconsider it now," he added with a laugh.

The children were still asleep when they arrived at the house so they just packed them straight into bed. Then Sue awkwardly asked Jennifer in a whisper about the sleeping accommodation for Ross and Christie, as she was not quite sure what to expect in these modern times. Ross gallantly solved the problem by announcing that he would sleep on the sofa in the den, while Jennifer and Christie took the single beds in her old room. Christie had a benign smile on her face as she kissed Ross goodnight and turned to follow Jennifer to her room.

The following morning the children were awake bright and early, tearing around the house chasing the pup which had been shut in the kitchen all night. Mike was up early as usual, and had the coffee brewing by the time the others were awake. Ross was the first to join him in the kitchen, and Mike immediately asked him what he thought Bill's prospects were.

"To be completely realistic, not very good," Ross answered with candour. "If that snowfall hadn't come when it did we might have had a chance to spot the plane, but once that covered everything with a white blanket it was like looking for a needle in a haystack. Bill's a tough character, well skilled in survival techniques, but it'll be tough for him to survive the winter out there, assuming he survived the crash. We have to take a realistic, and possibly fatalistic, approach in this business and Bill knew the risks. He was the most cautious pilot I know but sometimes the odds stack up against you. To be brutally frank, I think we should face up to the fact that he's dead."

Mike could not restrain the tears that flowed down his cheeks in an uncharacteristic show of emotion. "I thought of that boy as my own son, and that last summer I spent helping him build their house was unquestionably the best time of my life. It's going to be tough for Jennifer without him 'cause they were inseparable ever since college. However, she's a spunky gal too, so I'm sure she'll make it. Hopefully they'll stay here until she decides what she wants to do. We can help her financially since I know they were living right on the edge, and I don't suppose she'll get any insurance until they prove that Bill is dead."

Ross squeezed Mike's shoulder in a silent gesture of sympathy, and was unable to think of anything more to say that would provide solace for Mike's private grief.

After one of Mike's famous breakfasts, Ross asked if he could borrow Mike's car for an hour, as he had some business to attend to in town. The ladies were in deep conversation and they didn't notice Ross leaving until they came into the living room where Mike was sitting reading to the children.

"Where's Ross?" enquired Christie, trying her best to sound casual.

"He said that he had some business in town and borrowed my car."

"Typical bachelor," said Christie with a nervous laugh. "He has probably gone off looking for available females in the Mall."

"I doubt it. He seems to me to be pretty well hooked," Jennifer reassured her.

Despite the assurances, Christie paced around the house until she heard the car draw up in the driveway and tried to appear very nonchalant as Ross strode into the house, tousling the childrens' hair before greeting her.

"How were the girls at the Mall?" Christie asked casually.

"Stunning," Ross answered without hesitation. "Sure away better than the girls in Sioux Falls," he added with straight face.

"As a matter of fact, I looked at some brochures for exotic places in the South Pacific that I could escape to, but they wouldn't sell me a single ticket so I ended up having to buy two, and now I have to see if I can get someone to go with me," he said seriously. "Anybody interested?"

The children all chorused, "Yeah!" while Christie looked confused for a moment. Finally he handed her an envelope with a card and tickets inside for two weeks in Hawaii. She noted that they were made out to Mr. and Mrs. Stuart, and the tears welled up in her eyes as she ran forward and threw her arms around his neck. "Only one problem," Ross added. "You note that they're booked to leave on Monday and made out to Mr. and Mrs. Stuart, so if you want to be an honest woman, how about marrying me?"

Christie stood open-mouthed, totally incapable of responding. Ross added further to her utter shock by saying, "If you're interested, you might want to try this ring on or I'll have to take it back to the store."

"That is unquestionably the strangest proposal I've ever had," she finally gasped. "If you propose to all your ladies that way, no wonder you're still a bachelor."

"That's the way us bush pilots do things," he laughed. "But I can assure you there have been no other proposals and this is definitely the last for this cowboy."

Dianne finally broke the spell by shouting, "Say yes, Christie."

Jennifer quietly walked over to Christie and put her arms around her, tears of happiness and sadness welling up in her eyes. "I'm very happy for you Christie," she whispered. "He's a great guy, and Bill's best friend."

Finally gathering her composure again, Christie turned to Ross and said, "You really know how to sweep a gal off her feet don't you. Obviously you've been brainwashing the kids to support you, but since it's the best offer I've had in a long time, the answer is yes."

Ross grabbed her in a bear hug and swept her off her feet as everyone else clapped. The pall of sadness that had been hanging over the family was suddenly dissipated by this unanticipated turn of events, and temporarily diverted their attention from the loss of Bill. Christie was the first to inject a note of reality into the situation.

"How on earth could we possibly get married before Monday?" she said seriously.

"We'll all chip in," said Jennifer, all business. "Mom knows the minister at the church well and I'm sure he'll co-operate under the circumstances. If you get the licence, I'll bet he'd do the deed on Sunday." Nodding her head in assent, Sue was already looking up his number in the phone book. "Christie and I will go out and shop for her dress this afternoon while Dad and Ross go out and rent their Tuxedos," she added with a smile.

"TUXEDO!" exploded Ross. "You wouldn't find me dead in one of those penguin suits! I thought I was making a major concession bringing a tie to wear with my cowboy shirt, let alone a tuxedo," he said with mock disgust. "Actually, I did bring the only suit I own in the world and that will have to suffice for this bush pilot, I'm afraid."

Mike was roaring with laughter and agreed wholeheartedly with Ross who was obviously a kindred spirit, like Bill. He concluded that it must be the flying fraternity who were going to preserve their way of life at any cost.

Christie finally relented and said it was all a joke. In fact she was flattered that Ross was even making a concession and wearing a suit. "Well, now that we've decided on the dress code for this auspicious occasion, we'd better get down to the licence bureau and then you can drop me off to do some shopping. I'm sure that you and Mike can get into some mischief while I'm getting prettied up for my first marriage. Would you like to come with me Jennifer, and advise me what a bride wears for various occasions, especially in Hawaii?"

"I'd love to come and wander around stores for a while," Jennifer answered. "Shopping was quite limited in Buffalo Narrows and maybe it will do my morale some good. I'll leave the kids with you, Mum, or they'll hate every minute of it."

There was no objection from the children who were glued to the television watching cartoons with Buck sound asleep on Dianne's lap.

The ceremony was scheduled for ten a.m. the next morning and because of the circumstances only included the immediate family. Christie had had her hair done the evening before and in her new blue wedding dress looked stunning. Ross looked positively uncomfortable in his suit and tie and was incredibly nervous as the ceremony proceeded. Christie could actually feel him shake as he stood next to her and he fumbled for ages to find the ring and place it on her finger. He was taken aback when Christie also produced a gold wedding band and placed it on his finger. This symbol seemed to finally bring home to him the fact that they were now married and he looked at her in disbelief that she was his bride. After all these years of bachelorhood, he couldn't believe how quickly things had happened when he finally met the right girl.

After the ceremony they adjourned to a restaurant where Mike had reserved a private room, and the mood was joyful despite the loss of Bill. In his speech, Ross expressed confidence that Bill would be found and Jennifer assured them all that Bill was definitely alive and would come back to join them soon. She seemed to have taken on a new strength from that conviction and no longer wept as she had done regularly for the past two weeks.

That night Ross and Christie retired to a hotel where they could enjoy the privacy of their special moment, and the next morning they were escorted by the whole family to the airport where they received a royal sendoff on their honeymoon trip to Hawaii. Christie looked positively radiant and turned many heads as she and her tall mate left the lounge to board their flight.

Ross and Christie returned from Hawaii looking tanned, fit and happy. There had been a complete transformation in Ross who seemed more subdued and not as impulsive. He was most attentive to Christie and openly held her hand which he had never done before in public. Christie looked positively radiant and the pair brought memories of their own honeymoon rushing back to Jennifer and she could not hold back the tears welling up in her eyes even though she had felt completely under control for a while. It was painful to think that this entire crisis had its origins on their honeymoon down the Paradis River when they had fallen in love with Buffalo Narrows and vowed that some day they would build a house there. Now their dream was shattered and she did not know whether Bill was alive or dead.

After two days, Ross and Christie announced that they must get back to Sioux Falls, Ross to get ready for the winter's flying operations and Christie to the mining exploration. Jennifer and the children were most reluctant to see them go as they seemed to represent the last link with their former life. It was a tearful farewell at the railroad station but as Ross hugged Jennifer he whispered in her ear not to give up and they would keep searching until they found the answer to Bill's disappearance. "I know he's alive," she sobbed with conviction.

Chapter Eleven

Three weeks had passed since the crash, and Bill was regaining his strength slowly. The deep cuts on his face had healed well and he was able to hobble around the cabin on a pair of makeshift crutches that Willie Bearpaw had made for him. Suzanne had padded the arm braces with fur so that they were reasonably comfortable, and they gave him some mobility. His biggest concern was the broken leg which still gave considerable pain. Suzanne had fashioned a splint out of bark, strapped tightly with thongs made from animal sinew, but she was constantly concerned about gangrene so tried to inspect the leg every day to ensure adequate circulation. Although she tried to be as gentle as possible, Bill had to bite on a piece of rawhide to mask the pain. It was a small price to pay to try and preserve the limb until medical help became available.

One evening Bill could not restrain himself any longer and broached the subject of his return to civilization.

"What are the chances of me getting out before spring, Willie," he asked after the Indians had obviously had a good day of trapping.

"None, unless your buddies come in and get you, or you walk out," he replied brusquely. "It's pretty near fifty miles back to the reserve across the lake. At this time of year the lake ain't safe 'cause there's lots of air pockets in the ice 'til it's frozen thick. Even then there could be mush ice. One time we lost six guys from the reserve when they went through the ice on skidoos. Only way we could get you there would be pulling you on a travois. If the crash didn't kill you that sure as hell would," he added for emphasis. "Besides, what's the rush? It ain't many white men get the privilege of living with the natives and learning how to live off the land like we do, eh Paul?"

"That's for sure," answered Paul. "You white guys don't understand the Great Spirit that created this land. You just come in and take it like it was yours. He gave us Grandfather Sun and Grandmother Moon and they carpeted the earth with forests thousands of years ago. They made the trees to give us food, bark and shelter for the animals. Our ancestors have lived here for twenty five thousand years, and we treat the forests with respect and only take what we need to live, not like the white man who cuts them down and kills everything in sight. The white men have only been here a couple of hundred years, but now they figure they own everything. The Creator only allows us to borrow the land when we're on earth, but you guys grab it like it was your own. When our young guys reach puberty they go into wild places to learn all about the forest and animals, and how to look after them. That way the forest will always be there for our people just like our ancestors left them for us. When the white men came here, it was like we gave them a place in our house to live and the next thing we know they threw us out and took the house for themselves. Now they want us to ask permission to feed ourselves with fish and animals from our forest."

Bill felt thoroughly chastised and realized he had made a serious error in raising the topic and determined not to mention it again. He felt like an ingrate, and just had to accept the fact that he was lucky to be alive and would have to resign himself to his fate without question until spring, which seemed an eon away. The Indians and Bill had no further discussions on the possibility of getting him out to civilization, nor dare he even mention it to Suzanne who was also hurt by his question after all the care she had given him. The Indians' livelihood depended on their trapping during the winter months, and they could not afford to take time to make their way out for help.

Frequently, when the trappers were out on their traplines, they would hear the drone of plane engines in the distance but were never able to attract them, and would not bother to tell Bill about them in case of raising false hopes.

Apart from his physical injuries, Bill spent many agonizing hours worrying about Jennifer and the children, who undoubtedly had given him up for lost by now. Suzanne was a tremendous comfort and listened sympathetically when he became nostalgic and talked about his family, and a dream that had come to a literal crashing conclusion. He entered fits of severe depression and Suzanne would stay behind with him in the cabin although she should have been out on the trapline with the men. Willie Bearpaw and Paul were pretty empathetic with Bill, but the third male would not even speak to him or look at him, and kept to himself in a corner of the cabin, grunting only when spoken to, but rarely joining the conversation, particularly when Bill was involved. Finally, one day Bill asked Suzanne what his problem was.

"He was also taken away to Indian school when he was young and although he's never told us, they say that he was sexually abused as a boy until he finally tried to commit suicide in desperation. He was taken away and locked up in an insane asylum until he was twenty eight years old when the Mounties brought him back and just dumped him on the reserve. He scares people and everybody steers clear in case

176

he gets violent. Willie and Paul bring him out trapping with them to get him away from the taunts of the young kids, and some adults are pretty cruel with him too. His name, Mye-Ook, means grizzly bear, and he refuses to go by any other name. Although he speaks fluent English he won't speak one word, and has a violent hatred of all white men. That's why it's a good idea if you stay away from him."

"Don't worry, I've already learned that and wouldn't want to be left alone with him in the cabin."

"The guys will make sure he doesn't harm you 'cause they're always here when he is."

Suzanne spent many hours teaching Bill to scrape and prepare the furs of the animals that the men brought in from the trapline every day, and it helped to pass the time in addition to making him feel useful. He also helped Suzanne prepare some of the meals so that she jestingly referred to him as the camp squaw. At first the food made him nauseous, particularly the bear meat. It was extremely greasy, but Suzanne explained that the men needed the fat to combat the cold when they were out on the trapline. Bill's favourite was the fresh bannock that Suzanne baked every day, which was laced with raisins and molasses. The Indians dipped it in the bear grease which ran down their chins when they ate it. Bill surmised that they were prime candidates for heart disease, although Suzanne assured him that such a thing was a rarity. This was attributed to a diet heavy in fish and wild game, which was extremely low in cholesterol.

In the evenings when the men came back in from the traplines, invariably the discussion again came around to the injustice of the white men to the Indians in stealing their land, women and heritage. Bill found it extremely difficult to defend the white man's role, and he even felt guilty about moving into Buffalo Narrows and building his home in the midst of their land. The area was well known to the Indians, and their ancestors had hunted and trapped in the area long before it was taken by the white man, and they had been pushed back into the reserve. At one time they had called it

Klay-Ah-Kwohs and it had been almost sacred to them. As the stories unfolded, Bill resolved in his mind that if he survived this experience, he would return some of his land to the Indians, in gratitude to them for saving his life, and as a small token of penance for his fellow white man.

Bill was still wearing the same clothes he had on when he crashed, and even the smoke from the tin stove could not mask his odour. Finally, in desperation, he asked Suzanne if it would be feasible to have a bath and wash his clothes.

In response she broke out in gales of laughter. "I'd been wondering how much longer you could stand yourself, 'cause you're getting pretty gamy to be near. We've got an old tub that I'll fill with snow and put on the stove to melt and warm. I'll help you bathe yourself then wash your clothes in the same water. Only problem is, we've got no extra clothes for you to wear, so you'll have to stick to your bed 'til your clothes are dry again."

With Suzanne's help, Bill peeled off the offending clothes and Suzanne took a cloth and started to give him a bed bath with the warm water. At first Bill was embarrassed to expose himself to Suzanne, but she light-heartedly said, "I've seen all kinds of guys in the buff during my nursing days, not to mention the fact that I've been married, which stripped me of my last vestige of self-consciousness. As well, nude bathing in the lake at the reserve's an accepted fact, 'cause none of the houses have indoor plumbing."

Suzanne gently washed Bill, drying him with a towel as she went along. As she worked, her raven black hair fell over his face and body, and Bill could not disguise his arousal. They had lived in close proximity for many weeks, and Suzanne had nursed him back to health with her gentle, caring manner to the point where they had formed strong feelings for each other. Involuntarily, Bill reached up and drew Suzanne to him, gently kissing her on the lips. At first Suzanne resisted but then eagerly returned his kiss passionately as Bill pulled her on to the bed beside him. Even the pain from his leg was no deterrent as they locked in a pas-

178

sionate embrace and he ran his lips eagerly over her face and neck. Suzanne responded willingly as she rolled on top of him and the pent-up passion flowed between them in an uninhibited spasm of lovemaking. With their passion spent, they lay wordless, locked in each others arms.

Finally the pain in Bill's leg burned through the euphoria of the moment, and he gasped as Suzanne gently disengaged herself from him, kissing him firmly on the lips as she did so.

"My God, Suzanne, that was totally unpremeditated but I have absolutely no regrets. It was fantastic! Would you believe that you're the first woman, apart from my wife, that I've made love to? We met as teenagers and married young, so we didn't have the opportunity to explore the field like most people seem to do today. Until now I must admit that I haven't really looked for anyone else."

"I was the same, 'cause we were cloistered during my school days in the convent, and during my nurse's training. I'm afraid that making love with my husband wasn't what I'd expected 'cause he was pretty insensitive and rough. I guess he thought I was a savage and should be treated accordingly! For me that was truly the first time I've ever enjoyed making love and I too have absolutely no regrets. However, the guys'll be getting back soon and I'd be ostracized if they caught me making out with a white guy. Mye-Ook would even kill us, I'm sure."

Suzanne scurried around clearing up the cabin and putting Bill's clothing in the bath water to soak while he remained under the covers, feasting on Suzanne with his eyes. He felt a twinge of guilt when he thought of Jennifer, but quickly dismissed it when he justified his actions on the circumstances, and tried to convince himself that it was completely unpremeditated and might never happen again. Subconsciously, though, he was sure that he would not hesitate to do it again, although he shared Suzanne's concern about the reaction of the men. He'd have to completely mask his feelings for Suzanne and give no clue as to what had taken place.

It was almost dark by the time the trappers returned, which had given time for Suzanne to wash Bill's clothes and dry them by the hot stove. He was again fully dressed and feeling totally refreshed, spiritually and physically, but grateful for the dim candlelight in the cabin. He was certain the guilt would show on his face, so he remained in the shadows as much as possible. Suzanne hurried about getting dinner for the hungry men, and did not look at Bill at all, in order to avoid any inadvertent signs of their passionate interlude while the others were out on the trapline. She engaged them in small talk about their trapping in their native dialect which was still incomprehensible to Bill, although he was starting to recognize a few words, which he practised on Suzanne when they were alone. He soon found that the white man's tongue was not suited to the language, but he was determined to learn as much as possible.

After dinner the conversation again turned to the injustices that had been perpetrated on the aboriginal people by the white man, and Bill's sense of guilt was more acute than ever after the afternoon episode. He was subjected to yet another lengthy tutorial on the history of the aboriginal people and the social malaise that had been introduced by the white man. Although suddenly embarrassed to be a member of the race that had engendered this hatred, he was nevertheless fascinated by the stories that unfolded during the long evenings in the cabin.

One evening he asked Paul, "Is all this history written down anywhere?"

"Nope. We pass it on from generation to generation, but the trouble is the young bucks ain't interested any more, and they won't listen to the guys that know the history. The way it's going it'll disappear like our language."

"That would be a disaster, even for the white man, because they might have a better understanding of how you feel if they could read your side of it. Why don't you write it down, Paul, because you know it all."

"I never learned to write, and never went to school. What English I know I picked up from the hunters we used to guide."

"Do we have any paper in the cabin, and maybe I could start writing it down for you," Bill offered.

"I've got an old exercise book that I keep notes in, but you can have it if you want," Suzanne said, reaching under her pillow and handing Bill a child's school book.

"Would you mind if I start making notes, so that when we get out I could have it written down for you, and then it would never be lost?"

"Sure, go ahead," approved Paul. Willie Bearpaw also nodded his head in the affirmative while Mye-Ook just sat and rocked in his bunk, obviously furious that a white man would be writing down their history. Suzanne looked pleased that Bill was going to do something constructive for them, and it would keep him occupied.

The weeks flowed past and Bill had virtually lost track of time. One morning, however, Suzanne astonished him by presenting a gaily-wrapped parcel that smelled smoky, but felt soft. As he unwrapped it he discovered a beautiful pair of moccasins, all beaded and trimmed in rabbit fur, that were truly a work of art.

Overwhelmed, Bill exclaimed, "Thank you! But what's the occasion?"

"Merry Christmas," she responded as she kissed him gently on the cheek.

Tears welled up in Bill's eyes as a flood of memories of past Christmases with his family filled his mind. He choked out a feeble response, and fell into his bed as he thought of Jennifer and the children who undoubtedly were not aware that he was alive, which would subdue their normally boisterous celebration. He had no idea what they were doing, but he desperately hoped that they were with Jennifer's folks, and making the best of a grim situation.

Finally recovering his composure, Bill turned to Suzanne and said, "I'd completely lost track of time, and had no idea that it was Christmas. How on earth did you know?"

"I always bring a small diary with me on these trips and keep track of the date. The fellows don't celebrate Christmas, but I guess it's a leftover from my days in the convent and I always observe it as well as possible in these circumstances. We can't offer you turkey, but we've got half a dozen nice birch partridge that I'll be serving for dinner so that'll have to do."

Bill silently reached for his ring finger and pulled off his gold graduation ring that his father had given him when he graduated from Military College. "I'd like you to have this, Suzanne, as a small token of appreciation of all the care and love you've given me. I'm sure that if it hadn't been for your tender, loving care I wouldn't have survived this ordeal and I'll be eternally gratefully to you, regardless of what happens in the future. Please accept this with my best wishes for a Merry Christmas. Hopefully we'll be able to celebrate the next one in more traditional fashion. At least we can say we have a white Christmas, looking at the depth of snow out there. In fact it looks as if it'll never melt."

Suzanne silently took the ring and attached it to a gold chain around her neck on which Bill noted she also had a small crucifix. "I'll always treasure this," she said quietly with a catch in her voice.

It was dusk when the trappers returned but Suzanne had dinner all cooked and ready for the table. She had cooked the partridge with some of her valuable onions as stuffing, and made a rich gravy with flour. There were candles on the table, and she had hung some streamers from the rafters to add to the festive air.

"Holy smokes, Suzanne. What's the occasion?" asked Willie as he sat down and picked up his knife and fork ready to eat.

"It's Christmas Day. Happy Christmas."

Although Willie did not profess to have any Christian beliefs, he was always careful not to make light of the stories

182

he had heard from the priest and was very familiar with the story of Christ's birth. He always thought they were better off than Jesus, who had been born in a stable. By comparison they were in luxury in the cabin, especially with Suzanne cooking for them. Finally, he grudging responded, "Happy Christmas," although the other two remained silent.

"I guess this would've been a big day for you, White Man," Willie added to Bill.

"It is a big day, thanks to you guys. What better gift could anyone have than to have his life saved. Thanks to you all this is one of the most important Christmases I've ever had. I'm sorry that I don't have gifts for you all, but I hope we have a Potlach when we get out and I'll make sure everybody gets a gift. For the time being, I'm going to give back most of my land in Buffalo Narrows to the tribe so that you'll have Klay-Ah-Kwohs as your own again. That'll have to be my present for right now."

While the men started in to eat the feast, Bill noticed that Suzanne had her head bowed and he joined her in a silent prayer that his family was safe and happy, and that he would make it out to civilization in spring. Somehow he felt that he was communicating directly with Jennnifer, and believed that by ESP she would know that he was alive.

January seemed interminable. There were only about six hours of daylight, which was barely enough for the trappers to cover the entire trapline. They started from each end and met in the middle to return to the cabin at night, totally exhausted from walking through the waist deep snow. Even their snowshoes sank in the new snow that arrived in vicious storms, obliterating the trails, and made setting and finding the traps difficult. There were many days when the storms were so bad that they stayed in the cabin all day, which was uncomfortably crowded with the five of them packed in. Bill suffered periods of deep depression during those times, much worse than when he was alone or with Suzanne who frequently stayed behind to cook meals or prepare the skins when conditions were too bad for her to endure. Bill developed a new respect for these people who suffered great privation in order to reap the bounty of the forest.

To make the days more endurable Bill borrowed some sheets of paper from Suzanne's notebook, and made up a set of cards. He then taught the Indians a number of card games which they all, with the exception of Mye-Ook, participated in with great gusto. Mye-Ook sat on his bunk, rocking back and forward, all the while staring at Bill, which made the hairs on his neck stand up. Despite all his efforts, Bill could not initiate a dialogue with Mye-Ook who had obviously suffered a great hurt at the hands of the white man.

On two occasions the trappers were caught in blizzards and did not return at night which filled Bill with great apprehension. On these occasions he was tempted to initiate love making again with Suzanne, but she had remained deliberately aloof ever since their one unpremeditated episode. Sometimes he could not help but indulge in conjecture as to his fate if the men did not return, and he was left to fend for himself. Fortunately, the trappers were woods wise and had constructed the shelters on the traplines where they took refuge until the storms abated. They always carried a pocketful of pemmican for sustenance until they could return to the cabin. From their stories at night, when they chose to speak English, Bill formed a mental image of the traplines and tried to visualise where he had crashed in relation to the cabin. He was becoming quite adept at scraping the skins that the trappers brought in daily, and felt that they appreciated his limited help. In this way the days slowly passed, although at times they seemed endless, and Bill felt utterly devoid of hope that he would ever see the outside world again.

✝ Chapter Twelve

After Ross and Christie had left, Jennifer threw herself into a whirl of activity to keep occupied. First she had to get the children registered in a school, which caused considerable consternation. She then realized how they were lacking in social interaction after the isolation of Buffalow Narrows, and could see that no matter how idyllic their life had been, there were definitely drawbacks. She felt sad that they had to be rectified under such circumstances. Nevertheless, she anticipated that they would adapt quickly, as they had done when they were still in the air force and moved to a new base. In no time the children would be talking about their new friends and activities.

Jennifer was restless, and reluctant to accept financial assistance from her father, although she had no income whatsoever. She was not able to collect any insurance settlements until proof of Bill's death was established, and that could take months. Although she knew that Mike was willing to support her and the children indefinitely, she was too proud to accept charity.

Day after day she scanned the Help Wanted columns in the newspaper, and visited employment agencies until she was becoming totally discouraged. Then, one day one of the legal firms she had applied to called and asked her to return for an interview. She was so excited she could barely sleep the night before, and was up at dawn showering and fixing her hair and face. Selection of a suitable dress from her limited wardrobe consumed at least an hour, and she ended up having to rush to be on time for her appointment.

She was ushered into a fairly small office occupied by a man in his mid-thirties. "Hi, I'm Robert Cummings, and I'm one of the partners in the firm. What I'm looking for is a research assistant to help me prepare my cases. We're just starting to expand our practice and I simply don't have the time to do the research myself anymore. Have you done any similar work?"

"Not since university," Jennifer admitted, "and I hate to say how long ago that was."

"I'm sure you're much younger than I am," Robert said with a pleasant smile. "So it can't be that long."

Jennifer had taken an immediate liking to him and covertly admired his tall, athletic physique, open face and brown curly hair. He was impeccably dressed in a finely tailored suit.

"More than anything I would just like to try, and if you're prepared I would be glad to start on a probationary basis. I won't burden you with the reasons, but let's just to say I suddenly find myself a single parent and am too proud to accept charity from my folks."

"All right. May I call you Jennifer?" Not waiting for an answer he continued, "How soon could you start?"

"Would right now be satisfactory? All I have to do is call my mother to look after the kids."

"Great. How many children do you have?"

"Three. Two boys, ten and six and a girl eight. They're missing their father badly and trying to adjust to regular school again after the relative freedom of the wilderness."

"I'd love to hear all about your adventures some time, but meantime let's put you to work on a month's probation. You'll have the desk just outside my office. One of the girls will show you where the coffee pot is and then I'll give you your first brief."

Robert was a little doubtful about Jennifer being able to handle the work but was highly impressed by her attitude and willingness to learn. Jennifer shook his hand a little too enthusiastically and assured him that she would live up to his expectations. Cummings had a smile on his face as he watched this spunky lady leave the office and felt confident that she would work out well. As an afterthought he realized that they had not even discussed salary but he concluded that it would be a secondary consideration for Jennifer.

Jennifer plunged wholeheartedly into her new work and evening classes to learn about data processors. She even managed to squeeze in time to help out with the Brownie pack that Dianne had joined and participated in the home and school activities. For the first time in years, she started attending church with her mother on Sundays, along with the protesting children. Mike had enrolled the boys in junior hockey and the whole family became totally absorbed in their new lives to the point where they very rarely mentioned Buffalo Narrows or Bill, although each had private thoughts, particularly in the sanctity of the church on Sundays.

Time passed quickly with their full lives, and Christmas was upon them before they knew it. Although she was not disposed to celebrate, Jennifer knew that she had to give the children as happy a Christmas as possible. It was the first time they had spent Christmas with Sue and Mike for many years, and they were ecstatic. Sue baked and cooked for weeks while Mike disappeared into his workshop for hours manufacturing special gifts for the children. Woodworking had always been his hobby and he produced some beautiful toys that would probably be passed on to the children's children.

Robert Cummings' instinctive feeling about Jennifer was justified, and she quickly became indispensable to him. With her natural ability, she soon assimilated the word processor operation and the evening classes gave her an excellent grounding in data processing and retrieval. On many occasions the pair of them worked well into the night, preparing cases, and the client load expanded accordingly.

In the week before Christmas, Robert stunned Jennifer by inviting her out to dinner, as he had something important to discuss with her. She was in a total quandry, not wanting to become involved in any extra curricular activity, although she had become very fond of Robert. She had no idea what his marital status was, but she had carefully outlined her own situation.

"I have absolutely no ulterior motives, Jennifer, and I'm separated from my wife. I just thought it would be nice for us to get away from the office for a while, and I feel you've been working so hard that you need a break. In fact we both do!"

Jennifer was speechless for a moment, and then she realized how nice it would be to go out for a while as a break from her arduous routine. Reluctantly she agreed and called Sue to advise her that she would be late without offering an explanation.

Although she would have liked to change, Robert assured her they would go to a quiet little place where her dress would be quite appropriate. He also insisted that she drop everything and they leave right away.

Jennifer could not remember the last time she went out for dinner at a good restaurant, and had butterflies in her stomach as they entered the dark little bistro. They were seated in a corner and Robert ordered a good bottle of white wine as they sat making small talk while awaiting their order.

"This is part of your Christmas present," Robert announced. "But here's the second part," handing her an envelope. Jennifer opened it to find a cheque for one thousand dollars.

Jennifer gasped and effusively thanked Robert. "We've been taking advantage of you, and grossly underpaying you for your contribution so hopefully this will make up for it. Moreover, your probationary period is over. Let's just hope it's now a permanent arrangement 'cause I just don't know what I'd do without you."

Robert took Jennifer's hands in his and squeezed them. It was like an electric shock going through Jennifer and she quickly looked away as she withdrew her hands. She had never experienced such a response from anyone other than Bill, and she was overcome with a desire to get up and run out of the restaurant. As she withdrew her hands she said, "I'm sorry, Robert. I'm still married to Bill and I know that he's alive and will come back one day. I do hope that this won't affect our working relationship 'cause I love working for you and must admit a strong attraction to you, but I simply can't get involved in anything right now. Maybe you should take me home now."

"I'm sorry, Jennifer, I didn't mean to upset you. Be assured that I won't pursue this any farther, but if you ever change your mind, be assured that I'll be waiting. I'm a patient man and you're worth waiting for."

Jennifer got up and put on her coat as she headed for the door. Robert paid the bill and caught up to her outside, where she silently got into the car and he drove her to the house. As she got out Robert kissed her gently on the cheek. Jennifer did not look back as she entered the door and went straight to her room, totally flustered and confused about her feelings and the events of the evening.

Jennifer went to work the following morning concerned about how Robert would react, but she was relieved when he greeted her as he always had and gave absolutely no sign of reaction to the events of the previous evening. He was all business and they went right to work as if nothing had happened. Outwardly, Jennifer was calm and collected, but inside she was in a turmoil and could not banish the thoughts of the unexpected feelings she had experienced when Robert had touched her. She tried valiantly to clear the thoughts from her mind as she plunged into her work.

On Christmas Eve, Robert closed the office early and wished Jennifer a Merry Christmas with a gentle peck on the cheek. She was relieved that she would not have to come back for three days, during which time she hoped to regain her control. With the thousand dollar bonus she went out and bought expensive gifts for the children and her parents so that she could make her contribution to their happiness at their favourite time of year.

As usual, the children were up at the crack of dawn on Christmas Day, and finally managed to rouse the whole household to join them in opening presents amid much good-natured grumbling by Grandpa. They even had a big red ribbon tied around Buck's neck and parcels of treats under the tree for him.

It was as happy a day as they could have under the circumstances. At dinner time they set a plate for Bill as they all bowed their heads and said a silent prayer that he would be back with them next Christmas.

Chapter Thirteen

Spring was starting to manifest itself in a number of ways, and in particular by the warmth of the sun which was starting to thaw the snow off the roof of the cabin and surrounding trees. While the temperature still went below freezing at nights, it was sufficiently warm during the day for Bill to venture out of the cabin and bask in the sunshine for a couple of hours each day. He could almost feel the therapeutic value, and his strength was returning day by day. The only problem was that the sun also brought out hordes of black flies that attacked Bill voraciously on any exposed surface.

Suzanne jestingly said, "If Paul was here he'd tell you that the flies don't attack Indians. It's retribution sent by the Great Spirit to punish the white man for his transgressions." However, she finally took pity on him and gave him a solution made from skunk cabbage which they all applied freely to ward off the voracious insects in the bush. They had been known to drive both humans and animals mad.

"I'll also bring out a smoke pot 'cause the smoke has mystical properties that can get rid of all evil." She brought out a tin can with a smouldering rag in it that almost choked Bill, but he was relieved and grateful to see that it also dispersed the buzzing insects.

"You're starting to sound like Paul when you bring out folklore like that," Bill laughed.

"I've heard his stories so many times that I have them all memorised," she responded with a hint of sarcasm.

"This history of your tribe is marvelllous and that's why I'd like to record as much as I can so that it isn't lost for future generations," Bill said seriously.

"You probably just want to write a book and make your fortune, white man, and exploit us like all the rest of them."

"You can be sure that won't happen, Suzanne. After all these months I've developed a whole new outlook and respect for our native brothers, and I'll be dedicated to doing everything I can to rectify some of the wrongs that have been committed in the past."

Bill had changed a great deal over the past four months. He had grown a full beard, and his hair was now shoulder length. He had lost considerable weight and his skin had an uncharacteristic pallor with being confined to the cabin for virtually the entire period. His leg appeared to have knit together well and he spent many hours carving an elaborate walking cane to support himself when he felt he was able to discard the crutches. Willie Bearpaw guided him in incorporating many Indian symbols into the cane, and it was a genuine work of art when he completed it. He gave it a sheen by rubbing it with bear grease. Suzanne massaged his leg daily, and Bill undertook his own therapy by exercising the leg in an attempt to regain strength. Finally, Suzanne made him a short walking cast from birch bark and he tenderly tried adding a little weight each day. After a number of days he was able to limp around with the aid of his cane and it gave him a much greater sense of freedom, even to the point of venturing outside on his own while the others were out on the trapline.

It had been a good winter for trapping, and they had a number of bales of fine pelts ready to transport out to the reserve. The Indians were also in an upbeat mood as they started to make preparations to leave. The river had broken open but they would still have to wait until the lake opened enough for them to make the final leg of the journey home in their big freight canoes. Bill almost felt pangs of nostalgia as he had finally been completely accepted by the Indians, with the exception of Mye-Ook, who continued to look at him with dark hatred in his eyes. With Suzanne's tutoring, he had absorbed a fairly good grasp of the Indian dialect and was able to carry on a reasonable dialogue with Willie Bearpaw and Paul, which was particularly valuable when he was recording the oral history of the tribe and they were not able to offer an English equivalent of many of the words they used. Bill's notebook was packed from cover to cover with tiny hand-written notes that he intended to translate into a written history of the tribe when he reached civilization again. It was interesting to note that the history was a mix of legend and fact that had been passed down through the generations. Nevertheless, it was a priceless record for historians and Indians alike that Bill hoped would give the young native people a renewed interest in their heritage and a pride in their ancestry.

One warm, springlike day, Bill ventured outside on his crutches to bask in the warm sunshine on a rough-hewn bench that Willie Bearpaw had manufactured. The warmth of the sun was making the water cascade off the roof as the snow succumbed to the inexorable return of spring to undo the havoc of winter. It was so warm that Bill actually started to doze off, lulled by the drone of insects and the dripping water.

Through this peaceful aura, another, more ominous, sound penetrated his consciousness and awoke Bill from his reverie with a start. It was like the grunting of a pig and emanated from the direction of the meat cache in the limbs of a big spruce tree to one side of the cabin clearing. Fascinated, Bill hobbled on the unsure footing of the melting snow to investigate the source of the sound. As he rounded the corner of the

193

cabin he stopped dead in his tracks at the awesome sight that struck fear into his heart. Standing on its hind legs and reaching up into the tree was the biggest grizzly bear that he had ever seen. Bill quickly estimated that it was at least ten feet tall while it was ripping at the bark of the tree with its enormous claws, trying to get a grip to reach the remaining cache of moose meat hung there. It was obvious that the huge animal was ravenous after its winter hibernation, although its fur glistened and the silver tips reflected in the sunlight rippling as it clawed at the tree. Its grunts were turning to roars of rage and frustration that echoed in the still air.

Bill stood transfixed at the awesome sight before regaining his senses and hobbling at remarkable speed back into the cabin where Suzanne was cooking dinner. As he burst through the door he breathlessly described the scene to Suzanne who had not heard the sounds inside the cabin.

"Quick, have we got a gun, Suzanne, 'cause I'm afraid that he'll attack the cabin if he gets frustrated with the meat cache?" Bill asked breathlessly.

"Only Willie's old .22 which wouldn't be much good against a grizzly. Maybe if we beat on some pots and pans we can scare it away. The guys won't be back from the trapline for a couple of hours yet."

"We have to try something. Quick, get me Willie's rifle and all the ammunition you can find."

Suzanne scurried around getting the old rifle and a bag of shells and followed Bill outside to the corner of the cabin. Although reluctant to do so, she peeked around the corner and quickly withdrew her head at the terrifying sight.

"He hasn't noticed us yet," whispered Bill, his heart throbbing up into his throat. He thought how ironic it would be if he fell victim to a grizzly after surviving the crash and the winter in the cabin. "Quick, load the rifle and pass it to me when I'm set at the corner of the cabin, and reload it as fast as you can when I pass it back to you."

Bill hobbled to the corner of the cabin and leaned against the logs to steady himself before reaching back for the rifle.

Peeking around the corner he saw that the bear was still engrossed with the meat cache up in the tree. He grabbed the rifle and took careful aim at its temple. Although he was shaking like a leaf Bill managed to hold the rifle steady by exhaling all the air from his lungs and fired five shots in rapid succession before handing the rifle back to Suzanne to reload. The bear swatted at its temple with a massive paw as if brushing away insects, but remained erect at the tree by holding on with the other paw. It seemed forever before Suzanne handed back the reloaded rifle and Bill took careful aim again at the temple area, firing another five shots in rapid succession.

By now the grizzly was starting to swing its head from side to side, trying to shake off the effects of the bullets and making a much more difficult target. Bill held his breath until he thought he would burst, but still took careful aim each time the bear turned its temple towards him. He managed to fire another five shots and finally saw spots of blood appear on the white snow as the bear continued to shake its head more violently and slowly slide down the tree to a sitting position on its huge haunches. Bill could feel Suzanne shaking as she fumbled to continue reloading the rifle. He too was shaking as he reached for the rifle and was aware that many of his shots were now missing their mark as the bear continued to shake its head violently, spraying blood in an ever widening circle on the snow. Bill's leg hurt excruciatingly but he knew he had to complete the task as there was nothing more dangerous than a wounded grizzly. The roars of agony from the bear were terrifying but Suzanne stoically continued to reload the rifle whenever Bill handed it back to her.

Finally the bear's roars started to subside as it slid slowly down the tree, its claws leaving massive scars in the bark. The snow around the bear was turning blood red as foaming blood appeared from its mouth and nostrils. Bill watched in fascination as it slumped to the ground in slow motion in an inert heap. Bill and Suzanne let out whoops as they unrestrainedly hugged each other, despite the excruciating pain in Bill's leg.

"Suzanne, help me back into the cabin before I go into shock," Bill gasped. "Don't go near that beast 'til we're sure its dead. In fact we should leave it until the guys come back with the big rifle and they can make sure of it. A wounded grizzly is the most dangerous animal in the world."

"The guys will be some excited that we got a grizzly 'cause the Indians believe that there's a spirit in every bear. The gall bladder is potent medicine, and the claws are prized for our ceremonies. Its coat is beautiful after winter hibernation and the meat will be prime 'cause it won't have much fat on it. Mye-Ook will really be happy. He figures he's related to the bears, especially the grizzlies."

"Frankly, I've lost all interest in the beast and the only thing I want to do now is get back to my bunk. I've never been so mentally and physically exhausted in my life, even when I crashed, and that's saying something."

With Suzanne's assistance, Bill hobbled back into the cabin and collapsed on his bunk, falling sound asleep in minutes. His sleep was punctuated by wild dreams, and he involuntarily let out a scream as if he was being shaken like a doll.

It took a few seconds for him to gather his senses and to realize finally that it was Willie Bearpaw who was shaking him enthusiastically.

"Holy Jeez, white man, you just paid your winter's keep with that grizzly. We never heard of nobody killing one with a .22 before. He's one fine animal and the guys are busy skinning him out. The fur's beautiful and he's got one big gall bladder for medicine. You done good, guy." Bill noted with satisfaction that Willie had dropped the prefix white for the first time.

It was almost dark when Paul and Mye-Ook entered the cabin, and while Paul was not as effusive as Willie, he added his admiration of Bill's feat. "The Kwakwalas will be telling this story for a long time how a white man killed a grizzly with an old .22," he said with a look of satisfaction on his face that he now had another anecdote to add to his already extensive repetoire. Bill actually thought he detected a smile on Mye-Ook's face as he looked directly at Bill for the first time instead of averting his eyes as he usually did. Bill also noted that around his neck Mye-Ook wore a leather thong from which was suspended a small satchel that Bill had never seen before. He was not able to satisfy his curiosity until the trappers had eaten their meal and rolled into their bunks, emitting a chorus of snores in seconds. Since Suzanne was still clearing away the debris, Bill caught her attention and whispered his question about the talisman around Mye-Ook's neck.

"That's one of the bear's teeth," whispered Suzanne. "They're considered a very strong omen by our people and Mye-Ook can now live up to his name and get the respect of being a real hunter in the tribe. I made him the little pouch a long time ago out of the moose hide, but he's never worn it before. I'm sure that he'll carry it for the rest of his life now."

"I'm glad we've been able to provide him with a little happiness. He's a very disturbed guy," whispered Bill. He too rolled over in his bunk with a smile on his face feeling that he had finally broken down the barrier between him and Mye-Ook and he was confident now that they would ultimately form a close bond.

The final days were spent packing away any remaining foodstuffs in cans with tight lids to preserve them from the little animals that inhabited the cabin during the summer months. Spare bedding was hung from the rafters and the mattresses placed on edge and liberally sprinkled with pepper. Finally, the windows were boarded up as a deterrent to rampaging wolverines and bears. Suzanne busied herself scrubbing everything down and washing bedding so that she had little time for Bill who tried to help in any way he could.

After an inspection and great discussion, the men decided the river had gone down enough to safely make the trip down to the mouth, where they would camp until the lake opened up sufficiently for them to cross to the reserve. It took them almost half a day to pack the canoes, and Willie and Suzanne helped Bill to limp down the trail to the river. He asked them to pause at one point so that he could take one last, wistful look at the cabin that had been both his salvation and prison for more than five months. When they reached the river, he was suddenly lifted bodily like a rag doll into the lead canoe amongst the bales of furs, which still had a very strong animal odour. He was astonished to find that it was Mye-Ook who had lifted him. For a moment Bill felt apprehension, but then realized that Mye-Ook was being extremely gentle, as he was carefully deposited amongst the furs.

"Chyit, Mye-Ook," Bill murmured in Kwakwala, but Mye-Ook maintained his inscrutable look as he continued loading the canoes as if nothing had happened. Bill knew now that he had finally broken the barrier between them and no longer had anything to fear from Mye-Ook.

With the canoes fully laden, they moved out into the stream and started the outboards. Bill was able to breathe again as the wind flow dissipated the overpowering smell of the furs. Suzanne sat in the bow again to watch for hazards while Willie ran the motor. This time, though, the river was still in flood and the risk of hitting underwater hazards was much less than when they had arrived in the fall. There was very little freeboard remaining in the big canoe with the load of furs and an extra passenger. Suzanne thought back with nostalgia about wading into the icy river, half naked, to net the big fish that had helped to sustain them during the winter, and felt a strong kinship with the young braves who had to endure such hardships to prove their manhood.

The trip down to the river mouth was a wild ride as the river was still in flood and mostly white water. Bill gripped the gunwhales of the canoe until his knuckles were almost white, but the Indians seemed to take it in their stride, and wore complacent smiles. Bill took comfort in the thought that they would undoubtedly have white knuckles if they rode with him in his plane, particularly after his crash. Finally, after a ride that was probably twice as fast as the trip in against the current and in shallow water, they rounded a bend and saw the lake stretching before them with large expanses of open water punctuated by long fingers of ice.

They made camp in a small clearing at the mouth and it was without a doubt the longest night of Bill's life. Although he was given some furs to throw on top of himself, and the trappers built a good fire around which they made their beds, his teeth chattered with cold. He had lost so much weight that he was not able to maintain his body heat, and he now understood why the Indians consumed so much bear fat. They curled up and went fast asleep while he lay awake and shivered. He looked longingly at Suzanne, desperately wanting to go over and share her body warmth, but fought back the urge by anticipating the undesirable impact. He had come too far to risk losing all because of a few more hours of discomfort.

Finally dawn came, and they built up the fire to warm themselves and cook a meal before starting out on the final leg across the lake. Bill hadn't thought he would survive the night, but the roaring fire and hot tea brought life back to his aching bones. His teeth chattered against the tin mug of scalding tea that he gulped down. For the first time he felt excitement welling up in him as he could actually see the end of his ordeal in sight. At the same time he felt a strong nostalgia for the bond that he had formed with the Indians who had saved his life and were now delivering him back to his family, who had undoubtedly given him up for dead long ago.

After a quick meal eaten in silence, the canoes were loaded again, with Bill virtually buried in furs in the lead canoe as they headed out across the wide expanse of lake. "Well, this is it, buddy," laughed Willie as the loaded canoes were pushed off into the lake. It was obvious that even the trappers were looking forward to getting back to the reserve after their arduous winter. The expression on Suzanne's face masked her inner feelings about getting back to a normal life for a while. She sensed that her period of penance was over at last, and that she should be accepted back into the tribe without any further recriminations. Her visits to the river had seemingly purged her soul and she felt calm and serene.

Once again Bill was highly apprehensive as they threaded their way between massive ice floes, not wanting a watery grave after all he had survived, but the trappers guided the heavily laden canoes skilfully into open water and started to cross the final expanse leading to the north shore. Eventually, the buildings on the reserve came into view, and as they approached, the sound of their outboard motors attracted a crowd to greet them at the dock. They were led by the chief who was dressed in ceremonial costume to greet the trappers home as they traditionally had with a ceremony thanking the Great Spirit for the bounty of the land.

The hubbub of excitement suddenly subsided when they saw that one of the canoes contained a bearded white man that they had never seen before. The chief approached Willie Bearpaw with a look of bewilderment on his face, and Bill was able to understand enough of the conversation to realize that the chief believed they had brought a white alien back with them from the bush. In a gush of words and expressive hand waving, Willie explained how Bill had crashed his plane in the bush and they had found him and kept him in their cabin all winter while Suzanne had nursed him back to health. The chief regained his composure enough to turn to one of the children and send him running to bring the Indian Agent from his office.

As Bill was helped from the canoe, he was surrounded by a curious mob who stared at him as if he was from another planet. Some of the men were helping to unload the skins and piling them up on the dock while they excitedly checked the quality and the different species. They were particularly impressed by the grizzly hide and Willie kept pointing to Bill as he proudly recounted his heroic deed in shooting it with a .22. Bill felt very awkward and out of place as they discussed this Nito, white man, who had arrived in their midst with the trappers. Suzanne tried to remain aloof, giving no hint of her feelings as she chattered excitedly with some of the children and squaws surrounding her.

After a few minutes, a Jeep driven by a white man accompanied by the young messenger came bouncing down the trail to the dock. A wiry, bearded individual in his mid-forties, obviously of Scottish ancestory judging by the tartan tam on his head, jumped out and pushed through the crowd to Bill, offering his hand.

"Hi! I'm Angus Reid the Indian Agent for the district. This lad tried to tell me who you are, but he was too excited to make much sense."

"I'm Bill Headingly. I was flying out of Sioux Falls last fall and crashed on my way into Sustut. These people found me and kept me in their trapping cabin for the winter while I recovered from my injuries, including a broken leg. I have Suzanne Pierre to thank for nursing me back to health and the guys for finding me and keeping me in their cabin until breakup."

"My God! I heard about the crash and the search for you, but I heard that they'd given up the search without a trace. Apparently a snowstorm covered all the evidence and you were given up for dead. I guess the lakes were starting to freeze over too and even the local bush pilots had to give up. But I guess they kept looking all winter but didn't find a trace."

"Well, as you can see, I'm very much alive, but a little worse for wear. Suzanne made a makeshift splint out of bark and my leg seems to have knitted together pretty well. But now my first priority is to let my family know I'm alive. Do you have a phone out to civilization?"

"Normally I do, but the road and telephone lines have been washed out as they are every spring. But I do have a radio link with Sioux Falls if we can get it working."

"Good. Let's give it a try," said Bill limping towards the Jeep. He turned around to see Suzanne watching him wistfully so he called out to her that he would see her after he had contacted his family. She did not acknowledge his call but turned back to her animated conversation with the crowd around her.

Bill clutched his leg as the Jeep bounced over the potholed road towards the Agent's office. He could not help but notice the squalor on the reserve and the dilapidated state of the houses. When he remarked on it the Agent agreed with an air of resignation in his voice. "I'm afraid it's an all too familiar story of shortage of funds and the apathy of the natives, after years of frustration and succumbing to the social malaise introduced by the white man," Angus added. "I work my heart out to try and improve conditions, but it's pretty disheartening." There were empty bottles littered everywhere, testimony to the level of alcoholism prevalent on the reserve.

Finally they arrived at the Agent's office and he helped Bill up the steps into the building, which was sickeningly warm after Bill's months in the cool temperatures of the trappers' cabin. Bill also apologized for his obvious body odour which was triggered by the heat, but the Agent assured him that he was well acclimatized to it and promised him a warm bath and fresh clothes after they had made the radio call. For a moment Bill was torn over priorities between the two, but decided that the call took precedence.

The Agent switched on the radio and after a warmup period started calling Sioux Falls. Turning to Bill he asked him if there was anyone in particular he would like to talk to. "Ross Stuart, please," he responded.

Finally the train dispatcher in Sioux Falls answered and asked who they wanted to talk to. When the Agent requested Ross Stuart, the dispatcher advised him that they would have to send someone down to his trailer, which would take a few minutes.

While they waited for Ross to come to the radio Angus listened in fascination to some of Bill's account of his winter with the trappers. Bill could not disguise his feelings for Suzanne at which the Agent interrupted and asked, "Did she tell you any of her background?"

"Yes, I think she told me almost everything, and it wasn't a pretty story. It's almost inconceivable that we could have done such things to our aboriginal people. I would have sworn it was a direct excerpt from a Dickensian novel. By the way, she did mention how grateful she was to you for helping her regain her Indian status?"

The Agent interrupted the conversation about Suzanne, and served Bill the first real cup of coffee he had tasted in five months. The aroma was positively intoxicating. As they were enjoying it, Ross' familiar deep voice came on the air. "Someone calling Ross Stuart? Go ahead, over."

"Ross, this is Bill Headingly!"

There was deathly silence for a few moments before Ross came back on the air. "Is this a sick joke?" he exclaimed.

"It's no joke, Ross. It really is me and I'm alive and reasonably well."

"My God. Where the hell have you been?"

"It's too complicated to explain now. I'm on the Kwakwala Indian Reserve, so come and get me as soon as possible. But first, let Jennifer know I'm alive."

"I don't have floats on my plane yet, and there's nowhere to get in on skis once the lake is out. Are you injured so that they couldn't bring you out by road?"

"I have a broken leg which is healing, but I couldn't tolerate a trip out by road. Besides, apparently it's washed out and impassable."

"O.K., hang tough and I'll call the Search and Rescue people to see if they can bring you out in a chopper. Are you all right there for the time being?"

"Sure. I'm at the Indian Agent's house and he's going to get me a bath and turn me into a human being again. Just make it as fast as you can 'cause I'm running out of patience and dying to get back out to civilization."

"Hang on partner, I'll get back to you as soon as I can. Keep your radio on monitor."

"Roger, old buddy. This will call for a couple of brews when I make it out!"

"You can be sure I'll have a couple of cold ones in the fridge. Over and out."

Chapter Fourteen

Bill luxuriated in a warm bath to the point where he almost fell asleep. He had been absolutely shocked at his appearance when he saw himself in the mirror for the first time. His unkept hair and black, full beard seemed to emphasize the gauntness of his face and sunken eyes. The blue scars were clearly visible on his face where they had healed over during the winter. He involuntarily averted his eyes from the unfamiliar image staring back at him from the mirror, and felt embarrassed that others had seen him in such a state. The Agent had laid out a complete change of clothing, towels and lots of soap and shampoo which Bill applied liberally. While Bill was still in the tub, Angus came in and said, "Ross called back on the radio to advise that he had contacted the Search and Rescue Ops Centre and they're sending in a helicopter to pick you up tomorrow, since it is already getting dark. He had also telephoned Jennifer and she passed along her love."

"Thanks, Angus. I'd have loved to have been there when Jennifer got the call. I'll bet she, Mike and the kids were all set to charter a helicopter themselves, but we may as well wait for the SAR people to come and get me, even though every minute seems important to me now. You'd think after five months of incarceration I would be a little more patient. Not knocking your fabulous hospitality, but I'd like to be on my way right now."

"Patience, my boy. You're down to the short strokes now!"

Finally, Bill climbed out of the tub and scrubbed his head and body dry until they turned pink. He dressed himself in the fresh clothes that Angus had provided for him and concluded that the only destination for his soiled clothes was the fire.

"I'm not sure if I didn't bring out some cooties with me from the cabin so I think we'd better get rid of these clothes. The only thing I'll really miss is my old flying jacket that has been with me on many adventures, both in the air and on the ground. Probably it's very fitting that it be cremated after my resurrection."

"I agree wholeheartedly," laughed Angus as he took a pair of tongs and deposited the clothes in the stove piece by piece. When Bill was dressed Angus offered, "How about a drink to celebrate your homecoming?"

"Just a small one, thanks," Bill responded. "I never was a drinker and I'm afraid that even one might lay me low in my present condition." Nevertheless, he found that the drink relaxed him and he suddenly found himself talking non-stop about his experience.

Finally, Angus interrupted him to say, "We're invited to a native drum dance in the long house to celebrate the trappers' return and your arrival out of the blue. If you've never attended one before you'll find it a memorable experience. But it would be an insult to the chief and elders if we're late so we'd better get a hustle on."

Immediately Bill thought of his unkempt appearance and said to Angus, "Would you cut my hair and beard before we go so that I don't look like a hermit?"

"Not on your life," laughed Angus. "No one would believe your story if you turned up all neatly groomed. If you're thinking of impressing Suzanne you're wasting your time 'cause I'm sure she has seen you at your very worst. Besides, I would imagine she will try to ignore you as much as possible so that she isn't too closely associated with another white man. When I was trying to restore her Indian status I too became very close to her. As you can see, I'm a bachelor and thought she would make a perfect wife for me in this profession. However, when I asked her she ran away and avoided me for many months. She was so badly hurt by her experiences in the convent, and her marriage to a white man, that she wouldn't even consider it."

"That's too bad 'cause I've come to be extremely fond of her in our enforced intimacy, and I know she'd make a marvellous wife for any man of either race. But you're right that she's clinging dearly to her heritage now that she's regained it, and she'll be a great asset to the aboriginal people in their objective of self-determination."

"Come on, better get going or it would be an insult to the Chief if we're late."

As they entered the long house they were greeted by a crescendo of drum beats and dancers dressed in fur and feather costumes who escorted them to sit by the Chief and elders. Everyone was dressed in native costume and Bill immediately saw Suzanne, whose raven hair shone after she had obviously washed it, seated with all the women on one side of the room. He was tempted to wave, but resisted when he saw her avert her eyes and appreciated that he must disguise any feelings he had for her as she was obviously doing with him.

The Chief greeted Bill in his native tongue and was openly delighted when Bill responded in his limited Kwakwala.

"Chyit, hiwus," Bill thanked the chief.

Before them was a great feast of all the native delicacies including one that intrigued Bill, a large platter of moose nose. He noted that there were no alcoholic beverages, and the Chief explained that he was trying to eliminate alcoholism from the reserve, which he blamed for most of the social ills amongst his people, including sexual abuse and poor health.

The dancers performed ritual dances to the beat of the drums and Bill felt honoured to be able to participate in such a ceremony. Some of the food dishes he found too rich for his stomach, particularly those laced with oolichan oil, which brought memories flooding back of Suzanne nursing him back to health with large quantities of the oil when he was bordering on pneumonia in the cabin. He did try the moose nose, though, and was pleasantly surprised to find it highly edible.

When the feast was over, the Chief held up his hand and made a long speech in his native tongue. Since Bill was only able to understand a fraction of it, Willie Bearpaw came over and interpreted for the audience.

"The Great Spirit in his miraculous ways caused a big bird carrying a white man to fall from the skies. Our trappers were guided to the big bird by the spirits and saved the white man's life as white men would have saved ours. They kept him in the cabin all winter, and made him well again, so that he can return to the white man's world and help us get back our lands and save our culture. He is a brave man, and even though he had a broken wing, he killed a big grizzly bear with a little .22, which no man has ever done before. He is a true warrior like us."

The Chief paused for emphasis and there was a murmuring in the crowd as they listened to the story unfolding.

"When he was with our trappers he listened to Swakium tell the history of the Kwakwalas, and he wrote it all down in a little book. Now he's going to make it into a printed book so that all our young people will know and learn the history of the Kwakwalas so that it will never be lost. He has shown that he is a true blood brother and we're going to name him Tchim-Uhl-Kain, which means Broken Wing."

The drums throbbed to a crescendo as the Chief presented Bill with an elaborate fur and feather head dress, and gave him a carved talking stick. "This you will use when you tell

207

your white people about the Kwakwalas, and you will be our spokesman with the powers that be, and tell them of our problems and worries about losing our culture."

Bill was choked with emotion at the solemn significance of the ceremony, and when the Chief signalled for silence, he spoke partly in Kwakwala and partly in English, which Willie Bear Paw interpreted for the audience.

"Thank you brothers and sisters for this great honour. I'll always be grateful to you for saving my life so that I can go back to my family again. Now I have another family of all the Kwakwalas, and I'll be proud to be known as your blood brother. And I have a gift for you. I have a house and live in Buffalo Narrows, which was known to you as Klay-Ah-Kwoss, and now I'm going to give back to you most of the land that is traditionally yours, so that we can live together there in peace as a big family. We've found many signs of your culture there from ancient times. I'll keep our house, which is called Tohtohlah, because it means so much to my family and me, but the land I'll give back to you, as you deserve."

The whole assembly rose to their feet and started chanting "Klay-Ah-Kwoss" as the drums once again rose to a crescendo.

After the ceremonies Bill was utterly exhausted, and excused himself to return to the Agent's house with Angus. He was tempted to just roll into bed with his clothes on as he had done for the past five months, but finally summoned enough strength to put on the pajamas Angus had provided, and fell into a deep sleep in the delicious comfort of a real bed with sheets and pillows.

Bill slept uninterrupted for ten hours, until finally the combination of overburdened kidneys and the alluring odour of fresh-brewed coffee wakened him. He rolled out of bed and took a few minutes to collect his thoughts and realize where he was. He limped into the bathroom and then to the kitchen where he found Angus cooking an enormous breakfast of pancakes, sausage, bacon and eggs. The aroma was overpowering, and Bill's mouth watered at the thought of a real breakfast again after months of gruel made from cornmeal. Breakfast had always been one of his favourite meals, and this one looked like a gourmet special.

"How did you sleep?" asked Angus.

"Like a baby," replied Bill in a gross understatement. "I've always been a heavy sleeper, but that was one of the most memorable I'll ever have. I'd almost forgotten what it was like to sleep in sheets and on a mattress."

"Good, now let's see if you can do justice to a good old North American breakfast," said Angus, placing a platter loaded with food in front of Bill.

"Good grief, I doubt if I can handle all of this, but I certainly intend to try. And that coffee smells positively intoxicating."

"The way I make it will start your heart pumping, I can guarantee."

The two ate in silence until finally Bill had to push his plate away with only half of the food consumed. "I guess my stomach shrunk during the winter and I'll have to get back in practice. Normally your clothes wouldn't have fit me, but I guess I must have shed about thirty pounds. I'm sure I'll gain it back once Jennifer starts feeding me again. Cooking is her hobby and we all look it. Changing the subject, any news about the chopper coming for me?"

"Yes. Ross Stuart called while you were still sleeping and advised that they won't be able to get here before tomorrow. They have another search and can't spare a helicopter right now. I guess they figure they know where you are and know you're safe. The Search and Rescue people aren't familiar with this area so they're going to pick Ross up in Sioux Falls and bring him along as navigator when they come for you. He sounded delighted to be coming. He had also talked to Jennifer and Mike again last night to let them know what's happening. I guess he's having a bad time trying to discourage Jennifer and Mike from flying up here right away to meet you, but the SAR people are going to take you right to the hospital in Prince George. That's where they'll meet you."

Bill was crestfallen, but realized another day in his saga was minor. "We've been close friends for many years, and in fact it was Ross that arranged for me to fly the mining equipment into Sustut. After what happened I'm not too sure that I'm grateful about that, but he's a super guy! My children think more of him than they do of me I'm sure. Uncle Ross is their hero. He's a confirmed bachelor like you but loves children."

"I've a few things to do on the reserve and you're welcome to come along if you wish," said Angus.

"Where's Suzanne living?" Bill asked, trying to appear nonchalant.

"She lives with her uncle, Willie Bearpaw, but I think it would be wise if you didn't visit them in their house. First of all, I think they'd be embarrassed for you to see the run-down state of their house and, secondly, I'm sure that Suzanne wouldn't want to give the impression that she has any interest in a Nito. She's still pretty much on probation in the tribe after marrying a white man, and doesn't want to jeopardize her status again. If I see her, and the opportunity arises, I'll give her your regards. I talked to the Chief last night and he said he and the elders would like to have a discussion with you before you leave. If they're at the long house, I'll drop you off and pick you up later."

It was a spectacular spring day with a brilliant blue sky, punctuated by tiny wisps of white cloud. The cottonwood trees had come into leaf with their golden yellow hue and tassels of golden pollen. Even the squalor of the reserve looked much better in the sunlight as they drove to the centre of the village where the ceremony had taken place the night before. Everything seemed brilliant and new to Bill, as if seeing through the eyes of a child. He had read somewhere that all things and people became young again in spring, and he was now living those words. He could feel new life starting to flow through his veins again.

There was a small meeting room for the elders just off the entrance to the long house, and they found the chief and elders in deep discussion as they entered.

"Welcome, Tchim-Uhl-Kain," they all said in unison as Bill entered the room.

"Greetings, Hiwhihos," responded Bill in Kwakwala in recognition of their standing in the tribe as chief and elders.

They all beamed at being greeted in Kwakwala by a white man since even Angus Reid had only mastered a few words of their tongue, and had to find a translator to speak to many of the elders who had not learned English. They usually used Suzanne as an interpreter, but as the chief explained, they often had things to discuss that should not be heard by a slhanay, which Bill recognized as a woman.

They spoke slowly for Bill's benefit, and when he did not understand a word or phrase, they stopped and one of them would try and find the English equivalent. It was a repetition of what Bill had heard on many occasions in the cabin, but he listened patiently and respectfully as their story unfolded of their subjugation by the white man and the problems that had been introduced into their society. They complained bitterly of the introduction of alcohol, that had created other problems such as sexual and physical abuse of women and children. Although most had been converted to Christianity, they were incensed about the removal of their children to church schools where they were subjected to physical punishment if they used their native tongue. Few of the children came back to the reserve after this exposure and most went on to the cities to earn a living. As a result, the tribe was losing its ability to be self-sufficient, and their self-esteem was disappearing along with their language and culture. Since Bill was now a blood brother and a well-educated man, they pleaded with him to be their spokesman and work for change in the despised Indian Affairs Act.

Bill was extremely flattered that they considered him to be one of them now. "I'm not a lawyer or a politician," he explained. "Nevertheless, I'll be honoured to be your advocate when I get back to the outside world."

"We have no money to pay for legal expenses, but we hope you will be able to explain our problems to the powers that be," added the chief. Bill was embarrassed to note that most of them had tears in their eyes, evidence of their sincerity and dedication to their cause.

"Now that I've lost my plane, and with it my living, I won't have much money, but I swear that I'll do everything in my power to rectify the wrongs that have been committed against your people. I'll gladly be your voice and I'm honoured that you would ask me to do this on your behalf. I'll be your Wuwum Te Sch'en', your barking dog. I'll always be forever grateful to you for saving my life, and the honour of making me a blood brother in your tribe. Suzanne, Paul and Willie Bearpaw spent many hours in the cabin telling me your history which I've written down and will get printed for you. It will also help to prove some of the claims that you rightfully have." Bill could not control the tears welling up in his own eyes with the emotion of the moment as the chief and elders all came and embraced him.

They had talked through lunch time, so the chief invited Bill to accompany him to his home to eat with him. Although he was very tired after the meeting, Bill was very flattered to receive such an invitation, and willingly accepted. The chief's wife was a plump lady with a jolly round brown face, who was called Sarah, and she was honoured to have such a guest as she scurried around putting on a new tablecloth and her best dishes. Although she had no notice she soon had the table laden with smoked fish, canned moose and fresh-baked bannock, and kept piling food on Bill's plate, even though he protested that he could not eat as much as he used to be able to. All the while she chattered and showed pictures of her grandchildren and asked Bill about his own family. Finally she produced mocassin slippers for all of them which were beautifully hand decorated with beadwork. Bill felt embarrassed about not having a gift to give her in return, but assured her that as soon as he got home he would send them both a nice gift from the city. The chief's wife beamed with pride and took both Bill's hands in hers and held him tightly in a strong grip with calloused hands, the result of a lifetime of hard work, and made him promise that he would bring his squaw and children to visit her.

Bill was totally exhausted by the long discussions with the elders and the protracted lunch, and begged the chief to drive him back to the Agent's house in his battered old pickup so that he could rest for a while before seeing any more of the reserve. His leg was becoming very painful with so much walking and standing, and he was relieved to limp up the steps into the house and collapse on to the bed. He was asleep in minutes.

Bill was awakened by the gentle shaking of Angus Reid. He was bathed in perspiration and his heart was pounding, and his hands shook uncontrollably.

"You must've been having a dandy of a nightmare, Bill," observed Angus. "When I came back into the house I could hear you yelling bloody murder and I was afraid that Mye-Ook had got into the house. As you've no doubt found out, we can't trust him alone with white men, and I was afraid you may have crossed him while you were in the cabin."

"No, it's a recurring nightmare I've had since the crash in which I relive going into the trees, but in my dream the plane catches fire, which in reality was just a fire the Indians had built at the crash site. I've always had an obsessive fear of fire. I must have died at the stake or something in my former life. That's the one thing I remember vividly about the crash, and that was automatically turning off the fuel to the engine before I went in. When I went into the trees it fortunately tore off the wings so I was safely separated from the fuel tanks. I guess it'll take me a while to get over the trauma, but I'm sure that the memory will fade in time. How long have I been asleep?"

"I've no idea, but I just walked in from the office and it's after five o'clock. I checked at the long house but they told me the chief brought you here in his truck about three, so you must have been asleep a couple of hours."

"I was exhausted after our talks with the chief and the elders, and then the chief took me home for late lunch. It was more of a feast that Sarah laid on, and I just fell into bed when I arrived back here."

"I talked with the chief and elders and they're most impressed with you and your dedication to helping them out. I'm sure that you'll do much better than I can 'cause I get completely frustrated with the bureaucracy and lack of funds. As a lowly civil servant I don't have a very strong voice, but I'm sure that if you can go through the political channels you'll get more done than I can in years, particularly with your story and experience amongst the native people."

"I certainly intend to dedicate my life to their cause when I get back to civilization, and will publish the oral history of the Kwakwalas from the notes I took this past winter."

"How about some dinner after your long day? I can muster up some of my special bachelor's stew if it would interest you."

"I'm sure it's very good, but I'm afraid I ate enough stew made from every edible animal in the forest this past winter and I doubt if I'll ever eat it again. Actually, after that great lunch at the chief's house I'm not the least bit hungry, but will join you with a couple of scrambled eggs and toast if that's no problem. I desperately missed eggs in the bush and have a craving to catch up."

"Coming right up. Meanwhile why don't you relax and turn on the news on television. It should be on in a few minutes."

"My God, I can't remember the last time I watched television 'cause we didn't have it in Buffalo Narrows. In fact we did more reading that we have in years as a result of not having TV."

"It's a godsend for me being an old bachelor stuck out here. That's one thing I've managed to accomplish while I've been here. I got a television dish and most of the homes now have television which I think has cut down the vandalism and drinking in the evenings."

214

Bill watched in fascination as the news unfolded, describing events he had never heard of before. Although he listened to the radio religiously in Buffalo Narrows the television coverage of the news was much more comprehensive. Suddenly, he was shocked into disbelief when the story of his crash and resurrection were featured, and even more stunned when an interview with Jennifer and the children was included to get their reaction to the news of Bill's return from the wilderness. He shouted to Angus who ran in to see the end of the interview, as Bill unabashedly let the tears flow down his cheeks at the sight of Jennifer and the children. Jennifer and the children had let it be known unequivocally that there had never been a doubt in their minds that he was alive and they could not wait to see him again.

It took Bill a while to regain his composure, and he willingly accepted the glass of wine Angus offered him. He had totally lost his appetite, even for the scrambled eggs, and apologized to Angus for the trouble. "Good grief, man. I think I'd be whooping like an Indian warcry after an emotional experience like that. You certainly have a handsome family and they're obviously very loyal to you."

Bill was tempted to bare his soul and recount the story of his episode with Suzanne in the cabin, but decided that the secret should be locked in his mind alone.

After dinner Bill asked if Angus would mind driving him around the rest of the reserve. He was particularly interested in seeing where his cabin-mates lived, even though Angus discouraged his idea of visiting them. It was a total shock for Bill to see that Suzanne and Willie Bearpaw lived in a cabin not much larger than the one in which they had spent the winter, and he understood why Angus had discouraged him from paying a visit. As they drove past, Bill hoped for a glance of Suzanne, but she was nowhere to be seen. As an afterthought, Bill asked Angus to turn around and go back to the cabin. "I've something for Mye-Ook. Maybe I could leave it with Willie to get to him since we probably won't see him again." Taking off his wristwatch, Bill asked Angus to deliver

Stewart Dickson

it to either Willie or Suzanne to give to Mye-Ook as a gift from him. Bill was disappointed to see that Willie answered the door, but waved enthusiastically to him. Willie waved back and nodded his head as he took the watch and turned back into the cabin.

Chapter Fifteen

Bill was awake and prowling around the house long before dawn. Angus was still sound asleep, but Bill was simply too hyper to sleep in anticipation that this may be the day he would go back to his loved ones. His feelings were a mixture of sadness and elation, and he knew it was going to be a difficult transition going back to civilization after living the life of a semi-hermit. The television exposure was almost frightening and he was concerned how his feelings for Suzanne would affect his relationship with Jennifer. He had never encountered these feelings before in his married life, and worried about how he would be able to handle them when he returned to his family.

Finally, Angus awoke and came out to join Bill after putting on a pot of coffee. He could see that Bill was troubled and asked, "Would you like to talk your problems out with me, Bill? Or, if you wish, I can take you over to talk to the reserve priest who is a very kind and gentle man endowed with a lot of earthly wisdom?"

"No thanks, Angus. I think I have to work this out myself and I'm sure that things will settle into place again after I get back to my family. As you can imagine, it's going to be quite a transition, and I have to try and figure out what I'm going to do with myself now that my dream has gone up in smoke."

"Frankly, I don't envy you but you seem to be a pretty strong guy and I'm sure you will handle it all right. Meanwhile, I think a cup of coffee will do us both good," said Angus cheerily. "And then we'll see if we can get any news about your trip out of here. We'll call Sioux Falls about nine and get Ross to fill us in."

"Great. I can't believe that coffee could smell so good or taste so good. It's the little things that become important when you're deprived of them for a while. The Indians used to make an erzatz coffee out of oak acorns but I never did acquire a taste for it. The other thing I never did acquire a taste for was their oolichan oil, and I'm sure that I'll be nauseated every time I smell it again."

"Pretty powerful stuff, and you certainly couldn't get me to swallow it. They swear by it and credit it with saving many lives. However, how about some of those scrambled eggs you couldn't consume last night? Maybe a little bacon on the side."

"I'm really too nervous to eat, but I guess I should get something on to my stomach. Do you think we should call Ross yet?"

"Let's leave it until after breakfast, and then he'll probably have some news for you."

Bill reluctantly agreed and forced himself to eat the eggs and bacon set before him, but could hardly stop himself from getting on the radio.

"Okay. Let's give it a try now, Bill."

It took some time to get a response from Sioux Falls but when they did answer they had no news, but agreed to go and get Ross who had been talking to the Search and Rescue Centre the night before. Angus asked about the weather and

218

was assured that it seemed to be clearing off so they should have no trouble flying if they had a helicopter available.

About twenty minutes dragged past before Ross' cheery voice came on the radio asking for Bill, so Angus passed the microphone to him.

"I talked to the Rescue Centre a little while ago and they hope to get a chopper on the way within the hour. It's about three hours flying time up here and they're going to pick me up on the way to act as the local navigator. So, hang on pal, and we'll be in to get you as soon as possible. Did you watch the news report last night? You're an instant celebrity out here so be prepared for the VIP treatment."

"Thanks old buddy. Get here as soon as you can. And skip the VIP bit!"

"Roger and out."

Bill tried to busy himself by packing up his meagre belongings and kept pacing the floor and looking out of the windows for signs of the helicopter.

"For heaven's sake man, you're like a cat on hot bricks. Either sit down or I'll take you out on another drive to keep your mind occupied. Or you can even turn on television and watch the soap operas. I'm sure you'll have a lot of catching up to do on the current plots!"

"I apologize, but my nerves are completely on edge and I have a lot of adjusting to do before I can get back to normal again. However, I don't think that the soap operas are included in that adjustment so I'll take you up on your offer of a drive."

Angus drove to the local school and invited Bill in to meet the young students. At first he was reluctant but realized that he had to take every opportunity to increase his exposure to people as part of his readjustment. As they entered the big single classroom, a murmuring started up amongst the students who had been listening attentively to the nun that Bill was pleased to see was a native Indian girl in her twenties. She rapped the table with her cane and called out "T'us wus tuwixwal!" receiving an instant response as they all went silent. She came over and shook hands with Bill and asked in excellent English "Would you say some words to my students who are learning to speak English?" Bill immediately surmized that she had been educated at a convent school like Suzanne.

Looking down at the brown, eager faces Bill slowly said to them in Kwakwala "Greetings tuwixwal. I am now a blood brother even though my face is white," which caused a giggle to ripple through the class. "I have three tuwixwals just like you, and I hope that you'll all meet them and you can be friends and teach them the Kwakwala tongue and how to hunt and fish and trap like your ancestors. I haven't seen my children for a long time and I'm very excited to see them again. Some day we'll meet at Klay-Ah-Kwoss, which used to be your land, and now we're going to share it. I hope that you'll listen very carefully to your teacher because you have a heritage that you should be very proud of. While I was in the cabin this winter with the trappers they told me all your history and I wrote it down in a little book. Now I'm going to have it made into a school book for you so that you can learn all about your ancestors. It's very important that you don't forget who you are and be proud of your culture. Pretty soon a big helicopter is going to come and pick me up to fly me away to my family, but now you're also my family and I'll come back and visit you often. I hope that you'll also get a nice new school to learn in pretty soon. When I come back I'll bring my children and hope that you'll teach them some of your ways. Chyit, tuwixwals."

They all listened intently to what Bill had been saying, and as he said goodbye they all stood up and sang a native lullaby in Kwakwala that the nun had taught them. Tears clouded Bill's eyes as he turned to leave.

Bill was grateful to Angus Reid for providing such a welcome diversion, that was not as stressful as being with adults, and he concluded that Angus was a pretty special individual. He felt a twinge of regret that Angus had not been able to make an arrangement with Suzanne, as they were both special people and one would have complemented the other.

Back at the house Bill resumed his pacing and looking out of the window as Angus went about his chores. No longer having a watch, he kept going into the kitchen and looking at the clock while estimating the time the helicopter would be enroute. Finally, after a wait that seemed never-ending he heard the unmistakeable flop, flop sound of the big yellow Labrador helicopter which was approaching from the south. Picking up his bundle of possessions, he hobbled out on to the porch as Angus roared up in his Jeep to deliver him to the landing site on the ball diamond. Bill's heart was pounding as the realization sunk in that his ordeal was almost over.

The big Labrador helicopter hovered looking for the best space to land and finally chose the ball field in the middle of the reserve. As it hovered and descended it created a cloud of dust from those areas that had dried out in the spring sunshine and blew spray from the puddles over the horde of children that had appeared as if by magic. They thought it was a great joke and giggled as they were blown over by the force of the giant rotors. Angus drew the Jeep alongside the helicopter when the rotors stopped turning.

As soon as the door opened, Ross Stuart came bounding out looking for Bill but did not recognize him standing alongside the Jeep, leaning on his cane. The last time he had seen him, Bill was clean-shaven and well built. The bearded, gaunt individual before him now bore virtually no resemblance to the old Bill and Ross failed to respond until Bill called out to him. With that cue Ross ran forward and grabbed him in a bear hug, spinning him around in his usual exuberant manner. Bill gasped and involuntarily called out, "Watch for my leg, you big galoot!"

Ross set him down gingerly and stood back to look at him. "My God, I would've passed you in the street. Mind you, you look a lot better than you used to," he added, dodging the mock punch thrown by Bill.

By this time the helicopter crew had joined them and Ross introduced them to Bill. The Captain, Doug Stewart, stepped forward and shook Bill's hand warmly. "We're delighted to finally find you. We hate to lose a customer — it's bad for our statistics!"

"Let me assure you Bill, he's not a relative," Ross joked. "He can't even spell his name properly!"

"We've discussed that before, Ross, and you recall that you were the one with the oddball spelling. Nevertheless, it's a good name regardless of how you spell it."

By this time the whole tribe had assembled around the helicopter and the crewmen were giving children a tour of the interior, much to their delight. Bill noted that the Chief and all the elders were amongst the crowd and he finally saw Suzanne standing at the back, obviously wanting to avoid the spotlight. After a moment's hesitation, Bill pushed his way through the crowd and took her by the hand, leading her and Willie Bearpaw to the helicopter to meet Ross and the Captain. "These are the two people to whom I owe my life," Bill said with a catch in his voice. "We also had two other men with us but I don't see them right now. Suzanne was my nurse and Willie and Paul were my teachers in the Kwakwala language and the history of their people. Would you believe they made me a blood brother in the tribe last night so I'll have a lasting affinity with these people, quite apart from being indebted to them for saving my life."

Suzanne lowered her eyes and blushed but Willie was obviously enjoying his new-found fame and shook everyone's hand enthusiastically. He was particularly impressed when the Captain took him into the cockpit and showed him all the controls. One of the crewmen gave him his orange ball cap with the squadron crest on the front, which Willie was proudly wearing when he emerged from the back of the helicopter.

"Well, folks, I think we'd better get moving if we're going to make Prince George before dark. The hospital is alerted that we're bringing you in, Bill, and we have to drop Ross off in

Sioux Falls en-route. He's anxious to get back to his new bride, I think."

"His BRIDE!" exploded Bill. "Who would ever marry this reprobate?"

"You even know her, Bill. Do you remember Christie, the geologist who was going into Sustut? Well I changed her plans! We were married before Christmas from Jennifer's house and your family were the principals at the wedding. Young Keith was my best man on your behalf and Dianne and Jennifer were bridesmaids. David was the usher and, in spite of his protestations, really did a good job. Now, would you believe you're going to be an uncle about next November!"

"Wonders never cease, but congratulations, you old hound. I was sure that you were destined to be a perennial bachelor. I remember Christie well, and she's much more than you deserve, but I wish you both much happiness."

"I hate to interrupt your reminiscences but we really do have to leave. You can catch up on the news in the chopper on the way back to Sioux Falls. By the way, Bill, your family will be waiting for you at Prince George when we get there. We had a hard time persuading them to wait there instead of coming up here."

Bill suddenly realized that his odyssey was almost over, and he became highly emotional. Despite her resistance, Bill hugged Suzanne tightly in his arms and gently kissed her on the cheek, tasting the warm tears running down her face that she could no longer restrain. "I love you, Suzanne," he quietly whispered in her ear, and though she did not respond, he sensed her emotions through her body contact.

Quickly he turned away and shook hands with Willie Bearpaw, the Chief and all the elders, thanking them again for the great honour they had bestowed upon him and reassuring them that he was going to return some of their land and make a written record of their history for future generations. Finally, he turned to Angus, and thanked him for his hospitality and the clothes which he promised he would return as soon as he got out to civilization. Turning on his

heel he limped aboard the helicopter with his valued possessions under his arm. He took one last wistful look over his
shoulder and noted that Suzanne had left before the crew had
even closed the door. When he was seated by the window he
searched the crowd again but she was nowhere to be seen. He
was, however, astonished to see Mye-Ook standing alone at
the edge of the crowd saying an unspoken farewell with his
eyes. Bill responded by waving and giving a thumbs up sign
and was delighted to see a smile break out on Mye-Ook's face.
He lifted up his arm to proudly show his new watch on his
wrist. Now Bill was convinced that he had broken through the
barrier of silence with Mye-Ook, and was sure that their next
meeting would be on friendly and trusting terms.

"I would guess that you've got pretty strong feelings for
that lady," observed Ross as the engines sprang into life.
"Want to tell me about it?"

"Not really," Bill said quietly. "It's an impossible dream
that has ended forever. I suppose that I can lay most of the
blame on the circumstances, but regardless, it's finished and I
would really not like to discuss it any more, even with you
Ross."

For a while they were both silent but the mood changed as
they headed towards Sioux Falls and they started to act like
their old selves, joking and laughing while Bill recounted
some of the adventures of the winter. Ross enthusiastically
bared his soul about his feelings for Christie and his excitement about the forthcoming child. It was difficult for Bill to
accept the total change in Ross from the carefree bachelor to
the greatly enamoured husband who could barely restrain
himself from talking constantly about Christie.

The old Ross showed through when he suddenly interjected,
"By the way, you know you can no longer claim to be a
successful pilot 'cause you no longer have an equal number of
takeoffs and landings!" They both broke out in gales of
laughter, which broke the ice for Bill to talk about his accident that he had tried to push from his mind. From that point

on he poured out his story, including the episode with Suzanne, having sworn Ross to secrecy.

Time passed quickly and the pilot announced that they were approaching Sioux Falls and that they would like to spend minimum time on the ground before pressing on to Prince George. Bill suddenly felt a genuine pang of apprehension as he thought of being alone for the reunion with his family. He tried to persuade Ross to accompany him, but Ross pointed out that he had to get the 185 back on floats for the summer in time for a party of American bear hunters who were due the following week. He also reminded Bill that he was now a stable, married man and couldn't leave Christie on her own too long. Just as they were touching down Bill told Ross about giving some of his property in Buffalo Narrows to the Indians, but that he would retain the house and a few acres when he made the legal transfer to the Kwakwala band. Ross assured him he would go in and recover some of their personal belongings as soon as his schedule permitted.

The pilot did not shut down the engines, so as Ross left by the rear ramp, Bill accompanied him to the exit where they shared a bear hug. Bill could see Christie waiting by the hotel with Ross' Jeep, so he waved and gave her the thumbs up sign of approval. She waved back enthusiastically, throwing a kiss as the door closed, and Bill hobbled back to his seat as a wave of depression and apprehension surged over him. He was at least grateful to Ross for easing the transition from the wilderness but now he must face the next hurdle alone and it was a terrifying thought.

The rest of the trip to Prince George seemed endless, and a million thoughts raced through Bill's mind. He replayed the confinement in the cabin, and had flashbacks about the crash although he tried desperately to eliminate it from his mind. Throughout, Suzanne's face would reappear, and he had an ache in his heart for her future on the reserve. Then his thoughts would turn to his own future and his concern about fitting back into open society again. There was no doubt in his mind that his experience had changed him forever and he was going to face a difficult period of adjustment.

Finally, the twinkling lights of Prince George came into view through the gathering twilight and the helicopter flew to the northwest corner of the town where the hospital was located. As they started to descend on to the illuminated pad, Bill could see a mob of people and his heart began to race. He searched for Jennifer and the children but could not make them out in the milling crowd. The helicopter touched down without a bump, and as the rear ramp swung down one of the crewmen came to help him out. But first he made his way to the cockpit and shook hands with the pilots, thanking them profusely. "It's sure comforting to know that we have a bunch of people like you when we're flying in the back country. While you were a little delayed finding me I'm just as grateful." The Captain reached over to his shoulder and pulled off the 442 Squadron crest and handed it to Bill, jestingly reminding him that if he got into trouble again, this was the outfit to call for top service. Reluctantly Bill then limped to the rear of the helicopter and the bright lights of the hospital.

As he limped down the ramp with his meagre bundle of possessions, aided by one of the crewmen, he was blinded by the lights of television cameras and flashbulbs. He tried to push his way through the mob but was intercepted by a nurse with a wheelchair who insisted that he sit in it despite his protestations that he could walk. "Company rules," she laughed as an orderly tried to make a path through the mob of news media who were shouting questions in a jumble of noise that made Bill wince and shake. All the while he was searching the crowd for Jennifer and the children but it was not until they went through the emergency entrance that he saw them standing in a doorway with Mike. They all rushed forward spontaneously with tears flowing and smothered him with hugs and kisses. The only one who was at all reluctant was Dianne who stared at her father in disbelief with his beard and shoulder-length hair. The one who finally broke the tension was David who exclaimed, "Hey, neat Dad. You look like John Lennon!" The tears were streaming down Jennifer's face as she kissed Bill and hugged him. Mike had remained in the background but finally pushed his way through and gave Bill an enormous bear hug. "I thought I'd lost my old hunting partner for a while, but I knew you'd turn up again."

The nurse was finally able to push Bill into the emergency ward and transferred him to a bed where a young blonde doctor awaited him. "Hi, I'm Doctor Pace and I'll be looking after you until we see what needs to be fixed up. Meanwhile, I'll have to ask your family to leave us alone for a while until I check you over. My first diagnosis is that you need a shave and a haircut so that we can see what's underneath!" David immediately exclaimed, "Don't do that Dad, you look neat!" Keith playfully cuffed his ear and led him towards the door as the family all kissed and hugged him again and promised to be back first thing in the morning.

The nurse peeled off his clothing and Doctor Pace started her examination, carefully probing his leg, that had turned quite blue. "We'll get that X-rayed right away and see what's happening in there. We'll also get some blood tests done on you because it's apparent that you're anaemic and suffering from scurvy as a result of improper diet. You're certainly skinny, but apart from that seem to be in remarkably good shape. I'm afraid that it's too late to do anything about the scars on your face, but they'll give you character! Meanwhile, we'll get an orderly to help you have a bath and then we'll let you get a good night's sleep before you face that horde of newspeople out there. You've become quite a celebrity with your exploits."

"I neither feel or look much of a celebrity right now, and I'd be grateful if you can get rid of them. Tell them I died on the operating table or something!" exclaimed Bill.

The doctor laughed heartily as she gave instructions to the nurse. "See you in the morning, Mr. Headingly, and we'll see if we can get you out of here as soon as possible. I'm sure after your experience the last thing you want to do is hang around a hospital."

Bill agreed wholeheartedly as the nurse wheeled him off to the X-ray department to have his leg checked.

On return from the X-ray department and his bath, Bill was placed in a single room for which he was very grateful. He was in no mood for conversation and did not object when the nurse gave him a needle to help him sleep.

He awoke in the morning to the gentle prodding of Doctor Pace who was standing by the bed with a bundle of charts. A nurse was checking the I.V. tube that had been inserted the night before.

"Well, at least you're still alive and I think you're going to stay that way for a while. The I.V. tube is giving you some of the nutrients that you're lacking and that's the fastest way to give them to you. We've checked the X-rays of your leg and whoever set it for you did a remarkable job. It has knitted together well. There's quite a bit of blood clotting around the wound but we'll get rid of that. We're also going to put on a walking cast until it strengthens up again, but you can thank whoever looked after you that the leg won't have to be rebroken and reset. Otherwise, you seem to be in great shape. However, after the experience you've had I'm going to have the staff psychologist talk to you and he may be able to help with the part of you we can't see."

"I've probably needed to talk to a shrink for a long time," laughed Bill. "The one who set my leg was an Indian lady who was along with the trappers by a stroke of great fortune. She'd been educated in a convent and received nurse's training in this very hospital. I think I owe her my life and my sanity, presuming that is still intact. She was a terrific lady and I can't do enough to repay her."

"I don't have to be a doctor to understand your feelings for her. She sounds like a great lady and we could use her back here on our nursing staff."

"There's no likelihood of that," Bill said with authority. "Like many of the native people she wasn't well treated by the white man and will probably spend the rest of her life helping her brethren on the reserve."

"I'd like to hear your story sometime but meanwhile I have to minister to a few more broken bodies. Now that we have you pretty well fixed up we're going to have to expose you to that hungry pack of media people, so the Administrator has set up a news conference with them in the auditorium this afternoon. I wish there was some way we could protect you from them but you're big news and people expect to hear your story. They've specifically asked that you don't shave or have your hair cut until after the news conference so that you'll look authentic!"

"My God! That's the last thing I need, but if it's inevitable I'll have to suffer through it I guess. Hopefully it will focus credit on the deserving people."

Jennifer and the children arrived just after noon and Bill felt much more comfortable in their presence than he had the night before. They giggled and chattered until it was time for the news conference when it was agreed that they would all be present to lend moral support to Bill, who now had his cast applied. Jennifer combed his beard and hair so that he did not look quite so unkempt. The children thought it was a great adventure and were excited about the prospect of appearing on T.V.

For Bill the whole thing was a complete ordeal, and he was appalled at some of the questions that the news people asked about the most intimate details of his adventure. He very carefully avoided any direct reference to Suzanne as he was afraid that their probing questions would reveal his true feelings. Finally, the ordeal was over and he was wheeled back to his room utterly drained and exhausted. Jennifer sent off the children with Mike while she stayed behind to get Bill settled down again.

When they were alone again, Bill took Jennifer's hand and said, "There's something we must discuss and I'd prefer that we do it when the kids aren't here."

"Can't it wait until you're feeling better?"

"No. I'd like to get it over with now. As you can imagine, being cooped up for months with Suzanne and her nursing me back to health, I developed very strong feelings for her and I think she felt the same. However, she'd had such a bad experience with white men that it couldn't go beyond that point, so you've no fear that it'll threaten our marriage in any way. In fact I'd like you to meet her some time and become friends. She's a fine individual. During my winter with them I learned a great deal about the native ways and the injustices done to them by the white man. In fact, as you heard at the news conference they made me a member of the tribe, so I can feel a common bond with them. Amongst other things I found out that our property in Buffalo Narrows was a sacred place to them before the white man took it. It was known as Klay-Ah-Kwoss, and when I heard their story I decided we'd give part of it back to them in gratitude for saving my life. I insisted that we keep the house and a few acres around it, so we can visit when we want."

Jennifer caught her breath and started to weep. "Oh, Bill, that's our only home, and we've put our hearts and souls into it. The children will be shattered."

"Without my plane it'll be impossible to live in there full time. Besides, I've been thinking it over and the children should really be starting to attend a regular school or they're liable to become social outcasts. Maybe living in Buffalo Narrows was just an impossible dream, and it took this episode to make me finally face up to it. I made an agreement with the Kwakwalas that we could go back in there to our cabin any time we wanted for vacations and they'll respect our rights. I'm just sorry that I didn't have the chance to discuss it with you and the kids first. The other thing I did was to agree to build a new house on the reserve for Suzanne and her uncle, Willie Bearpaw, when I saw the squalor they were living in. We'll use part of the insurance claim from the Beaver to pay for it. By the way, I arranged for Ross Stuart to fly in and pick up some of our personal things when he gets time."

"I'm in full support of what you've done, but how will we survive? We don't even have a home now."

"Hopefully, we can live with your folks for the time being. If necessary I'll sell real estate," he added with a laugh. "We've had some tough times before and we'll make it again from scratch."

Jennifer looked very grave, but volunteered to break the news to the children, who were going to be inconsolable. "Meanwhile, you'd better get some rest so that you can get started on the real estate course! I'll start advertising to take in washing and the kids can all get paper routes," she added, showing the spunk that had attracted Bill to her in the first place.

After she left, Bill collapsed into a deep sleep, totally exhausted from the strain of the news conference and the discussion with Jennifer. In fact he slept right through the night and was astonished when the nurse, Kathleen, brought his breakfast.

"While you were making like sleeping beauty you had a phone call from a Miss Brittney Wooding, who urgently wants to talk to you. She said she was flying right up from Vancouver and would be here some time this morning. She certainly was anxious to see you, so I'll bring her right here when she arrives."

"I don't know any Miss Wooding, unless she's from the accident investigation board. Otherwise, I haven't got a clue what it can be about."

"She's probably one of the groupies that've been hanging around here since you were on television!" joked Kathleen.

It was almost noon when Kathleen arrived with a smartly dressed young woman in her early thirties carrying a slim briefcase under her arm. She was beautifully coiffed and exuded confidence and efficiency.

Bill certainly didn't recognize her, and when she introduced herself as Brittney Wooding he was no wiser.

After shaking Bill's hand with a firm grip, she went on, "I'm a writer and publisher. We saw your interview on TV and all agreed that you had a fabulous story to tell, so I flew up here this morning to see if we can interest you in letting us do your story in book form. I'd work with you on the book and we'd undertake to publish and distribute it. We do enjoy an excellent reputation in the industry, and specialize in books with a native Indian or wilderness theme. Our company is Talking Stick Productions. You may have heard of us or read some of our books."

"I must plead ignorance on both counts," Bill admitted. "But I must also admit that I'm a Louis L'Amour fan and any spare time I have I get into one of his works. I'd have given my right arm to have a stack of them in the cabin."

"Well, you certainly have lots of company since he's one of the most prolific writers of our time. Wouldn't we love to have the publishing rights! Right now I'd be basking on a South Seas island instead of downtown Prince George if we had! However, back to business. As I mentioned, either I or one of our other writers would work with you and hopefully tell the story the way you want it. I've been authorised to offer you one hundred thousand dollars advance on royalties, and five per-cent on gross sales thereafter. Needless to say, the essence is to get this type of a story on the market as soon as possible while it's still fresh in people's minds, and certainly in time for the Christmas market. So, it would mean getting started pretty well right away if you're interested."

"I must admit that you've taken me completely unawares although I have been thinking over such an idea. You're also the first on the scene, and presumably there may be other offers. However, I've always been one to follow my instincts and I like the cut of your jib, if you'll pardon the expression. There are two things I'd like to stipulate though: first of all I have a friend in town who's a lawyer, and I'd like him to check over the contract; and, secondly, I've promised the Kwakwala tribe that I'll publish the history of their tribe from notes I took all winter from their oral recitation. If you'll agree to print and publish that for me gratis I think we can make a deal."

232

"That's certainly the first time anyone has called it my jib, but I'll take that as a compliment!" Brittney laughed. "How long would it be and would soft cover be adequate? The history I mean," she added with a benign smile.

Bill had established an immediate rapport with this obviously highly intelligent and successful lady, and knew he could work with her comfortably. "I have a book crammed full of notes, but my guess is that it would translate into about a hundred printed pages. Much of it is myth, of course, but that's an integral part of the history that has been passed down orally for centuries. The elders are afraid it'll disappear because the young people are more interested in watching television than listening to some old men rambling on. Their culture will disappear if we don't try to preserve some of it now."

"Of course I'll have to discuss it with my partners, but I'm sure they'll go along with it. Why don't I go call them while you check out the contract with your lawyer friend. As I mentioned before, time is of the essence with this type of story so we'll have to get right at it. In fact I have my recorder and laptop computer with me so I could even stay on for a few days to get started."

"I'm virtually certain that my answer will be positive, but I'd like to check it out with my wife and lawyer. Jennifer and I were just sitting here in despair last night wondering how we'll survive now that I've lost my livelihood and I was even joking about selling real estate as a last resort. This would certainly help us get started again."

"Good. Well, I'll go call my partners and have a bite of lunch while you think it over. How would it be if I come back about two and get your answer?"

As soon as she had left the room, Bill called for the nurse to bring him a phone and the number of Jennifer's motel. He felt a surge of excitement at the prospect of the book, and the money which would get them re-established until the insurance money for the Beaver came through. He was almost breathless as he recounted the story to Jennifer and asked her opinion.

Always the cautious one, Jennifer immediately asked if they shouldn't wait and see if they had any better offers before deciding, but Bill told her he had a good feeling about it, so she gave her blessing. Next Bill called Pete Richards, an old college friend, who was now practising law in town and asked if he could come over and check over the contract.

"Gosh, Bill, I'd love to, and to see you again, but I'm tied up with a client right now. However, I've had dealings with Talking Stick Productions before and they're a first class organization. So, if you're happy with the money they offered you I wouldn't worry about it. As soon as you get out of the hospital we'll have to get together."

"Thanks, Pete, you've eased my mind just talking to you and I think I'll accept the offer."

"Save me an autographed copy of the book when it comes out," Pete added as he hung up.

It was just after noon and Bill didn't know how he would fill in the time until Brittney came back to confirm acceptance of the offer when the nurse came in with the phone again.

"Another call for you. You're a pretty popular guy right now, but this one's a man. I hope your wife knows all about this," she added with a smile.

"I tell her everything I do," Bill responded.

"I'll bet!" was her parting shot as she left the room.

Picking up the phone Bill was greeted by an effusive voice who identified himself as the Federal Minister of Indian Affairs, Pierre Lapointe, calling from Ottawa.

"I saw your press conference, Mr. Headingly, and was most impressed by your exploit. But above all I was impressed by your obvious empathy with the native Indians, and your understanding of their claims and problems. We desperately need people like you to negotiate land settlements and redress other grievances. What I'd like to do is to employ you as a consultant for the Department on an indefinite basis. I'm sure we have enough to keep you busy for years if you're interested."

"Good grief, Mr. Minister, it never rains but it pours! Yesterday I was desperately trying to figure out how I was going to make a living after losing my aeroplane and almost my life. Now I have a book offer plus your most interesting challenge. Without hesitation I'll tell you that I'm most interested and will accept without reservation. I have very strong feelings now about our native people and this will afford me the opportunity to do something about it."

"Wonderful, Mr. Headingly. I'll have one of my deputies fly out there and finalize the details as soon as possible so that when you're fully mobile again you can get to work. It would be ideal if you could take up residence in the Prince George area since that is pretty well the focal point of our current negotiations."

"Thank you, Mr. Minister. I do have a commitment to the publisher to work with their writer, but hopefully that won't be a full time job, so I'm prepared to start any time."

"Nice talking to you, Mr. Headingly, and I'm sure we'll meet before long. Goodbye."

"Goodbye, sir," responded Bill as he hung up the phone.

There was no answer at Jennifer's motel room, so he assumed she was enroute. He was pacing the halls impatiently when she finally came into sight with the children. He virtually ran down the hall to meet them and bundled them all into his room to tell them the good news. "Better start house hunting right away," he blurted out. "Looks as if we're starting a whole new life along with my resurrection. Little did I think when I was lying in that cabin in the wilderness in the depths of despair that this is the way it would all turn out. If Paul had been here he would've said that it was the Great Spirit looking after us, but I think the Good Lord must have had a hand in it too. I suspect they're one and the same, but in any event we should be grateful to both of them."

True to her word, Brittney arrived back right at two and Bill introduced her to the family. "I discussed your proposal with my partners and they're in full agreement with printing the Kwakwala history as long as we can use our name on it. Unfortunately, I also have to get back right away for other important business, so I'll send up one of our best writers to work with you. She should be here in a few days if you're prepared to sign the contract."

"It's certainly the best offer we've had so far, and Jennifer and the kids are in agreement, so it's a deal."

"Fine, Mr. Headingly, I'll get a cheque in the mail to you as soon as I get back." She shook hands all around and bustled out of the door.

Epilogue
Chapter Sixteen

Bill was released from hospital on the sixth day as an outpatient, on the understanding that he would return each day for therapy. Jennifer and the children arrived in a taxi to take him to the motel where she had been able to get a small suite with cooking facilities. Enroute Bill observed, "The first thing we have to get is a vehicle to drive, although you'll have to be the chauffeuse until I get this cast off. What kind do you think we should get, kids?"

There was an immediate chorus of opinions ranging from a BMW to an open Jeep, so Bill asked Jennifer for her opinion before giving his. "Something easy to drive," was her immediate choice, so Bill asked the driver to take them to the nearest dealer that sold four-wheel drive vehicles since that was going to be the most practical for them. The driver took them to the Jeep Eagle dealer and deposited them, instead of returning them to the motel.

As they entered the door, with Bill bringing up the rear, hobbling on his cane, the sales manager came forward to greet them. "Hi, I'm Tony Burton. You're the guy who was lost for the winter aren't you?" he said to Bill who had not yet had his beard and hair shorn. It was his intention to visit the barber shop as his next stop.

"I'm afraid so," responded Bill. "I'm beginning to develop a new respect for dignitaries who have to put up with this constantly. Some of them obviously enjoy their notoriety but I'm dying to slip into anonymity again. Maybe if I get rid of this hair I'll be less obvious."

"No, don't Dad!" David exclaimed. "I think it looks great on you."

"So do I," said the sales manager diplomatically. "But what can I do for you?"

"We need a vehicle that can transport this mob and we need a four wheel drive since we'll spend a lot of time in the bush. My new job will also take me down some bad back roads to Indian reserves."

"Here's just the thing for you. The new four wheel drive wagon. As you see, it has tons of cargo space and seats for eight so it'll accommodate all in comfort."

Bill was immediately sold, but there was much grumbling from the children, who thought it was pretty mundane and they should be getting something much more sporty. Jennifer was concerned that it be automatic if she was going to drive it. The major concession Bill made to satisfy the children was that it had to be cherry red in colour.

"How soon could you provide one, seeing that we're totally without transportation?"

"I can have one to your specifications within a few days, but in the meantime we'll be pleased to loan you a vehicle. In fact to please this young lady, we just happen to have a used BMW on the lot that we'll give you to drive until your own comes in."

Dianne's eyes sparkled at the thought, and even the boys were impressed by the prospect of driving around in a BMW, so everyone was happy as they drove out with Jennifer at the wheel and Bill trying to figure out the switches and controls.

"First stop the barber shop," Bill commanded much to the dismay of David who still thought his father looked neat. Bill noted a smile of relief on Jennifer's face who was not at all impressed by his hirsute appearance. The change was nothing short of dramatic as the locks and beard began to fall to reveal a much thinner Bill, and the family were quite shocked by the scars criss-crossing his face. Bill was equally shocked but tried to pass it off lightly and agreed with Dr. Pace that the scars certainly gave him character.

"Don't worry about it," Jennifer reassured him. "When I get some of my home-made soup into you and fill those cheeks up you'll look human again." Once again the strength of character that had attracted Bill to her in the first place was showing through and he knew that his rehabilitation was already well on the way.

Arriving back at the motel, Bill was not prepared for the welcome he received when they opened the door and a half-grown golden retriever pup came bounding out. In its enthusiasm it knocked Bill over and then proceeded to lick his face as he lay on the ground.

"What on earth is this beast?" he gasped as Jennifer helped him back on his feet.

"This is Buck," Keith shouted as the children chased the pup around the courtyard. "Uncle Ross brought it for us when you were missing."

"Good old Ross!" exclaimed Bill sarcastically. "Just the sort of thing he would do."

"It was a Godsend for the children when you were missing and he really is a nice little guy. He just needs a bit of discipline if he's going to live in society. We were waiting for you to come back to train him properly," added Jennifer diplomatically.

Although Bill feigned annoyance, he was secretly delighted as he had always wanted a dog but circumstances were never right. "Well, now we've got him I suppose we'll have to find a proper place to live where he'll have room to roam. Which brings me to the next subject. I think we'll have to have a family meeting to decide what we'll do."

After they were all settled in the motel, Bill laid out all the options for them. "Okay guys, I know how much we all love Buffalo Narrows, and nothing would make me happier than to go straight back there now. But we have to face reality and accept that it's impossible under the circumstances." He looked around the family to see tears starting to roll down the children's faces, but he continued. "Without my plane we couldn't live in there and I'd have no way to make a living. I promise you that some day we will go back there to live, but right now I've been offered a job with the Department of Indian Affairs here in Prince George. I think we should be grateful that I survived and we're all together again, which is the most important thing. So, if you'll just support me the way you all did when we built our house and moved to Buffalo Narrows, we'll make it again."

The children sat in silence, tears welling up in their eyes, and Keith immediately exclaimed, "I don't want to live in a city."

"Neither do I," agreed Bill. "That's why I asked your Mum to see if she could find us a place in the country. I also thought it would be great if we could have a horse too," he added diplomatically.

"Oh, Daddy, could we?" Dianne exclaimed, brightening up immediately.

"Can we each have our own?" added David in his usual grandiose way.

Bill heaved a sigh of relief as he had agonized for hours in the hospital about how he would break the news to them about no longer living full time in Buffalo Narrows.

"In fact," he added, "your mother has been talking to the real estate people and they're coming this afternoon to show us a place in the country that sounds like just what we're looking for. So, take that hound out for some exercise while I have a rest and you can come with us to look at it."

"Yeah!" they responded as they bounded out of the door with Buck hard on their heels.

"Phew!" exclaimed Bill. "I thought it would be harder than that."

"It was the horse that swung it," Jennifer observed with a smile on her face, as she kissed Bill gently.

Promptly at 2 p.m. a large station wagon drew up outside the motel, and a salt and pepper-haired woman in her late forties came to the door. She introduced herself as Vivian Johnson and confirmed that she had come to show them the property they might be interested in. It was Bill's judgement that the pup should stay home but he was soundly outvoted and they ended up loading it in the back of the station wagon.

Vivian drove south on the highway for eight miles, and then turned onto a gravel road for another three miles, before turning into a long driveway leading up to a cluster of buildings. The dominant building was a large barn, about eighty by forty feet, with a rail corral alongside. About fifty yards away stood the house, which turned out to be made of logs which were well weathered, and dated the house. It had a shake roof and a large picture window that looked out on a small lake. The upper windows were set back into dormers that were obviously looking from bedrooms.

The first impression was that the whole place was run down, and obviously in need of a good overhaul and renovation. Nevertheless, it had a rustic charm that immediately attracted them all. As soon as the car door was opened the children and Buck spewed out and immediately headed for the barn where they were delighted to find a good stock of hay, and in no time they were climbing up the beams and leaping into it. Bill and Jennifer, with a critical eye, were more interested in the house and were greeted with a strong, musty odour as if it had been closed up for a while. It was completely furnished, but most of the furniture was well worn and much of it ready for the scrap pile.

The main floor consisted of a large living room with a view of the lake, a large country-style kitchen and the master bedroom with an ensuite bathroom. Upstairs were three smaller bedrooms, each with a dormer window looking over

241

the lake, and a big bathroom with an old-fashioned claw-foot tub. The plan was well laid out, and the whole place was lined with cedar. A large stone fireplace dominated the north wall of the living room, and a wood heater stood in one corner.

Vivian broke the silence by explaining, "The house was owned and occupied by an old man who had lived alone after his wife died. That's why it looks a little run down. It has actually stood vacant since the old man died five months ago. The children are long gone and scattered across the country, some as far away as California. None of them are interested in living here any more and are anxious to sell it to settle the estate. Although there was over four hundred acres at one time, the old man had sold most of it off when he could no longer manage to run it, but there are still fifty-five acres left with the house. There's some uncut timber, and it's all enclosed with snake fencing to keep in livestock."

Jennifer was not enthralled with the state of the house although she did like it and could see the potential. Bill was busy checking the structure with a critical eye, having built a log home himself, and was impressed by the workmanship. Next he went and joined the children in the barn, where they were excitedly swinging on ropes and leaping into the hay. "Let's buy it, Dad," Keith shouted, even though they had not set foot in the house. The barn looked sound, and only needed a few sheets of tin replaced to make it fully waterproof. At the end were stalls for livestock if they decided to get horses, which was inevitable if they purchased the property.

Bill rejoined the ladies in the house and asked Vivian for details of the listing, after getting a reluctant nod of approval from Jennifer.

"As I explained, the house has been empty since the owner died and we haven't had much interest at the price the heirs were asking. Now, however, I think they'd be interested in any reasonable offer to get rid of it and settle the estate. I should add that the furniture would go with it if you wanted it."

"Most of it would have to be junked, but since we don't have any furniture here, and it wouldn't be worth moving any out of Buffalo Narrows, it would do us for a start. But first, how about school for the children?" enquired Bill.

"The school bus picks the children up at the end of the driveway, and the junior children go to the local school while the high school students go into Prince George. There are a number of children living in the area so there'd be no problem with friends."

"Well, what do you think, Jennifer? I've already had a full vote of confidence from the kids, who are only interested in the barn. By the way, there's even a toy for me in the barn — a dandy old tractor that looks as if it still runs. It would be great for clearing the driveway in winter, if nothing else."

Jennifer did not want to appear too eager, although she could see that it would be an ideal transition from Buffalo Narrows, and she certainly could not entertain the thought of living in a city again. "Well, it would take a lot of work but the potential is there if the price is right," she answered.

"Alright Vivian, what's the lowest price you think they'll take, as is, with immediate occupancy?"

"Well, they were asking two hundred thousand dollars, but I'm sure they'd accept considerably less now just to get rid of it and settle the estate."

"Let's offer them one hundred and fifty thousand, and see what they say. Can you get in touch with the executor right away 'cause we'd be anxious to consummate the deal as soon as possible and move in immediately. I have a friend in town who's a lawyer and he could handle the transfer."

"As soon as I get back to the office I'll phone the daughter, who's the executrix, and should have an answer for you this evening."

Bill and Jennifer felt a surge of excitement at the prospects of owning the property, and were both already mentally making plans for the renovations that would be needed. The children were so excited they could hardly contain themselves, and Buck even showed his approval by racing around the yard, barking furiously.

It was a long wait at the motel for the answer, and the phone did not ring until almost nine o'clock. Bill grabbed the phone and was delighted to hear Vivian's voice, although he did not want to appear too eager.

"Sorry it took so long Mr. Headingly, but the daughter was not home, and she had to discuss the offer with her siblings. Very reluctantly they agreed to the offer, so if it's not too late I'll bring over the paperwork tonight."

Bill tried his best to sound nonchalant, but as soon as he put down the phone he let out a whoop and hugged Jennifer and the children in a mass hug. Even Buck started barking, and they had to quieten him before the neighbours complained. Bill went to the fridge and brought out a brown paper bag from which he produced a bottle of champagne he had bought in anticipation. He raised his glass, and they all joined in a toast to the start of their new life in what they had already agreed would be named Tohtohlah Two.

The days following the purchase of Tohtohlah Two were a blur of activity. Jennifer flew back to Edmonton to pack up their belongings from her parents' house, and get transfers for the children to their new schools. Sue and Mike were shattered that they were moving away again, as they had grown accustomed to them being around. They were nevertheless happy for them and their new house, and Bill's work. They agreed to come and visit them as soon as they were settled.

The most difficult thing for Jennifer to do was to resign her job, since she had felt she was really accomplishing something useful. She and Robert had become a team, and he had been shattered when he heard the news that Bill had returned, and surmised correctly that Jennifer would be leaving. While she was unwilling to admit it to herself, Jennifer had become extremely fond of Robert, and he made no secret of his feelings for her. She was the epitome of efficiency in the office and he had managed to persuade her to join him for dinner on a few occasions when they were working late. Notwithstanding her feelings, she was always a model of propriety with Robert, both in and out of the office, and never allowed anything more than an innocent peck on the cheek after an evening out. Even so, she felt a sense of guilt that she had never experienced before in her married life. Sometimes she even allowed herself the fantasy that if Bill did not return she would turn to Robert at the appropriate time. Now it was an impossible dream, and she knew she had to sever all connection with Robert and resume her old life as soon as possible. As a parting gesture, Robert gave her the name of an old classmate in Prince George, and virtually assured her of work if she so desired. Although she resisted at first, Robert hugged her tightly and kissed her firmly on the cheek when she turned away her face. Flustered, she said a quick goodbye to the other members of the firm and was relieved to pass through the door.

Meanwhile, Bill was fully occupied with moving into the new house, and with the writer, who had arrived as promised. She came equipped with a laptop computer and tape recorder. Bill found that he could only tolerate about two hours each session with her, as she was a very intense young woman and did not consider Bill's feelings when she was prying the story out of him. He regretted that Brittney had been unable to stay on as she was easy to work with, and they had established an immediate rapport. He became incensed when the writer kept probing him about his relationship with Suzanne, telling him that the book would be no good without a love story in it. In the end he resigned himself to the fact that she was going to invent the love scene if he did not tell her the facts, and thought it would be better this way so that he could pass it off as fiction. After their daily sessions she would return to her hotel room to transcribe her notes and recordings to the computer memory. It was obvious that the book was going to be highly dramatized, but Bill had to accept the inevitable and the fact that the book had to appeal to the public, whereas the real story would undoubtedly be dull by literary standards.

Bill was stunned one day when the writer announced, "Okay, it's obvious that your memory is being selective, so I've reached the point where I have to see the actual venue in order to really paint a word picture. I just can't proceed until I actually experience it. How do we get there?"

"Access to the area is pretty well limited to helicopters, canoes, or a long bumpy road after a train ride," Bill answered, hoping to deter her from making an actual visit to the cabin. He was virtually in shock at the prospect of going back to the scene of his adventure.

"Fine, let's hire a helicopter as soon as possible. Can you arrange it?"

"Sure, but it'll cost money," he answered, unable to think in the grandiose terms of the commercial world. He reflected on how he would have loved to get a contract with people like this when he had his plane.

"That's our problem, Mr. Headingly," she answered brusquely.

Reluctantly, Bill called Skookum Choppers and booked a Bell Jet Ranger to leave at seven the next morning to fly them directly to the Kwakwala reserve. He was astonished when they told him that they could be there in under two hours, but then realised that the Jet Ranger was virtually twice as fast as his old Beaver.

Jennifer arrived home that evening so that she was able to look after the children while he was away. He anticipated the trip with some trepidation when he thought of going back to the place where his adventure had taken place, and Jennifer expressed her serious reservations in no uncertain terms. But the writer was not to be deterred. Bill was also somewhat disturbed at the thought of flying again, but realized he had no option and that he would have to face up to it again sometime. He even started to have some misgivings about the whole project, but resigned himself to the fact that it was giving them a whole new start after a disaster that had virtually wiped them out.

246

The Jet Ranger was incredibly fast, and Bill actually started to relax and enjoy the trip. They arrived at the reserve just before ten, and their arrival caused a stir, with a curious crowd assembled around the ball park to see who was arriving. As soon as Bill stepped out of the chopper he was recognised, and people started shouting "Tchim-Uhl-Kain" as they came up to shake his hand vigorously. Bill was grateful when Angus Reid arrived in his Jeep to welcome them.

"It didn't take you long to get back, Bill. Obviously you missed us all and liked the place so much you wanted to show us off."

Bill introduced the writer and explained the reason for the visit. This caused great excitement amongst the Indians, expecially when they learned that there was going to be a book and maybe even a film about the Kwakwalas. The chief and elders joined the throng, and Bill was careful to ask permission to visit the trapping area before explaining that he hoped it would benefit the whole tribe financially. He added that the writer would also be producing from his notes their tribe history after the book was finished.

Meanwhile, the writer was snapping pictures all over, and stunned Bill when she asked to see the cabin and crash site. Bill protested, "I couldn't possibly find it again. It would be like a needle in a haystack."

Not satisfied, the writer asked, "Aren't there any of the trappers around who could show us where it is?"

Turning to Angus Reid, Bill asked if Willie Bearpaw was around, and learned that he was fishing down at the dam. Angus offered to drive him down there, which gave Bill an opportunity to ask about Suzanne.

"She's thrown herself full time into work on the reserve and she's helping out at the school right now. She has never mentioned your name again, and I'm sure you can appreciate why."

They bumped over the road to the dam and found Willie pulling in his net full of big carp, which the Indians considered to be a delicacy. His eyes opened wide when he recognized Bill and came running over to the Jeep, enfolding him in a bear hug.

"Holy Jeez, buddy, how come you're back?" Willie enquired.

"How'd you like a ride in a helicopter Willie?" Bill asked, as Willie stood open mouthed. "We have to take somebody in to the cabin and the place where I crashed, so we need you to guide us."

"I never flew in my life!" Willie exclaimed.

"There's nothing to it," Bill reassured him. "Come on, let's go 'cause we've got to go back tonight."

Willie reluctantly climbed into the Jeep and they bounced back to the waiting helicopter.

As Willie was strapped into the front seat of the helicopter, Angus took off in the direction of the school. Bill mentally visualized Suzanne working with the children at the school, and hoped he would see her before they left.

The pilot headed out over Tatlatui Lake, with Willie clutching his seat with both hands. When they arrived over the river mouth that Bill recognized immediately, it brought back a flood of memories of his cold night and the trip on top of the furs. Following Willie's pointed directions, they quickly came to the clearing where the cabin stood. It gave Bill a totally different perspective of the area since he had previously only ventured as far as the door of the cabin. There was ample room in the clearing in front of the cabin and the helicopter landed, blowing clouds of leaves and dust in a whirlwind that obscured the cabin. Bill had a strange feeling in the pit of his stomach when he saw the cabin again that had been both his salvation and his prison.

When the rotors had stopped, they all piled out and Willie opened the door of the cabin, which was dark with the shutters boarded over the windows. He left the door open and lit a lamp so that they could see the interior. "It's certainly no Hilton," observed the writer as she unslung her camera with a wide-angle lens and started flashing pictures from every aspect. She planned to use some of the photographs in the book. Bill was reluctant to even step through the door, but finally did, and a wave of nostalgia swept over him as he saw the familiar bunks, table and stove, and sensed the old familiar smells. The old blanket was still hanging over Suzanne's bunk just as she had left it, looking as if she planned to return the next season.

Next they walked down the trail to the river, and saw the place where Suzanne had netted the fish, and where they had embarked for the return journey. Bill had an immediate flashback of Mye-Ook lifting him into the canoe as his first gesture of reconciliation.

"Well, let's go see the plane," the writer announced matter-of-factedly.

As they climbed back aboard the helicopter Bill's stomach knotted up at the thought of seeing the crash site, and his faithful old Beaver a crumpled wreck. Once airborne, Willie pointed toward Goat Mountain and vivid flashes of memory raced through Bill's mind. With the fresh leaves on the trees, Willie had difficulty spotting the wreckage, but finally they all saw the swath cut through the trees near No Name Lake and a yellow object pointed down into the heavy timber. Bill's heart leapt when he saw the wreckage, and couldn't conceive how anyone could have survived the crash. The odds of the Indians finding him there were one in a million, and the prospects of finding the wreckage from the air virtually nil unless the searchers had passed directly overhead in the tangle of forest.

The pilot indicated that it was impossible to land anywhere near the wreckage, so the writer took a whole roll of film as they hovered overhead. Bill had an almost fatal fascination with the wreckage as he thought of all the hundreds of hours he had flown in the Beaver, and the vivid memory of the last few moments before the crash flashed through his mind. He could almost hear the rending of metal as he went into the trees, and started shaking uncontrollably.

Bill felt a great sense of relief when the writer finally indicated she was satisfied and motioned for the pilot to return to the reserve. To Bill it was almost like burying an old friend and he knew that he would never see it again. Nevertheless, he felt it appropriate that the final resting place of the old bird was in the forest over which it had flown for many thousands of hours. Bill was silent all the way back to the reserve, trying to regain control of his emotions.

Back at the reserve Bill saw Angus standing beside the Jeep with a woman, and his heart leapt when he saw that it was Suzanne. He was glad that she did not leave before they landed, and immediately ran over to her and took her two hands in his, squeezing them tightly. He was cautious not to make any overt show of affection with the writer present. Suzanne responded by looking into his eyes and exclaimed, "My God, I'd forgotten what you looked like without all that hair and beard."

"I still have a few scars as a souvenir, though," Bill observed. "And by the way, the doctor said that you'd done a fantastic job of setting my leg. They didn't even have to reset it. The doctor says they have a job for you anytime you want to go back."

"No way! My place is here with my people and I'll never leave again. They also need me to help nurse them, and I'm helping to teach in the little school we've started ourselves. No more kids are going to leave this reserve while I'm still alive, and I'm trying to get back the ones that have already been taken to residential schools."

"Maybe I can help you Suzanne, 'cause I've been asked by the Minister of Indian Affairs to work with them, and I intend to make sure the Kwakwalas get priority treatment. I guess Angus has told you all about the book, and I've got an agreement that your history will be done at the same time. Hopefully, if we make any money, it'll be donated to the tribe."

"Good lord, man, here I slave my heart out to get things done and in a few weeks you've got everything organised.

How about putting in a good word with my bosses when you meet them in Ottawa," Angus interjected.

"With great pleasure, Angus," Bill replied as he gripped his hand firmly.

The writer was anxious to get on her way, so they bade their farewells and promised to be back soon. Willie was still starry-eyed over his helicopter ride, and obviously the local hero as he recounted the trip, trying to sound nonchalant. Bill shook hands with Willie and desperately resisted the urge to hug Suzanne. Again he gave her hands a firm squeeze in a symbol of unspoken affection as she turned her head away.

Once airborne, Bill asked the pilot if he had enough fuel left to overfly Buffalo Narrows, but when he studied the map he concluded that it was too far out of his route. In a way Bill was relieved, since he felt more at peace with himself than he had since he returned to civilization.

Chapter Seventeen

Bill was highly relieved when the writer finally decided that she had enough material to work on, and left with a briefcase full of notes, cassettes and her laptop computer programmed with essential information. She would now prepare the manuscript without any further reference to Bill, or any other characters, until the final product. It was quite obvious that the manuscript would not necessarily follow the original story line, but she kept explaining that it had to be made dramatic to hold the readers' attention. Despite his and Suzanne's objections, she was going to insert a love scene in the cabin. She kept repeating with a smirk, "Sex sells!"

Since nothing more had been heard from the Department of Indian Affairs, Bill was beginning to discount it as just another political promise unkept. He was actually grateful for the interlude to do some renovations on Tohtohlah Two and between him and Jennifer the house was beginning to take on a new atmosphere. Even the boys were put to work, after much grumbling, oiling the logs outside, and renewing the original lustre to them. They ended up with more oil on themselves than on the logs but it gave them a sense of accomplishment. Dianne, meanwhile, helped her mother with the interior redecoration.

After their hard work Bill thought the children deserved a reward, and he visited one of the local ranches, unbeknown to them. One day when they were out playing in the barn they heard a horn honking in the yard. Overcome with curiosity they all went to investigate. A pickup truck with a horse trailer hitched to it was parked in the middle of the yard with a large florid man wearing a cowboy hat leaning through the window and blowing the horn.

"You the Headingly kids?" he asked brusquely.

"Yes, we are sir," Keith responded politely.

"Good, I thought I was gonna have to wait here all day," he grumbled.

"Is it a horse?" Dianne asked timidly.

"No, it's an elephant, what did you expect?"

Although they had taken an instant dislike to this man, they were consumed with curiosity. "Can we see it, sir," David chipped in.

"Well, I guess so 'cause I ain't gonna hang around here all day," he groused.

They all walked around the back of the trailer as the driver undid the chains and let down the tail gate, revealing a jet black horse, already saddled. He pushed alongside the horse and untied the bridle, backing the horse down the ramp until it was fully visible.

"Wow," shouted David. Dianne added, "It's the most beautiful horse I've ever seen. Look, it has a white star on its forehead. We should call it 'Star'".

"You're too late missy. That's been her name ever since she was born. She's an Arabian".

"She's gorgeous," gushed Dianne. "How old is she?"

"She's three, and when she's a bit older we'll breed her with my good stallion. Then, she'll have a little foal and you'll get two for the price of one," he added with his first sign of a smile.

"Can we ride her though?" interjected Keith who had been standing back reservedly.

"Sure, right now if you like," the driver added with a chuckle. Already the children were beginning to warm to him.

"I'm first," they all shouted in unison.

"I still figure it's ladies first around these parts, so come on missy." He lifted Dianne up into the saddle where she clung desperately to the pommel.

"Let's go show Mum and Dad," said Keith, taking the reins and leading the horse to the house. Bill and Jennifer had intentionally been watching through the drapes to see the reaction of the children, but now they emerged to be assaulted with a flood of gratitude.

"Now, it's your horse so you have to look after it every day, rain or shine. The first sign of neglect and it'll have to go."

"We promise," they all chorused.

"Okay, put her in the coral and we'll go get her some oats from the feed mill."

"And a brush so I can groom her every day," added Dianne.

"See that you keep that promise," Jennifer admonished. "You don't do that great a job on your own hair right now!"

"Kids, this is Mr. Jim MacIver," Bill added as an after-thought.

"Folks hereabout call me Jim Bob, so you young uns can do the same."

"Thank you, sir," Keith acknowledged, to the amusement of Jim Bob.

Star kept the children amused day in and day out, and they didn't notice that summer was disappearing. With great reluctance, they were enrolled in the local school, and Jennifer and Bill were pleased to find that they were well up to their peers after their correspondence courses and five months in Edmonton. They even found a family living about a mile away with children in the same age brackets, so Bill also bought each of the kids a new bicycle to visit back and forth. Despite Bill and Jennifer's fears about them becoming anti-social in the protected environment of Buffalo Narrows, they adapted very quickly and soon made fast friends, especially amongst the exuberant group on the school bus. Bill and Jennifer could hear when the bus had arrived, even though the house was a couple of hundred yards from the road.

Bill had given up ever hearing from the Department of Indian Affairs when he was astonished to receive a phone call from a deputy minister one day. "I must apologize for not getting in touch sooner, but we're in the midst of negotiations on land claims and have been extremely busy. There's a conference scheduled in two weeks in Ottawa and we'd like you to attend. You can give us your first hand account of your experiences, and your opinion of the situation in the west, plus any recommendations you might have on ways to settle the various outstanding native issues."

Almost instinctively Bill asked, "Can I bring along another expert in the field who has experienced the old ways and is now working to rectify the old evils left over from the earlier days?"

The minister agreed immediately, and assured Bill that tickets and per diem expenses would be put in the mail right away.

As soon as Bill hung up, he briefly explained to Jennifer what was happening, and placed a call to Angus Reid, hoping that the phone lines had been restored. He was delighted to hear Angus's cheery voice respond immediately.

"Angus, I've just been talking to your boss in Ottawa and he had nothing but good to say about you," Bill joked.

"Moose droppings, my friend. Those guys in Ottawa don't even know I exist, and I'm astonished that my meager pay turns up from time to time. I send letters there that just disappear into the bowels of bureaucracy, never to be seen again. As I told you, if you go the political route you'll get fifty times the response I do. However, what can I do for you?"

"It's most urgent that I speak to Suzanne, so can you get her to call me back as soon as possible? It's for the good of the whole tribe, or even the whole aboriginal brotherhood, so try to convince her to call me."

"I'll try my best, but you know what she's like, and I can't guarantee that she'll even call you back. I'll turn on my Scottish charm and see what I can do, although she rejected my last offer out of hand. I'll call you back, friend, one way or the other."

"Thanks, Angus. By the way, did you ever get your clothes back that I sent to you. I would have kept them but I've put so much weight back on that they no longer fit."

"Yes I did, thank you. They were much cleaner than when I gave them to you, so I suspect Jennifer had something to do with that. Cheerio and I'll call you later."

Jennifer had been listening to the call and had a quizzical look on her face. "Do you intend to take Suzanne to Ottawa with you?" she asked with a hint of jealousy in her voice.

"If she'll go, which is doubtful. What better spokesperson could we find since she's experienced the horrors of residential school and trying to live amongst the white people. Now she's back amongst her own people and knows exactly what is needed to give them independence and regain their native pride. By the way, you don't have to worry about anything untoward 'cause she's too proud of her heritage to become involved with a white man again. Besides, I have all the family I need and love." He gave Jennifer a reassuring hug and kiss, and she busied herself with housework.

Many hours passed before the phone rang, and Angus gave his usual cheery greeting. He deliberately chatted small talk until finally Bill, in desperation, asked if he had contacted Suzanne.

"I had to use every ounce of my persuasion to get her to agree, but here she is in person," Angus concluded, passing the phone to Suzanne.

Bill explained what he had in mind, but she immediately refused, saying that she did not want to get involved with those big shots in Ottawa. He tried every manner of persuasion but she seemed steadfast in her refusal. "Listen

Suzanne, there will be representatives of tribes from right across the country, so you could benefit the whole native population, not only the Kwakwalas."

There was silence for a few moments until finally she reluctantly said, "Okay, I'll talk it over with the chief and elders, but don't hold your breath."

It was the next day before Suzanne finally called back. "I've talked it over with the chief and elders and they figure it would be a good thing, even though I'm a slahnay. I don't mind telling you I don't want to come and talk to all them big shots in Ottawa, but if it'll do us any good I guess I could do it. They said because I could speak such good English I'm the one to go. But I don't have anything to wear and my hair's a mess." Bill recognized the concerns of a woman of any race.

"Just a minute. Here's Jennifer, and she can talk to you and help you with all those things. Meanwhile, we want you to come here early and stay with us for a couple of days so that Jennifer can take you shopping."

The two women talked for ages, until finally Bill interrupted to talk with Angus again and explain how he was to issue funds to Suzanne for her train trip. He asked him to get Ross Stuart to fly her out to Sioux Falls when she was ready. He put down the phone, elated at the prospect of Suzanne meeting his family, and accompanying him to Ottawa. He could anticipate the impact her testimony would have on the conferees.

The whole family was at the train station to meet Suzanne, and they would probably have recognized her from Bill's description. She was prettier than they had imagined, and her long, raven-black hair framed her tanned native features. She was wearing a beautiful buckskin jacket embroidered with intricate beadwork, and a blue jean skirt with a checkered shirt.

Bill ran forward and embraced her, and then turned to introduce the rest of the family. "I would've known you all anywhere," said Suzanne as she hugged each of the children and shook hands with Jennifer. "This guy used to talk about you day and night in the cabin, so I feel like we've met before."

The two women walked down the platform arm in arm, engaged in deep conversation as if they were old friends, while Bill and the children followed along behind carrying Suzanne's only bag. When they reached the station wagon the two women climbed in the back together, and no one else could get a word in as they talked incessantly. The children shrugged their shoulders in mock resignation and Bill winked at them knowingly. Finally, he was able to interject a question during a pause in their chatter.

"How was the trip, Suzanne?"

"I was scared when Ross picked me up in his plane 'cause it was the first time I'd ever flown, but he seemed to be a good pilot. When we got to Sioux Falls we had a lot of time 'til the train came, so he took me down to his trailer to meet his new wife. She's one nice lady and is going to have a baby in the fall. He's all excited about it. The train trip down was the first time since I was nine years old, and brought back bad memories of going to the Indian school here in Prince George. It was a lot more comfortable though, and I could go to the bathroom whenever I wanted. I was so scared the first time that I wet my pants."

The children all giggled, but Bill told them how serious it was at the time, and added that it hadn't hurt Suzanne. They could see she had turned into a fine lady. By this time they were entering the driveway of the house, and Buck came racing down to meet them, barking as he ran alongside the wagon. As they drew up in front of the house, Suzanne was delighted to see the name that Bill had carved on a piece of cedar. "Tohtohlah. That's a good Indian name, and I sure hope that it brings you good luck."

"It already has," said Jennifer, squeezing her hand. "We've all been dying to meet you, and we can see now why Bill has been talking about that fabulous lady who saved his life. We'll all be forever grateful to you Suzanne for bringing back our loved one." Suzanne averted her eyes, part in embarrassment and part to hide her feelings.

They still had two days before leaving for Ottawa so Jennifer and Suzanne spent virtually the whole time shopping. At first Suzanne was reluctant to buy anything, as she had very little money, and did not want to spend the money that Angus had given her for clothes. Jennifer finally convinced her to let her pay for the clothes on her credit card after explaining that the money was coming from the book they were making and that she had made it all possible. With Jennifer's guidance, Suzanne was equipped with a whole new wardrobe that had to be modelled every night for the family. She looked positively stunning in some of the outfits, and Bill could not help but think of the influence she would have at the conference, between her native good looks and her eloquent speech. That was one residue from her Indian school education that would now benefit the whole tribe, in fact the whole Indian nation.

When Jennifer drove them to the airport, Suzanne was extremely nervous and began to have second thoughts about the whole venture. Both Bill and Jennifer kept reassuring her of the benefits that would accrue, and tried to convince her that she was representing her whole race in redressing past wrongs. Jennifer hugged her tightly as they boarded the plane, and Bill held her hand reassuringly as they were shown to their seats. Again it was a first for Suzanne to travel on a commercial airliner, and the experience was intimidating. She was grateful for Bill's comforting presence as they started the long flight across the land that had once been populated only by her ancestors.

Arriving in Ottawa they were met by a civil servant from Indian Affairs and driven to the Embassy Hotel where they had adjoining rooms. Suzanne had never seen such opulence, and the bathroom was something out of a magazine. She immediately excused herself and started drawing water in the deep tub while Bill showed her how to operate the jacuzzi, before leaving her to luxuriate in the hot water. It was hard to comprehend the difference between such luxury and the squalor of the reserve where she lived. She stayed in the hot water until her skin actually started to wrinkle like a prune and she panicked that it might stay that way. After a brisk rub with the thick, fluffy towels she was relieved to see herself return to normal as she gazed at her reflection in the full length mirror.

Bill's knock on her door brought her back from her reverie and, as she answered the door in her housecoat, Bill told her that she looked positively radiant. "If I ever get a house of my own I'm going to have a bathroom just like that. The trouble is that I'd probably spend all day in there."

"Now that you've had your fun, we have some work to do. We're scheduled for a one hour presentation tomorrow morning at eleven o'clock, so we have to decide what we're going to say. Why don't you get dressed and we'll have dinner and talk while we eat."

"Oh, God. You don't expect me to stand up and talk in front of a crowd of people do you? I'd faint."

"Suzanne, you're a gutsy lady and some of the things you've done in your life are hundreds of times worse that that. I can't imagine wading into a river in mid winter and catching fish like you did, so you don't have a thing to worry about. Don't forget too that you're representing your people and they're a proud and brave race. You have a lot more education than a lot of the people who'll be in the audience and you speak English beautifully. I'll be right there with you too, so we'll do it together."

Suzanne fretted all through dinner and slept fitfully but she got up refreshed from her sleep in the luxurious bed and had a shower to waken her up. She was all dressed when Bill came to take her to breakfast, and was much calmer than the night before. She did not tell him that she had been tempted to come to his room when she couldn't sleep, but was glad now that she hadn't. They had agreed that Suzanne would tell her story exactly as she had told it to Bill in the cabin, and then he would describe his impressions of life on the reserve and make recommendations to redress the wrongs that had been perpetrated on the aboriginal people. He had made excerpts from the notes he made in the cabin so that he could trace the history of the tribe, particularly the loss of their land and their traditional hunting and fishing rights.

Suzanne fidgeted through the first few presentations and went to the bathroom at least five times before she and Bill were introduced. She was extremely nervous at first, but calmed down as she recounted her story of being taken from the reserve and her family that she never saw again. In a calm and deliberate voice she described the conditions in the Indian residential school, and the denial of speaking her native tongue. Finally, she told of returning to the reserve and finding that she had lost her Indian status, and of being ostracized by her own people because she had married a white man. The audience listened in rapt attention and broke out in applause when she had finished her presentation. Bill then briefly recounted his adventure, and the dramatic experience of a white man being thrust into the native environment and conditions. He concluded by making a number of recommendations on how the white man could help to mend the social malaise that they had introduced into the Native culture. As they left the stage they were given a standing ovation, and Bill squeezed Suzanne's hand as he told her how well she had done.

At the lunchtime break the Minister of Indian Affairs sought them out, and magnanimously told them what an impression they had made on the conferees. He invited them to his office at the end of the day so that he could discuss urgent measures with them. In typically political fashion he added, "The Kwakwalas have received a lot of publicity because of Mr. Headingly's exploit, so we should capitalize on it. What we should do is make the Kwakwala reserve a model, and negotiate a satisfactory land claim with them as soon as possible while they're still in the spotlight. Everybody's short of funds, but I'm sure that I can find enough to make good on our promises and use it as a model for dealing with other

261

bands." Bill felt somewhat nauseated by the deliberate manipulation of a situation, but nevertheless hugged Suzanne unabashedly when they understood the benefits that were going to accrue from their efforts.

At the end of the conference the Minister summarized the presentations, complimenting Suzanne in particular for her excellent contribution. An aide came and fetched her and Bill and ushered them into a luxurious office, lined with oak and filled with beautiful furniture. For a fleeting moment Suzanne thought of the irony of this man deciding their fate from such opulence while they lived in such squalor. These were the perks of political life but she did not envy him in any way, nor did Bill.

"How about a drink?" the Minister offered sliding back a panel to reveal a well-stocked bar.

"No thanks," responded Suzanne without hesitation. "I've signed a pledge and so far we've got more than fifty percent to do the same on the reserve. Booze is behind most of the problems we've got on the reserve, including sexual and physical abuse. My own parents became alcoholics after being provided with liquor by an American hunting party they were guiding. Finally, they deserted me and went to the city and I've never seen them since."

The Minister sheepishly closed up the liquor cabinet and apologized. Bill sat back with a benign smile on his face to see him thoroughly chastized by this spunky young lady who a few days ago would have been embarrassed to even speak to him. Notwithstanding being a woman, there was little doubt that Suzanne would become a leader in the tribe, and he could predict that she would stand for chief when the old one stepped down.

Regaining his composure, the Minister said, "As I mentioned at noon I think we should capitalize on the publicity the Kwakwalas are getting right now, and especially with the book being published soon. I'd therefore like to appoint you two as special consultants to make recommendations on what we need to do to settle all the outstanding claims and other problems areas, such as housing and schooling. I'd also like your recommendations on how the tribe can become self-sufficient and self-governing. Before you leave my aide will give you a letter of authority from me to enable you to act on my behalf. I'm sure that you both have strong ideas so I expect great progress in making the Kwakwalas a model band that we can use as an example in negotiations with other tribes. And I won't even offer you a drink on that!" he added sardonically.

They shook hands all around and as they were leaving the office, Suzanne turned to Bill and said jokingly, "To think, white man, that this all started because you couldn't fly a plane without crashing into our trapline!"

Bill roared with good natured laughter while the aide looked on bemused. "I'll get the Minister's letter over to you at the hotel tonight so that you can carry it back with you. As you can see, the Minister's a man of action so I'm sure he'll be expecting great results from the pair of you. You should be flattered that he's entrusted this to you, since it's highly politically sensitive, and it will enhance his image if you can come up with an agreement satisfactory to all. As you know, successive governments have been trying to accomplish it for years so it would be a great coup. Good luck to you both!"

Back at the hotel, Bill placed phone calls to Jennifer and to Angus Reid on the reserve telling him the news, making sure he gave credit to Suzanne and suggesting that the chief should consider getting her elected to the band council, the first slahnay in the band's history. Angus was highly sceptical as the chief was one of the old guard who felt that women should not become involved in running the tribe. Bill pointed out that he would have little option after Suzanne's coup in Ottawa, and the tribe would have to accept modern ideas if they were to achieve independence. Afterwards, they celebrated by going out to one of the best restaurants in town, and Suzanne felt quite at home in one of her new dresses. They turned a lot of heads but Bill was not sure whether it was because Suzanne was an Indian, or because she looked stunning, but he didn't care. Nothwithstanding Suzanne's pledge, he celebrated with a good bottle of white wine.

Arriving back in Prince George, they were met once again by Jennifer, who tried to persuade Suzanne that she should stay with them for a while but she was anxious to get back to the reserve and get started on her project. She tried to convince Bill to come back with her, but he demurred as he wanted her to get full credit for the negotiations in Ottawa, but agreed that he would join her in a few days. Again he arranged for Ross Stuart to meet her off the train and fly her back to the reserve from Sioux Falls.

Ross Stuart had telephoned ahead to Angus Reid to give him an arrival time at the reserve, so that when they pulled up to the dock virtually the whole tribe was waiting to greet Suzanne. She had deliberately worn her buckskin jacket, jean skirt and checked shirt in case they thought she had become white again while she was away. In fact she had left most of her new wardrobe with Christie so that she could pick it up again on the way out if she had to go out to conferences or other band business.

The reception was reminiscent of returning from the trapping trip, and the drummers and dancers led the natives in a ceremonial dance of celebration. The chief and all the elders were there in their headdresses and beaded shirts and welcomed Suzanne back with great formal dignity. The chief held up his talking stick and announced that there would be a ceremony in the lodge that night and Suzanne would tell her story about her visit to the Great White Chief in Ottawa.

It was the first time that a woman had been invited to join the elders at the head table, and Suzanne felt just as uncomfortable as she did at the conference. This time, though, they were all faces of her own race and family, and she quickly calmed as she started to tell her story to a hushed audience. They listened in rapt attention when she told of flying in a big aeroplane that carried them right across the vast country that at one time had been populated only by Native people. "The land was so big it filled the sky from horizon to horizon.

We talked to aboriginal people from all across the land, and met the Big Chief himself, who has chosen the Kwakwalas to be the leaders in deciding our own destiny and making claims for recovery of the land and fishing and hunting rights that we lost over a century ago. Our blood brother Tchim-Uhl-Kain spoke for us as if he truly is one of us, and being a white man everybody listened to him. He told them of him being a white man who was now ashamed of the treatment the Indians have received. The Big Chief even offered us a drink in his fancy office, but I refused 'cause I told him I've taken the pledge like most of our tribe. I told him that booze caused most of our troubles after the white man brought it. The Big Chief said good, and hoped everybody would sign the pledge." This was met with stony silence but she continued, "We should be honoured that the Big Chief has chosen the Kwakwalas as the leaders in getting our lands back and becoming self-governing."

When she sat down, the chief made a long speech about their heritage and concluded that the Great Spirit was responsible for their resurrection, and that he had made the white man fall from the sky. They had welcomed him as a blood brother and given him an Indian name, Tchim-Uhl-Kain, meaning Broken Wing, and he was going to guard over them from now on. They were going to rename No Name Lake where the white man had crashed Tchim-Uhl-Kain Lake so that their descendants would always remember story.

The chief then stunned everyone by announcing, "I'm getting too old and tired to preside over such big changes that needs somebody young who understands the ways of the white man. So, I'm going to step down in favour of somebody younger who can speak the white man's tongue and can negotiate self-government for the Kwakwalas. Although she's a slahnay, she's best qualified of us all, and the Gods must have chosen Suzanne Pierre, who used to be known as Washababino, to be our leader. I'm going to nominate her to replace me as chief."

A hush fell over the crowd in the lodge for a long time before they started to murmur and finally the chant "Washababino, Washababino," rose to a crescendo which filled the room, the cadence being set by the drummers. Suzanne's eyes filled with tears as it was the first time she had heard her Indian name since she was a little girl, when her grandmother used to call her by that name all the time. It suddenly brought back the poignant memory of her grandmother calling to her in broken-hearted distress when they took her away to the Indian school. She thought with sadness how proud her grandmother would have been of this historic moment.

After the demonstration subsided, one of the elders stood up and said that he didn't think an election was necessary, and that he supported the chief's decision to elect Suzanne chief by acclamation. Once again all the elders called Suzanne's name, one by one, and she was installed that same night as the first woman chief of the Kwakwalas. As a final gesture, the old chief handed Suzanne his talking stick, saying, "Use this when you speak for our people."

Although her voice was choked with emotion, Suzanne made a stirring speech. "We're a proud people, and I'm greatly honoured to be chosen as your leader. I'll work long and hard on your behalf, and I'll make sure that we regain that which is rightfully ours. I'll also make sure we build a school on the reserve so no more of our children are taken away to the white mans' schools like me. They'll stay here and learn the language, skills and history of our people and be proud of their heritage. They'll learn to trap and hunt and fish like our ancestors, and they'll sustain us like they did for centuries. The women will be taught to produce their crafts for sale, and they'll all be provided with proper housing and sanitation like the white man. Finally, the men will carve a big totem pole to tell the story of our emancipation, and the path to self-determination that is starting at this historic moment. This totem will be seen for centuries to come by our descendants, and they will know the story of how we became a proud people again."

As soon as the opportunity arose, Suzanne left the long house and ran over to the agent's house where she asked Angus if she could make a call to Bill. When he answered, Suzanne said, "Tchim-Uhl-Kain, this is Washababino, Chief of the Kwakwala tribe. You were sent to us by the Creator God Huhk-Ahls and I was chosen to mend your broken wing. Now in return I'll need your help to make all our dreams come true for the Kwakwalas, blood brother."

"Chyit, Washababino," Bill responded as tears of happiness welled up in his eyes.

Chapter Eighteen

With typical enthusiasm, Bill threw himself wholeheartedly into his new work, and after considerable research, he laid out a plan for visiting all of the reserves in northern British Columbia. This required extensive travelling and time away from the family; however, they were all thoroughly settled into their new home and life, so that he did not worry about them when he left on trips. Although they frequently discussed Buffalo Narrows, it was not with the same sadness, but rather with nostalgia, having resigned themselves to the impossibility of living there under the circumstances. It was difficult to believe that a full year had passed since Bill's return.

It was on one such trip that Jennifer and Dianne were left alone while the boys were playing hockey in a weekend tournament in Prince George. Dianne went out to the barn to brush Star, which had now become a daily ritual. Buck accompanied her as usual, and as they were about to enter the barn, the dog began to growl, and the ruff on the back of his neck stood up. Dianne's heart skipped a beat, but she had no idea why Buck was growling. Suddenly, she looked up and was petrified to see a large animal crouched on the roof of the shed, emitting low-pitched screams. Turning on her heels, she ran as fast as her legs would carry her back to the house, shouting at her mother as she ran.

Jennifer heard the screams and ran out of the house, her heart pounding up into her throat when she detected the urgency in Dianne's voice. "Mummy, mummy, there's a big animal up on the shed roof that looks like a big cat."

From the brief description, Jennifer correctly surmised that it was a cougar, and grabbed Dianne by the hand as they ran into the sanctuary of the house. Buck stayed behind growling and barking at the animal. They could also hear Star whinnying in fright and kicking the stall as she sensed the cougar's presence.

Jennifer's immediate reaction was just to lock the door and hope the animal would go away, but she also realised that both Buck and Star could be in mortal danger. Although she still hated guns, in desperation she took down Bill's hunting rifle from the horns above the fireplace, and went to the desk to search for ammunition where she knew Bill locked it up. She fumbled with the key for ages before she finally got the drawer open and found the box of shells and a full clip. She was shaking so badly that she dropped the clip a dozen times before she managed to get it inserted into the rifle the right way around.

"You stay in the house and phone Jim Bob MacIver to come right away. His number is on that pad by the phone." Jim Bob, the man who had sold them Star, lived about a mile down the road.

With the rifle in her hands, Jennifer crept towards the barn until she finally saw the big cougar, still on the roof of the shed, spitting and snarling at Buck down below. She continued to edge forward until she was about thirty yards from the shed, before she raised the rifle to her shoulder. Jennifer had never fired a big rifle in her life before, and was shaking like a leaf. Try as she might, she could not see anything through the scope, and finally had to open both eyes to point the rifle. Aiming it in the general direction of the cougar she squeezed the trigger, but was stunned to find that nothing happened. Taking the gun down from her shoulder she looked to see what she had done wrong, suddenly realizing she had not taken off the safety catch. This accomplished, she once again raised the gun, and this time was even able to look through the scope with one eye. Finally, she moved it around until all she could see in the scope was the tan coloured fur and quickly pulled the trigger.

The results were electrifying, as the gun recoiled into her shoulder and the scope hit her with a terrible impact in the eye. Little did she know that she was supposed to grip the rifle tightly, and hold it to her shoulder to absorb the recoil of the powerful shell. The cougar leapt into the air and let out a bloodcurdling scream as it slid off the roof where Buck immediately pounced on it, his fur standing on end and teeth bared. Although the rifle was an automatic and already had another shell in the chamber, Jennifer was terrified to try another shot, especially with Buck tangling with the cougar. The two of them were locked in deadly combat, and Jennifer saw that blood was spurting on to the ground. She could not tell which animal it was coming from. She stood transfixed, unable to even move, until finally she saw the cougar relax its grip on Buck and drop on its side. Buck continued to worry at it, sinking his teeth into the cougar's now exposed throat. Finally, the cougar lay inert and Buck limped towards Jennifer, with an ear torn and bleeding from other wounds, but still wagging his tail.

Just at that point Jennifer heard a truck come roaring up the driveway and skid to a stop beside her. Jim Bob MacIver jumped out with a rifle in his hand, and cautiously approached the motionless cougar. He poked it with the barrel of the rifle and satisfied himself it was dead.

"My God, lady, you've got yourself a hell of a cougar, but it looks like your dog took a beatin'. I'll bet that thing is eight feet from nose to tail and could've taken on a horse. In fact I'll bet it was after Star."

Turning his attention to Jennifer he saw that her right eye was swollen and bleeding. "Holy smokes, how'd that happen?"

"I guess I'm not very good with a rifle," answered Jennifer in a shaking voice. "The scope kicked back and hit me when I fired."

"You were good enough to shoot that beast, but we'd better get you down to the hospital and get you looked at. You're some gutsy lady. We'd better get your dog to the Vets as well 'cause he looks pretty beat up."

Seeing Jim Bob, and sensing security from his presence, Dianne appeared from the house and timidly approached the others.

"Oh, Mummy, look at your eye," she gasped. "And look at poor Bucky. He's bleeding and his ear is torn."

"Don't worry, missy, we'll take them both into town and get them fixed up right away."

In contrast to his gruff exterior, Jim Bob picked up Buck very tenderly and laid him in the back of the pickup on a bale of hay that he split open. Jennifer ran over to the house and left a note for the boys in case they came back before she did, and climbed into the front of the pickup with Dianne.

"I'll skin that beasty out when we get back. He'll make a beautiful rug." Jennifer wondered how he could think of such things at the moment.

It brought back a flash of deja vu as they drew up to the emergency entrance of the hospital where Jennifer had seen Bill for the first time after his resurrection. She thought it ironic that this time it was she who needed their ministrations. Interestingly, the nurse on duty recognised Jennifer immediately.

"Good grief, what have you been doing?" she asked. "That guy hasn't been beating you up I hope," she added in jest.

She had been joined by a young resident who asked the same question, but with a serious demeanour. He explained later that it was common practice to determine the source of any facial damage in case of abuse.

"You'll probably never believe this but I guess I'd better tell you my implausible story." Jennifer then went on to recount the episode with the cougar, and her amateurish efforts with the rifle.

"Good grief, that family of yours really knows how to hit the headlines. Wait 'til this one makes the news. 'Plucky housewife takes on Cougar and wins'," the nurse said with a smile.

The doctor did a thorough examination of the eye and announced with relief that there did not appear to be any serious damage, but there would be considerable swelling and discolouration for a long time. He covered it with a pad and taped it shut.

Meanwhile, Jim Bob had taken Buck to the Vet and Jennifer did not have long to wait before he returned. "They're going to keep Buck in for a couple of days and get him all stitched up. They were worried the cougar might be rabid so the Vet is coming out to check over the carcass. It's a good thing none of you were bit."

They were just pulling into the driveway when the boys returned from their hockey game and were shocked at their mother's appearance. "Holy mackerel, who gave you the shiner?" asked David without thinking.

"Just like you," huffed Dianne. "While you guys were away playing we had to defend the place," she said, continuing breathlessly with the rest of the story in a haughty air. Finally she had got one up on the boys who were constantly teasing her about being a girl. They looked at her and their mother with a new, grudging respect, especially when they saw the carcass of the cougar still lying by the barn.

Consumed with curiosity the boys went to examine the cougar. "Don't touch it boys. It might have rabies and the Vet's comin' to check 'er out. You might have to get a bunch of painful needles in the bum if it's got rabies," Jim Bob cautioned. "Your buddy Buck was a real hero, but he'll be laid up for a while."

It was two days before Bill got home and he was shocked when Jennifer met him at the airport with her eye all bandaged up. He sat in stunned silence as she recounted the episode.

"Good grief, I could have expected anything in Buffalo Narrows, but I didn't think this would happen in relative civilization. I guess the first thing I have to do is teach you to shoot a gun properly."

"No thank you," countered Jennifer. "I think I've had enough of guns for the rest of my life. I'll stick to my broom from now on!"

Fall turned into winter again, and the farm was a picture postcard with the fresh white snow covering up the debris of the falling leaves. The family had fallen into a routine and rarely even mentioned Buffalo Narrows any more. Christmas was creeping up on them, and they decided to invite Mike and Sue to spend the Festive Season with them. Jennifer's eye healed without complications, and Buck was back to normal, except for the partial loss of one ear and a few scars that did not show under his fur. The cougar was not rabid and Bill had quietly taken it to the taxidermist to have the pelt tanned and made into a rug as a gift for Jennifer.

* * *

Christmas Day dawned clear and crisp. After the usual breakfast feast cooked by Mike, the whole family decided to go down to the lake to try out their new skates. Before they left, however, Dianne reminded them that they had not taken Star her Christmas breakfast. Jennifer made her a hot mash with oats and the three children ran over to the barn with it. David was back in minutes shouting at the top of his voice to come to the barn to see Star. He was forever crying wolf and they were not sure whether to respond or not, but the urgency in his voice convinced them there really was something wrong, so they all put on their outerwear and hurried to the barn.

273

The sight that greeted them stopped them all in their tracks. There, lying on the straw beside Star, was a newborn foal, and Star was licking off the placenta. The foal was honey- coloured, with a blond mane, and was struggling to get up on its feet. Bill grabbed a sack and wiped the foal dry before lifting it up on its feet and guiding its mouth to Star's teats. Instinctively it started sucking as it stood on its wobbly legs.

Everyone was standing in awe at the sight, and Jennifer and Dianne had tears rolling down their cheeks. Dianne finally broke the spell. "Is it a boy or a girl?" she asked her father.

"It's a little filly, just like her mother. I can't believe Star delivered it on her own 'cause I didn't think she was close. It's a blond Arabian, just like Jim Bob's stud. She's going to be a beautiful horse."

Star looked proudly over her shoulder at her new offspring which was sucking furiously as if it was starving.

"Good work old girl," Jennifer said with a soft voice that only another mother could emulate. "Now it's your turn for a treat," she said as she held the bucket of warm mash for Star to eat.

"What're we going to call her?" Dianne interjected.

"Well, she was born on Christmas Day, so how about Mary or something?" offered Keith.

"No, that's not a horse's name," said David in disgust.

Sue had been standing back observing the scene and spoke up for the first time. "I've a suggestion for you. Seeing that her mother's name is Star, how about Twinkle, Little Star?"

There was silence for a moment until everyone absorbed the idea, and suddenly there was a chorus of approval. "Good old Grandma did it again," added Keith.

Plans for skating were forgotten as the children spent virtually the whole day in the barn gazing in wonder at the beautiful creature that was so self-sufficient after only a few hours of life. In fact Bill had a hard time getting them to come in for Christmas Dinner. Dianne held his hand tightly as they walked back to the house and said, "Daddy, this is the best Christmas day of my life."

As the winter was drawing to a close, Jennifer became concerned about Bill. It was almost two years since he had returned from the wilderness and he seemed to enter long periods when he withdrew into himself. Jennifer was not able to communicate with him for the first time in their married life. In fact she became so concerned that she telephoned Doctor Pace who had treated him when he first returned and with whom he had established a strong rapport.

"I'm afraid that I'm not a psychiatrist, Jennifer, but I'll be pleased to refer him to one if you wish. Often people who have undergone a severe trauma as he did will experience fits of depression long after the event. Do you think you can get him to come and see me and we'll discuss it?"

"I'll try, but it's going to be difficult 'cause even I have trouble talking to him."

When Bill came home that evening, Jennifer told a little white lie to say that Doctor Pace had called to see how he was doing and suggested that he drop in for a checkup. Bill did not respond and instead went off into the barn to tinker with the old tractor.

Spring arrived, and Jennifer could tell that Bill was becoming even more troubled. She had hoped that the reawakening of the earth would have a therapeutic effect, but he was still moody. She was totally baffled, as things were going well. His job was challenging and interesting and they had finally received the insurance settlement for the Beaver. The book had been launched and was an instant success. In fact, he was in demand to attend signings and interviews in various places and he spent quite a bit of time away from home. As promised, the publishers had printed the history of the Kwakwalas. He called Suzanne from time to time, but even his discussions with her were strained.

It was early May, and the trees were in full leaf again. Star and Twinkle spent most of the days outdoors as the foal raced around the paddock, chasing her mother and kicking up her heels. The ice had all gone out of the lake and Bill had gone to Vancouver for a book signing and an interview on radio.

Just after lunch one day, Jennifer was startled by the sound of an aeroplane buzzing the house, and when she ran outside she saw a red and white Cessna 185 on floats making passes at low level over the house. She immediately assumed it was Ross Stuart coming in for a visit, and watched as the plane skimmed low and landed on the lake below them, taxiing up to the beach where the engine was shut down. Jennifer went into the house to get the binoculars to identify the figure walking up towards the house and gasped in disbelief when she saw that it was Bill. She put down the binoculars and ran down to meet him.

As they met he scooped her up and swung her around with a show of enthusiasm she had not seen for a long time.

"How do you like my new plane?" Bill asked, his face beaming. "I picked it up from a friend of mine in Vancouver for a song and it's in super shape. It's more like a sports car than my old Beaver," he bubbled. "I've been thinking about it for a long time but didn't know how I'd be flying again after the crash. Now I know I have no problems and can satisfy my lifelong love again. You probably remember my old motto 'Per ardua ad astra'- through toil to the stars. I figure I've done my toil and now I can head back for the stars again."

Jennifer was silent for a few moments before venturing, "You're not thinking of trying to make a living that way again surely?"

"Not on your life," he answered with conviction. "I think we can afford to have it as a luxury now, although I'd be prepared to do the odd charter if it came up. I can also use it for trips into some of the reserves and charge it off as a business expense."

Jennifer heaved an audible sigh of relief and the realization of what had been bothering Bill came to her. He had been missing his first love, and inwardly pining to get into the air again after the trauma of his crash had receded. She was grateful that that was all that was involved, and didn't mind sharing him with that mistress.

As they strolled hand in hand back to the house Bill said, "First trip we'll take will be back to Buffalo Narrows for the weekend. Maybe we could keep the kids out of school for an extra day and blame it on a serious sickness that their father has."

When the children came home from school they were just as excited as Bill, and had to go for a trip immediately. Even Dianne was enthusiastic as she had grown to love flying, and wore a smug look when she was allowed to sit up front and handle the controls, despite the mock screams of terror from the rear seats.

On Friday morning they loaded up the Cessna with sleeping bags and supplies for the weekend and took off for Buffalo Narrows with a great air of anticipation. Bill was in his element, beaming as he handled the controls as efficiently as he ever had. Jennifer knew looking at him that his problem had been solved, and wondered why she had not thought of it herself.

It was a beautiful clear spring day, and they could see Buffalo Narrows from ten miles away. As they drew closer the cabin presented a tranquil vista, and the lake was like a mirror. As Bill skilfully set down the plane and taxied towards the dock, they were all silent, buried in their own thoughts, remembering the last time they had seen Tohtohlah.

Bill and the boys busied themselves taking down the shutters and uncapping the chimney, to get a roaring fire going to air the place out. It had a decidedly musty smell after being closed up for so long. Jennifer dusted and swept out cobwebs. Dianne helped for a while, and then lost interest as she wandered outside to visit some of her secret places. She had been gone for about twenty minutes when she suddenly came racing back to the house, shouting at the top of her voice. Bill rushed outside to see what was happening, and had to hold her tightly to get her to calm down enough to tell him what it was.

"It's Molly," she gasped. "And she has a little baby with her."

"Where?" Bill asked.

"Down by the stream where we first found her."

By this time everyone was outside and following Dianne back down to the stream. As they approached, a young cow moose emerged from the bush and came directly to them, followed by a calf just a few weeks old.

As they approached, Bill cautioned them to go slowly as Molly had been living wild, and would be protective of her calf. Without fear, Molly walked right up to them and accepted the grass that Keith had pulled for her. She allowed the children to rub her snout, but the calf stayed behind her out of reach.

"My gosh, it's a miracle," said Jennifer. "Imagine her remembering us after all this time. It's as if she was here to welcome us back to Buffalo Narrows."

"She is," Bill answered quietly, as he took her hand. "All looked lost for a while, but we should be thankful for another chance to start a new life, just as Molly's calf is doing."

They all walked back to the cabin hand in hand where their adventure had begun, and was now continuing on such a happy note.

The sun was descending in a huge crimson ball over the mountains, and it reflected in a perfect mirror image on the glassy surface of Buffalo Narrows, casting a magic spell on the little group. Bill finally broke the spell by asking, "Well, guys, what would you think if we moved back here for the summer? I don't think we could survive for the winter, and we're all settled in our new Tohtohlah. So, if you're all in agreement, this way we can have the best of both worlds."

There was a chorus of approval as they all went back into the cabin that symbolised an interrupted dream.